Acknowledgements

Researched, walked, photographed, compiled and written by
Peter Gerard-Pearse and Nigel Matheson

Additional research
Jo Carroll
Osterley Park Walk
Peter Kendall

Maps, illustrations, layout and paste-up
Bill Goodson

Cartoons
Peta Maughan

Travel research
Martin Hitchcock

Editor
Nicola Hodge

Introduction

THE DRINKERS' GUIDE TO WALKING: LONDON AND THE SOUTH-EAST is a complementary edition to our nationwide book, THE DRINKERS' GUIDE TO WALKING, and is a lively and essential travelling companion for anyone in London and the South-East of England. We shall shortly be bringing out some more regional guides and an updated edition of the first book.

Once again we hope that we have taken into account a wide range of interests as this is not a book purely for the hardened drinker nor the hardy hiker – it's crammed with anecdotes, ghostly tales and informative snippets of natural history.

It is important to read through the talk-round before starting out, by this I don't mean to suggest that you won't be in a fit state to do so 'en route', but it's sensible to get an idea of the mileage involved, the public transport available and the overall difficulty of the walk. Although we have started nearly all the talk-rounds at the pubs, the walks are all circular and therefore it is possible to begin at any point and even to treat the pub as a well-deserved reward after a hard day's foot-slog. The maps should be seen as a supplement to the detailed talk-round, which is designed to direct you, right down to the last hedge.

Our researchers have asked me to stress the advisability of warm and protective clothing, namely wellingtons and kagoules, along with a few points of protocol on arriving at the pub; please don't eat your own sandwiches in the pub and take off your muddy boots outside. As we stated in the first edition, we have tried, wherever possible, to make these walks suitable for young children and/or grannies and, as a result, the average walk in this book is between three and four miles. As far as the pubs are concerned, children and dogs are probably less trouble in the summer months, as most of our featured pubs have gardens.

As the words in this guide are not timeless, the countryside and its landmarks both man-made and natural, being subject to change, we would like to ask for a certain amount of common sense and co-operation from our readers. Don't write and tell us if Mrs Brown of Rose Cottage has painted her door yellow, but do write and tell us if you find that footpaths have been closed or if cliff edges have crumbled into the sea.

Finally I'd like to draw your attention to The Drinkers' Guide Country Code.

1. Guard against all risk of fire, especially in, or near woodland.
2. Fasten all gates that you open securely and, if you climb a gate, climb at the hinged end, not the latched.

THE DRINKERS' GUIDE TO WALKING

LONDON AND THE SOUTH-EAST

PROTEUS

PROTEUS BOOKS is an imprint of
The Proteus Publishing Group

United States
PROTEUS PUBLISHING CO., INC.
733 Third Avenue
New York, N.Y. 10017
distributed by:
THE SCRIBNER BOOK COMPANIES, INC.
597, Fifth Avenue
New York, N.Y. 10017

United Kingdom
PROTEUS (PUBLISHING) LIMITED
Bremar House,
Sale Place,
London, W2 1PT.

ISBN 0 906071 73 9 (p/b)
     0 909071 74 7 (h/b)

First published in UK 1981
© 1981 Proteus Publishing Group
All rights reserved.

Printed and bound in Great Britain by
The Anchor Press Ltd. and William Brendon & Son Ltd.,
Tiptree, Essex.

3. Keep dogs under control. Farmers have been known to shoot even friendly ones.
4. Keep to the path when crossing farmland.
5. Respect other people's property and privacy.
6. Litter is matter in the wrong place; keep yours with you.
7. Avoid damaging hedges, fences and walls.
8. Don't contaminate streams, rivers, ponds or lakes.
9. Protect wildlife, plants and trees.
10. Please walk and drive with special care on narrow country roads. *Never* drink and drive.

Nicola Hodge
February 1981

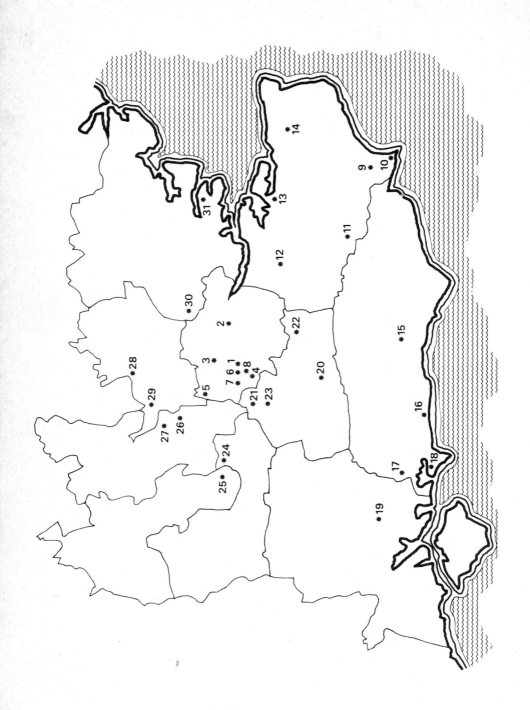

The Index to the Walks

Titles in the series

The 'National' Drinkers Guide to Walking
(80 walks)   £6.50 (h/b)

The 'National' Drinkers Guide to Walking
(80 walks)   £3.95 (p/b)

London and The South-East
(31 new walks)   £3.50

The South-West
(38 new walks)   £3.50

Key for the Maps

THE ROUTE:

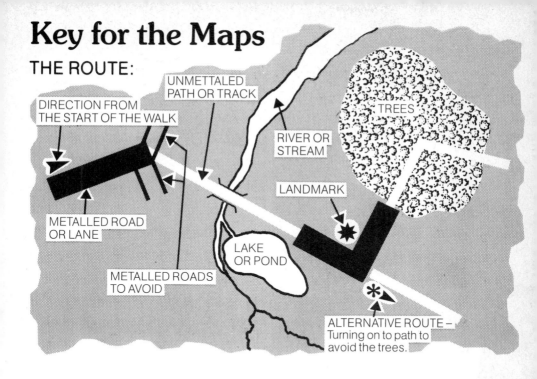

UNMETTALED PATH OR TRACK

DIRECTION FROM THE START OF THE WALK

RIVER OR STREAM

TREES

LANDMARK

METALLED ROAD OR LANE

METALLED ROADS TO AVOID

LAKE OR POND

ALTERNATIVE ROUTE – Turning on to path to avoid the trees.

THE SYMBOLS:

 INN, PUBLIC HOUSE

 SCENERY

 FARM

 HOSPITAL

 HOTEL, HOUSE, COTTAGE, ETC.

 CASTLE, FORT

 LARGE HOUSE, MANSION

 RUINS OF CASTLE

 WATERMILL

 RUINS OF CHURCH

 CHURCH, ABBEY, ETC.

RUINS OF FARM

 — — — — — — — RAILWAY STILL USED

 —▪—▪—▪—▪—▪—▪—▪—▪— DISUSED RAILWAY

MAPS NOT IN PROPORTION – BUT COMPASS DIRECTION CORRECT.

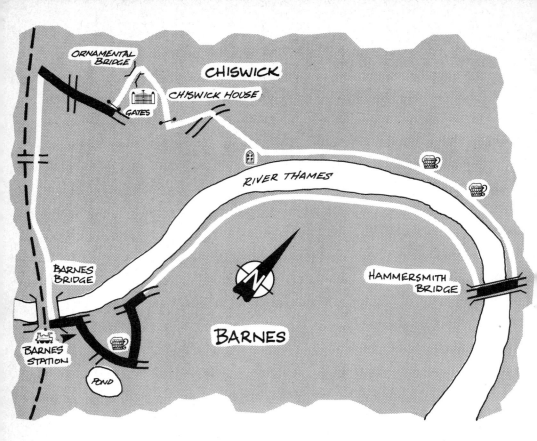

1   Barnes

APPROXIMATELY 4¼ Miles

The District

The population of Barnes has doubled over the last ten years causing the original 'village' to bulge at the seams. Nevertheless there is still a green, a pond, some ducks and some quaint old shops tucked in between the ubiquitous health food stores and scrubbed pine centres on the High Street. Look out for Barnes Terrace, overlooking the river, as it contains many fine old houses.

Hammersmith, although only the width of the river away, has none of the village atmosphere of Barnes. Densely populated and bisected by major road routes it seems far removed from the times when it was renowned for its market gardens, orchards and dairies. However there is a thriving sense of community here amidst the concrete, and arts centres such as the Riverside Studios in Crisp Road have done much to reinforce this.

The inhabitants of Hammersmith have apparently always displayed great loyalty and affection towards one another and one of the best-loved of past residents was Queen Caroline who married the Prince of Wales and came to live in Brandenburgh House in 1820. The marriage was doomed from the start, the Prince reputedly only having married her for financial reasons and then forbidding her to see their daughter born nine months to the day from the wedding ceremony. Scandalous rumours eventually forced Caroline into exile in Italy where she rejoiced in the salacious company of her handsome servant lover, Bergani, until her husband was crowned King in 1820. She then moved back to Hammersmith where she was regarded as something of a local heroine and was immediately faced with divorce proceedings on the grounds of adultery. During this time the smuttiest details of her rampageous sex life were made public and yet demonstrations of her popularity continued and eventually the bill of adultery was dropped. Soon after being denied a coronation she died unexpectedly in Brandenburgh House and Hammersmith went into mourning – two people were killed in the uproar of the funeral procession.

Chiswick too has had its share of colourful residents. Georgiana, Duchess of Devonshire in the late 18th century lived at Chiswick House where she was involved in a bizarre menage à trois with the Duke and Lady Elizabeth Foster. Both ladies bore the Duke children and Georgiana also had a child by the future Prime Minister, thereby ensuring that they were all at the forefront of local gossip for at least 20 years. Perhaps there is something in the water in this part of the world, for yet another female resident, Lady Castlemaine, lover of Charles II, was renowned for her infidelities. When Charles eventually complained, she retorted "as to love, one is no mistress of oneself" and retired to ruminate over her ebullient life in Walpole House on Chiswick Mall.

Chiswick House was originally a Jacobean mansion but was given an Italian facelift after the Earl of Burlington spent a holiday there. The gardens are said to reflect the character of that naughty lady the Duchess of Devonshire; they were laid informally to provide surprises with statues appearing unexpectedly amidst the trees and shrubs. The bridge was built for Georgiana by James Wyatt.

How to Get There

By road Barnes lies on the intersection of the A205 South Circular Road and the A306.
By rail to Barnes Bridge from Waterloo.
By bus numbers 9, 72 and Green Line 710, 714, 715 and 716.

The Inns

The Sun Inn, Barnes

Inns have stood on the site since the 14th century though the present building was constructed in the mid 1700s. Classically situated by the pond on the village green it is well equipped to deal with those hot summer Sunday lunchtimes. The bars are on different levels and feature exposed beams and an open fire.

It is a popular and very busy pub renowned for its fresh salmon salad, home-made pies, and sandwiches. Beers include popular Taylor-Walker Bitter and Burton Ale.

The bowling green, still in use behind the pub, is reputedly where Drake taught Elizabeth I to play. Believe it or not Dick Turpin is popularly supposed to have used it as a hideout, watching for the Bow Street Runners from a top window. Another feature is an active pub ghost, old Charlie Owen – a past tenant departed in all but spirit.

The Dove, Hammersmith

The Dove has become world famous over the past 50 years, perhaps this is because it seems to epitomise the London riverside pub. Built in the 17th century the front opens into a narrow passageway surrounded by Georgian

11

The Barnes Walk

For those dependent on public transport, Barnes Bridge Station serves as the starting point, whilst those with motors (or cycles) can strike out from **The Sun Inn**. From Barnes Bridge Station turn right onto The Terrace and follow the road round to the right into Barnes High Street. The blue plaque fixed to No 10 The Terrace attests to the residency of composer Holst between 1908 and 1913.

To digress . . . in the early part of the 19th century The Terrace was colonised by a settlement of French émigres. Living in a small house at the upper end were the Count and Countess D'artraignes. They were murdered there in 1812 by their Italian valet who stabbed and shot them, leaving the Countess to stagger into the road and die on the pavement. The valet then killed himself in an upstairs room leaving no explanation for his behaviour, although it was rumoured that he had heard them discuss his dismissal the previous evening.

At the end of the busy High Street lies Barnes Green. Opposite the pond, to the left is The Sun Inn, ideally placed for those whose idea of the good life is fresh air, pleasant scenery and good beer, as drinks are best enjoyed from the green opposite in fine weather.

Turn left out of the pub and take the next road left – Nassau Road. At the end of Nassau Road cross Lonsdale Road to the footpath by the river and proceed to the right. Continue along the public footpath where 340 years ago Donald Lupton mused "This is a long, broad, slippery fellow". A pleasant tree-lined pathway now leads downriver to Hammersmith Bridge. This is a dirt footpath and may be muddy if wet, so if it's wet come prepared. Real ale buffs will notice the famous Fullers brewery across the river, blending in comfortably with the old river barges and syncopated shouts of the rowing crews, who seem to train in even the bleakest of weather. The Thames here is known as Corney Reach, and the twin arches of Hammersmith Bridge, a ➤

houses, whereas the back overlooks the river. Its history is naturally tied in with the river, being used by watermen since cargo was offloaded at nearby wharves. A brass plaque in the small public bar shows the level that the tide reached in 1928 – the highest tide ever recorded. It is classified as a building of special architectural and historic interest.

Historic associations go back to the 17th century, though its exact origins are uncertain. Legend has it that Charles II and Nell Gwyn drank here together. It also has endless associations with literature and the stage, not least the writing of Rule Britannia in an upstairs room. Past landlord George Izzard, portrayed in a painting in the bar wrote, 'One for the road' here and many say that he now haunts the pub.

The Dove is essentially a 'beer house' selling two draught beers – London Pride and ESB. The lagers are bottled only. A special meal is on offer daily, such as casserole or curry. Alternatively there is a good cold buffet.

familiar sight since 1887, soon heave into view.

At the bridge take the path to the right to gain access to the footpath over the Thames. Once across the bridge take the first staircase down to the left, turn back towards the river and proceed right along the Lower Mall. Continue along into Furnivall Gardens, named after Dr Furnivall, a white bearded Victorian gentleman who pioneered the first women's sculling club, which roused great local opposition. Following the path to the right at Dove Marina (Hammersmith Pier) take the narrow passageway on the left. This leads to **The Dove**, one of the most famous of all riverside pubs. Its diminutive size undoubtedly helps to maintain its charming character but it can get very crowded. The back terrace is a popular vantage point for the boat race, if you can get anywhere near it, that is. The houses around The Dove are Georgian and were built around 1879. From The Dove continue left along the riverside, passing through an archway to **The Old Ship**, another infamous boat race landmark, acclaimed 'Evening Standard Pub of the Year' in 1978. After suitably acquainting oneself with The Old Ship continue up the river terrace. At the end of Upper Mall carry straight down Hammersmith Terrace West and into Chiswick Mall, passing close by Chiswick Eyot.

At Chiswick Mall Public Drawlock, bear right by the church of St Nicholas. Notable inhabitants of the graveyard include William Hogarth, Whistler and two of Cromwell's daughters in unmarked graves. It's also believed that Cromwell's own remains were secretly interred here after the Reformation.

Circle the church to the front, walk through the graveyard, bearing right into Powell Walk and away from the river. At the end of Powell Walk turn left along Burlington Lane. Cross at the traffic lights and follow the walk through the grounds to Chiswick House. Enter by the first gate encountered and bear left. Follow the path to the right and through the white stone gateway to Chiswick House (open

The Old Ship, Hammersmith

One of the oldest pubs in Hammersmith, The Old Ship overlooks the Thames close to Chiswick Eyot. At one time it served as a haven for smugglers engaged in illicit activities on the Thames. Nowadays somewhat more respectable it attracts many TV characters and has itself starred in a film.

The walls inside are cluttered with interesting, riverside curiosities — antique lamps, brasses and among the various ships wheels is one from the Royal Yacht Britannia, presumably donated after an over-indulgence on the draught Guinness. There are also collections of wind instruments and an oar from each riverside sailing club from Barnes to Hammersmith.

In 1978 it was voted 'Evening Standard Pub of the Year' and the food is indeed consistently excellent. There is a choice of twelve salads on offer each day until 21.30.

The Bulls Head, Barnes

The Bulls Head is a large Victorian fronted pub overlooking the Thames. For many years it has been known as the best pub in London to hear live jazz. The reputation is well deserved and the list of notables who have played there would fill the page, but includes Ronnie Scott, Humphrey Lyttleton and Nucleus. There is live music every evening and week end lunchtimes. As well as the usual Youngs beers, hot and cold food is available as well as wine by the glass.

to the public all the year round although from 16th October to 14th March it is closed on Mondays and Tuesdays).

From the other side of the house walk along the avenue of statues, then take the left fork at the end to go down past the pond to the left. The grounds are peppered with various ornamental bits and pieces. Here you are likely to hear the sound of a violin. This is the fiddler who has practised here most afternoons for seven years or more. A lover of classical pieces, Sid says he is inspired by the trees and claims the birds join in.

Cross the fairytale bridge and take the path second from the left. At the stone pinnacle leave the park through the gate on the right. Cross Burlington Lane and continue down to the right, crossing Stavely Road and Wilmington Avenue. Turn left down the public footpath opposite the phone box before the row of shops. Follow this path to the end, looking out for the path to the bridge on the right, as the road runs to the left. At the river ascend the steps to the right over the bridge. Entry to Barnes Bridge Station is directly adjacent to the bridge on the other side. Walk back up The Terrace to where the High Street curves round to the right. Cross the road and on the right facing the river is **The Bulls Head.**

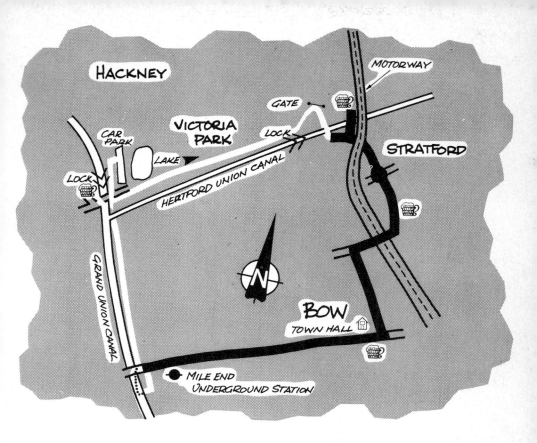

2   Bow

APPROXIMATELY 3¼ Miles

The District

If you're born within the sound of Bow Bells you can consider yourself a true Cockney and not merely an East Ender. Bow Bells aren't in Bow however, but in nearby Aldgate. Their most famous association is, of course, with Dick Whittington, who was trying his hardest to get out of the metropolis when the big bells 'told' him to return to become Lord Mayor of London.

To the north of Bow is Victoria Park, whilst somewhat of a poor relation to the likes of Hampstead Heath and Richmond, this unassuming expanse of green has a gay and colourful past. In the eyes of the East Enders the exceptional feature of the park used to be its bathing lake where, in 1895, twenty five thousand bathers were counted before eight o'clock one summer's morning! Rumours of water being turned into wine are, apparently, entirely unfounded . . . Mixed bathing was considered sinful at this time, and it was a while before women were allocated a separate bathing area.

The most famous aspect of the park however, was its use as a public forum — a bread and butter version of Speaker's Corner. The emphasis here was on earnest political discussion, and speakers ranged from early socialists such as Bernard Shaw and William Morris, to devotees of Oswald Moseley's 'Union of Fascists'.

➤

15

Nowadays the canals which link the East End docklands with the built-up areas on either side of the Thames are used more for recreation than for commercial enterprise.

How to Get There
By road Aim for Victoria Park (south-west), taking the A11 (Mile End Road) north-east from central London. Then turn left onto Cambridge Heath Road and right onto Old Ford Road.
By rail to Bethnal Green or Mile End.
By bus from Bethnal Green the 8 or 106 and from Mile End the 106 or 277.

The Bow Walk
This is a walk to acquaint you with London's canals. Not only have they been instrumental in the industrial development of London, but they have also given rise to a good number of ale houses, many of which are still with us today. One of these is **The Royal Cricketers**, overlooking Regents Canal, in Old Ford Road.

London's waterways have been neglected somewhat over recent years and though most canals do have towpaths, in varying states of repair, they are often inaccessible. An excellent pathway has however, been provided along the length of Regents Canal, from Regents Dock to Hammersmith and beyond. Access points should be open between 9.00 and sunset. Angling is restricted to members of the London Anglers Association (details on 520 7477). Anyone interested

in cycling the towpaths should ring 286 6101 to apply for a permit.

A striking aspect of walking canals is the relative speed with which you seem to get from place to place. This walk incorporates the comparative peace of the canal banks, and provides a fairly typical glimpse of the East End environs.

We start from the car park, between the large boating lake in Victoria Park and the Grand Union Canal. From the Grove Road roundabout, enter the gates giving the view of the lake and drive, or indeed, walk along to the end of the lake, to where a clump of trees and bushes stand on the left-hand side. You should also see a set of black cast-iron steps, where a path leads up to the canal. From here, the lake and islands look surprisingly beautiful, inhabited as they are by various ducks and swans. It is worth checking closing times, on your way in, though its usually 16.30.

Following the path up to the canal side, turn left by the lock. On the other side of the canal, the terrace of The Royal Cricketers should be visible. The quickest way to the bar (providing the gate is open) is up the steps to the left and across the roadbridge, but if the gate is locked, which is more than likely, go under the bridge, to pick up the path leading back to the road.

From The Cricketers, head back to the canal, and walk down the lane from the bridge. Go through the gate, down the slope to your left – here there is a little bridge and you should now be on the left of this. Along this section, the Hertford Union Canal (or Sir George Ducketts Canal), is a good paved towpath, to be followed the length of Victoria Park. The first road bridge is Grove Road, the second Old Ford Road. The bank opposite, is for most of the way, occupied by scrapyards and derelict factories, and one wonders at the great human effort that must have been involved in smashing every window in every derelict warehouse. Moored by the timberyard, near the next flight of locks, are old Thames lighters, the sort which regularly ploughed up and down these canals in the heyday of water transport.

At the locks, turn left along the path away from the canal, to the left of the white fence, and through the black door-

way. Cross the canal to the right, and the junction of Jodrell and Parnell Road and bear left along Jodrell Road. At the end, turn left to **The Top o' the Morning**. Then retrace steps back down Wick Lane under the bridges. Passing UKAY, the huge discount warehouse on the right, turn left at the roundabout, into Old Ford Road. Follow Old Ford Road round to **The Iceland**, which stands on the corner of Iceland Street. Continue to the junction with the motorway and cross straight over.

This side of the motorway seems to be a land of scrapyards, some specialising in washing machines and 'white goods', others in iron fencing and drainage pipes, and the biggest of them all in mangled cars.

The Inns

The Top O' the Morning, Victoria Park

The Top O' the Morning, apparently a unique pub name in Britain (there's one other in Majorca), is on the corner of Victoria Park on the banks of the Hertford Union Canal. It has been a pub since 1920 and is therefore contemporaneous with the park. In Victorian times the upstairs doubled as a music hall and the area was a hive of activity; people spending leisurely days in the park before enjoying a good old knees-up in the pub at night.

There's a gruesome story behind this pub's benign Victorian facade – a certain Thomas Briggs was murdered by a German named Muller on a train and thrown onto the track running behind the pub. His body was then brought into The Top O' the Morning (or the Midford Castle, as it was then known). However the crime did not go undetected for long; Muller made the mistake of putting on his victim's hat as he left the train and the law managed to track him down when they discovered his own hat still in the compartment.

There's a panelled bar decorated with stuffed pheasants, a vixen and German beer mugs – and a pool room. There are tables, chairs and umbrellas outside for use in the summer, when landlord Oliver Donnelly gets into his other interest – Gaelic football. The Top O' the Morning is wholeheartedly recommended, not least because of its amazing choice of beers – there's hand-drawn Courage, John Smiths, Watneys and Ben Truman and keg Tartan Bitter, Harp, McEwans, Carlsberg and Guinness and, somewhat unusually for a London pub, draught Murphys. There's a wide variety of bar food with sandwiches, pies, pizzas, soups and salads numbering amongst the ranks. ▶

▶

Cross Wick Lane into Tredegar Road, and take the next left opposite the advertising hoardings, down Fairfield Road. Walk under the railway bridges, passing on your left London Transport's Bow Garage, and at the end cross over to **The Bow Bells**. Continue along Bow Road, under the railway bridge, past the police station. Further up is Bow Road Underground and, further still, the ornate Victorian edifice of the Stepney and Bow Foundation Coborn Girls School. Opposite this, is an example of the somewhat uninspired and dull contemporary architecture typical of the East End. Next on the left is St Clements Hospital.

Bow Road now becomes Mile End Road, and further up on the left is Mile End Underground. At the major junction, go straight across Grove Road, and continue up Mile End Road. Eventually, just before the bridge is a Whitbread's House – **The New Globe**. The landlord here is as likely to serve you a mouthful of abuse, as a pint of beer, so enter at your peril!

At The New Globe cross over to the left into Canal Road, by the large open ground space – King George's Fields. Follow Canal Road as far as the bridge at Solebay Street. A black gate leads off to the left, which in turn leads to another black gate, leading onto the towpath. Turn right, and pass under the bridge. The next bridge is very low as it is actually the Mile End Road. Carry on past the old wharves, under the railway bridge to the next road bridge, and Roman Road. Continue following the path, to the point

The Iceland, Bow

The Iceland sits amongst a jumble of factories, office blocks and scrapyards – a welcome place of refuge in a somewhat dreary landscape. The pub is 130 years old, and was originally a beerhouse . . . sawdust on a white wood floor, buckets of water to keep it clean, you know the sort of thing . . . but then came lino and eventually, carpets. Heavy red velvet curtains and red lamps make for a cosy intimate atmosphere which is reinforced by the friendliness of both staff and the local customers. Beers include Watneys, Ben Truman and Special, with hot pies, sandwiches and rolls to soak it all up. Apparently Glenda Jackson and Oliver Reed shot a scene from a film across the road on the rubbish tip.

The Bow Bells, Bow

An old coaching inn, there's a stableyard out the back where robbers used to hide. Before it was rebuilt in 1865, the pub used to look out onto meadows and cornfields – nowadays its prospect is the busy Bow Road and Bow's Registry Office. The church bells of Bow are located in Aldgate . . . the historic chimes that called Dick Whittington back to London to be inaugurated as Lord Mayor. Another less pleasant 'historic' association is the ghost of a woman who died in the toilets – the poor lady keeps coming back to pull the chain!

Inside, the pub is typically Victorian with red mahogany panelling, tall mirrors and lamps behind the bar, an Adam fireplace and a couple of toilets coyly labelled 'Victoria' and 'Albert'. The atmosphere is friendly and jokey with a Sunday lunchtime piano player and discos in the evenings. The pub serves Taylor Walker (an East End brewery that has recently been revived) and Burton ale on handpump and keg Guinness, DD, Skol and Long Life. Food is cheap and plentiful and includes steak, lamb chop, scampi, cold roast pork, ploughman's and salad, along with the ubiquitous sandwich.

where the Hertford Union Canal joins the Grand Union/Regents Canal. Looking at the Royal Cricketers from here you'd swear it was about to fall over, though its noticeable slant probably evens up a bit after a few pints.

Royal Cricketers, Hackney

In times gone by, landlords had trouble keeping their beer clear in The Royal Cricketers. No matter how carefully they stored it, there were frequent complaints of cloudy beer. Eventually, it was discovered that it was caused by barges, banging up against the canal wall. The pub has always been very closely associated with the canal, and this tradition is upheld by the present landlord Jim Smith, who was a Thames lighterman, and also worked the barges on the Regents Canal. He is now a Freeman of the River Thames. Hopefully by the date of publication of this book, hand-drawn traditional beer will be available, as well as the usual Whitbread Trophy and Tankard.

The hot and cold snacks include sandwiches, home-made steak and kidney pies, oxtail and dumplings. The canal patio and downstairs bar, are only opened in the summer months, except on special occasions. The downstairs bar is known as the Butty Bar, after the barges, whose nameplates are fixed to its walls. Entertainment is provided in the summer by the Mikron Theatre Company, who travel by 'monkey boat', between the canal side pubs.

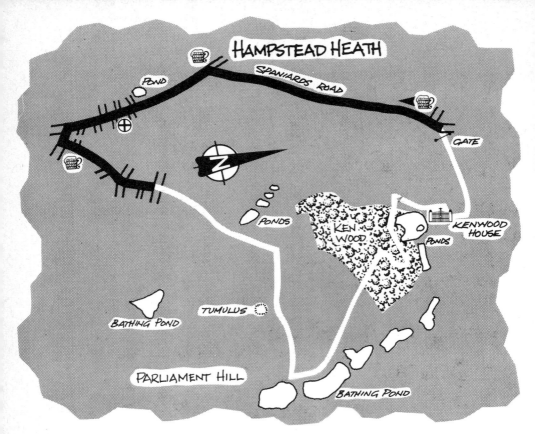

3   Hampstead

APPROXIMATELY 4½ Miles

The District

Hampstead is perhaps London's most infamous village with its fantastic display of 18th century architecture. Nowadays its fashionability is the butt of endless jokes – you are, apparently, a true Hampsteadite if you own a Range Rover, an Afghan hound and play frisbee with the kids on the heath. The first seeds of sophistication were sown in the 18th century when the miraculous powers of the chalybeate spring in Well Walk were advertised. The waters were freshly bottled each morning and sold for 3d a flask at The Eagle and Child in Fleet Street.

The village also has a long tradition of popularity with artists and writers. Notables would descend on the village in droves, equipped with brush or pen – a practice that John Constable observed, and which led him to remark "I love every stile and stump and lane in the village, and, as long as I am able to hold a brush, I shall never cease to paint them". The original street pattern of Hampstead has been largely retained and consists of a tangle of narrow streets, courts, steps and cobbled alleyways. Church Row, a tree-lined avenue teems with some of the finest examples of 18th century architecture, and one-time residents include H G Wells, Gracie Fields and Peter Cook.

The Heath covers about 800 acres of rough grassland and woods and is home to a myriad of animal and plant life. It *is* still possible to 'get away from it all' on the heath although most of the paths are extremely well-trodden. There is a lovely story in Neville Braybrooke's *Book of Hampstead* of a Second World War pilot who made a crash landing, saw a badger waddle across his path and was astounded to discover on checking his instruments that he was less than five miles from Charing Cross. Unsurprisingly legend and folklore abound – including the unlikely siting of the grave of Boadicea under a tumulus, a little to the east of Parliament Hill.

How to Get There
By road Hampstead lies on the A502 Haverstock Hill Road, north of Camden. It can also be reached by turning right off the A41 onto the B511 and A502.
By rail West Hampstead or Hampstead Heath from St Pancras.
By tube to West Hampstead.
By bus numbers 187, 268 and 210.

The Inns

The Hampstead Walk
A walk in this area would not be complete without a visit to Kenwood, which can be made either at the beginning or end of the walk, depending on personal preference. For convenience sake we'll start at **Spaniards Inn** and leave Kenwood until

Spaniards Inn, Hampstead
The Spaniards Inn lies close to Kenwood next to an old toll house which narrows the road, creating a sharp corner. Perhaps its most famous historic connection was its part in preventing the destruction of Kenwood by the Gordon Rioters. Kenwood was the summer residence of Lord Mansfield, Lord Chief Justice of England. His town residence in Bloomsbury was ransacked by the rioters, who then intended the same treatment for Kenwood. They made the mistake of stopping off at the Spaniards Inn for an invigorating quaff 'en route'. Realising their objective, the landlord, Giles Thomas, kept them drinking until the arrival of the military.

The pub is an early 18th century building, thought to have been commissioned originally by James I as a house for a Spanish Ambassador. Dick Turpin (yes, the omnipresent highwayman) was at one time a regular and today his pistols hang on a wall in the bar.

The atmosphere is cheered by the three open coal fires and the low beamed ceilings. Outside is a rose garden with tables and chairs for use in the summer, and an aviary – a delightful setting chosen by Dickens for the arrest of Mrs Bardell in *Pickwick Papers*.

the end. From the inn turn right between the pub and the old toll house. Continue along Spaniards Road, a busy through road across the heath.

At the end on the right, behind the war memorial, is Heath House. This is a fine 18th century house once inhabited by Samuel Hoare and later the Earl of Iveagh who eventually moved into Kenwood and preserved it for the nation. Opposite is **Jack Straws Castle** which has been sharply described as looking like a "grounded Mississipi paddleboat". A little further along is Whitestone Pond, popular with model boat enthusiasts of all and often surprising ages, some of the boats are undoubtedly more sophisticated than many a passing car.

Continue down the hill into Heath Street. Towards the bottom the wine bars, restaurants and boutiques of trendy Hampstead life begin to predominate. The more interesting side of the village lies in the side streets. An example of this is Golden Yard a small picturesque courtyard on the right-hand side of Heath Street.

At the bottom of the hill there is a junction, turn left here into Hampstead High Street. Take the next left into Flask Walk, a narrow lane which once had an arched entrance. Past the shops and on the right is the Flask, an unpretentious pub for Hampstead, with a reputation for wholesome no-frills lunches. It's a Youngs house, which in winter means a quick pint of Winter Warmer before muffling up for the Heath.

From The Flask walk straight on down

the hill and at the end continue along Well Walk, across Christchurch Hill and past the Wells Hotel.

At the end of Well Walk cross East Heath Road onto East Heath. Follow the gravel path straight on along the avenue of lime trees. The path leads down and then up again and is eventually crossed by another gravel path. Walk on past this and the football pitch and then turn right along the path at the cycling prohibited sign. Bear left at the next fork and follow the path down to the ponds – the pond to your right with the high diving board is the mens bathing pond. Take the path left by the ponds to a fence at the end. Bear left along the iron fence then take the next right fork. From the higher part of this path you can just see the secluded ladies bathing pond. At the end of the path go through the gate into Kenwood Woodland Area, a surviving part of the old Forest of Middlesex, which at one time covered most of what is now north-west London. Take the fork to the left and follow the path uphill, taking the second right turn. Bear left at the bottom of the slope and go straight through the arcade of holly bushes. Bear left at the gate and again at the brick shelter, then right at the fork. Turn next left and after a little way a good view of Kenwood House can be seen through the trees. Bear left at the next path and go across the bridge to the right. There, stretching in front of Kenwood, is the lily pond.

Follow the path a little way, then cut across the grass to where the steps can be seen to the left of the house. From here is a good view of Kenwood's two swamp cypresses standing in front of the lily pond. One of these is spire shaped with upsweeping branches. At the top of the steps go left away from the house, taking the path to the right at the end of the grass. Bearing right, the path leads past Barbara Hepworth's well-positioned, if oddly named, sculpture – Monolith-Empyreon (1953). At the end of the path go right where you can see, a little further up in the bushes, Dr Johnson's Summer House, restored in 1967. Continue through the ivy-covered passage to the front of the House.

It is estimated that over half a million people visit Kenwood annually, the star attraction being the splendid library – of Adam design with magnificent columns and a painted ceiling.

Kenwood houses a stunning art collection including Rembrandt's 'Self-Portrait', Stubbs' 'Whistlejacket', Vermeers' 'The Guitar Player' as well as paintings by Reynolds, Turner and Gainsborough.

Back outside Kenwood, follow the gravel roadway to the left and through the gate onto Hampstead Lane. Turn left here to return to the Spaniards Inn.

Popular with the regulars are the famous Spaniards Inn sausages, of which I was proudly informed nearly 12 tons are sold per year. Upstairs is a wine bar where live music is performed during the week. A good selection of food is also available here. Among the regulars are TV and film personalities, many of whom live locally.

Jack Straws Castle, Hampstead

Standing close to the highest point in London, Jack Straws Castle has a unique history. There was never a castle however, and Jack Straw himself lived in a hut close to the present site. He was second in command in a peasants revolt in 1381 against heavy taxation and local inhabitants chose to honour his memory after the revolt by romanticising his hut, lending to it the status of a castle. The title was taken up by inns which have stood on the site for at least three centuries.

Yet again folks, local legend has it that Dick Turpin was a regular, and a hiding place behind the inn was used to tether his infamous mare Black Bess. Another famous past patron was Charles Dickens, who often stayed for long periods, and who is said to have recommended it to a friend as follows: "I knows a good 'ouse where we can have a red hot chop for dinner and a glass of good wine".

The inn was largely destroyed by bombing in the Second World War and its present shape is the result of rebuilding in 1962. The battlements and weatherboarding caused quite a controversy at the time, as they were considered perversely inappropriate. The architect described his work as 'Georgian-Gothic'. Standing about 440 ft above sea level, it offers impressive views over London and on a clear day the reflections from cars on Blackheath can apparently be seen flashing in the distance.

Three times a year (Easter, Whitsun and August Bank Holiday) the Hampstead Fairs are held on the heath opposite. There is a restaurant upstairs but good home-made food is also available in the downstairs bars.

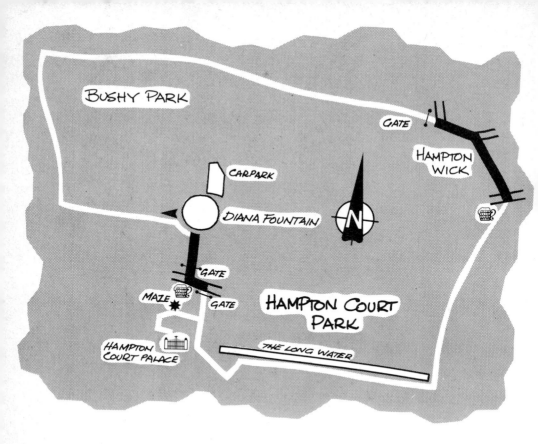

4   Hampton Court

APPROXIMATELY 4¾ Miles

The District

Arriving by road through Kew and Richmond, Kingston comes as something of a shock . . . as it is a very busy built-up area with a one-way system every bit as challenging as Marble Arch. A short walk over the river to the grounds of Hampton Court and the wilds of Bushy Park should transport you back to the days when motor cars were not even a pipe-dream. Hampton Court is perhaps the most emotive of all of London's historical sites; indeed London without it would be like Moscow without the Kremlin! Thomas Wolsey, son of an Ipswich butcher, later to become Cardinal and Lord Chancellor of England and Henry VIII's right-hand man, started work on the palace in 1515. Of Tudor design, the palace was lavishly decorated and furnished – there were, for example, 280 silk beds prepared for guests. Wolsey had a staff of five hundred here, indeed his wealth was said to have been greater than King Henry's, which goes a long way towards explaining his rapid decline and fall. When Henry VIII took over the palace he greatly enlarged it, added some beautiful flower gardens and lived there in great style with his various wives, coats of arms and innumerable courtiers. After Henry, little further work was done until William III and Mary moved in and employed Christopher Wren to start work on the fountain court and the state apartments. The death of

Mary of smallpox in 1694 and William's fatal encounter with a molehill whilst out riding in the park four years later curbed building activity for a while – however the next resident, Queen Anne, was responsible for the infamous maze. Although the maze may seem a desirable place for a quick stroll, if you are hoping to hit the pubs before nightfall it might be as well to forego the temptation . . .

However the attractions of Hampton Court today are as endless as the intrigues and tragedies of its past, the gardens in particular owing something to the grandeur of Versailles.

The known history of Kingston goes back to the 10th century when Saxon kings were crowned here. In the middle of the 19th century the actual coronation stone was rescued from ignominious use as a public mounting block for horses . . . (people?) and was suitably mounted on a stone plinth, restoring it somewhat to its former glory. Kingston has a particularly poor record as regards the preservation of its heritage; in 1971 it was discovered that the borough had fewer historic buildings than any other south of the Thames. Of 28 listed items, two were merely lumps of stone . . .

How to Get There

By road Hampton Court can be reached from the A3 by taking the A308 southwest from London.

By rail to Hampton Court from Waterloo.

By bus numbers 111, 113, 216, 152 (regular), 201, 215 and 211 (irregular) and 715, 716, 725, 718 and 726 (Green Line).

The Hampton Court Walk

This walk combines the mildly rigorous aspects of the deer parks with the beauty

The Inns

The Old Kings Head, Hampton Wick

The Kingston Gate to Home Park stands behind The Old Kings Head, providing easy access to its avenues, ponds and ultimately the grounds of Hampton Court. The pub undoubtedly has a long history though not much is known about it since the rebuilding in the late 19th century. A print on the wall of the bar shows the building as it was around 1895. It was probably an old coaching inn and functioned as a hotel for many years.

A ghost is known to visit the building on occasions, popularly believed to be a witch who drowned on the ducking stool in Hampton Wick Pond. The pond lies just inside the Home Park behind the pub. Model ships decorate the walls of the bars, which are unfussy though comfortable. The lunches are good value and feature traditional English food such as roast beef and Yorkshire pudding, roast pork, home-made savoury pie, or egg, chips and beans. Sunday lunchtime features Big Al on the piano, banging out those old favourites.

The Kings Arms, East Molesey

A choice of seven traditional real ales makes The Kings Arms almost as big an attraction as the Palace itself. The line up

25

of the royal gardens and palace of Hampton Court. Parking can be a problem, but is most easily overcome by using the space available in Bushy Park. This is reached via the gate at the Hampton Court end of Hampton Court Road from Kingston Bridge. Walk back to the fountain from the car park, crossing the road and following the shale path down to the water's edge. There is a good view from here down the length of Chestnut Avenue, which is made up of no less than 274 chestnut trees spaced 42 feet apart.

Walk round the pond as far as the road leading back to the gate, then continue round along the road so as not to miss the next path to the left. This leads into Lime Avenue, where another impressive vista opens out from The Fountain. Bushy Park covers roughly 1100 acres and contains ten miles of lime trees alone. Whenever a tree falls it is replaced. The actual avenue is off this path to the right, so stray off the path and walk on the grass. You'll undoubtedly notice the great abundance of deer, some of which are the ancestors of those introduced by Henry VIII in the 16th century. Other wildlife includes the occasional fox, and as many as 82 species of bird in one year; amongst them are tits, doves, swallows, kestrels, sparrow hawks, owls and woodpeckers. A wooden fence follows the avenue over on the right, keeping the deer out of the woodland gardens. When you reach the break in this fence cut across the grass towards the red brick bridge on the right.

There is a pathway, though it isn't always distinguishable. Cross the bridge and carry straight on, following the wooden fence to the left. This section of the walk can be very muddy in the winter and lethal when mixed with the mounds of dung. Stay on this path, skirting a small brook at the end of the fence, continuing to the right of the hawthorn bushes along the tyre tracks.

At the end are two paths. Take the gravel one to the immediate right. Continue along this track past the car park, and along the road to the T-junction at the main road (Chestnut Avenue). Turn slightly right here and look for the path on the opposite side of the road, going left at the fork. This is Cobbler's Walk named after Timothy Barnet a singleminded 75 year old Hampton Wick shoemaker who prevented Bushy Park from being swallowed up into the private estate of Lord Halifax. Follow Cobblers Walk past the house on the right to the end and go through the gate. There is an interesting inscription on a memorial stone here that reads: "I am unwilling to leave the world worse than I found it". Noble sentiments! From here turn right down Park Road following it round to the right into Park Grove. At the end cross the main road to **The Old Kings Head**.

When you leave the pub go round to the right and through Kingston Gate into Home Park. Follow the road straight ahead and you will see Hampton Wick pond to the right. Bear right at the first fork and left at the second. When you reach a gate walk up the bank to the right to see the magnificent view the length of The Long Water to the Palace. Go through the gate and turn sharp right to walk along The Long Water towards the Palace. On reaching the fence at the end of the canal, head for the large black iron gates to the left. Go through the gate and over the bridge, heading towards the Palace. Walk across the front of the main doors and take the next green gate on the left. Take the path straight ahead. At the first green gateway turn left, following the sign to the State apartments. At the end bear right and then left to the front entrance. Enter the Palace through the red brick arched gatehouse. I'll leave it to you which parts of the palace you visit! On leaving, retrace your steps to the

includes Sam Smiths Old Brewery Bitter, Ruddles County, Wessex Devenish, Everards Tiger, Hall and Woodhouse Badger, Godsons Black Horse, and lastly Watneys London Bitter. The pub stands right next to Lion Gate and overlooks the maze at the back.

Of indeterminate age, The Kings Arms has naturally had close connections with the Palace, not least the sharing of a ghost. The identity of this nocturnal visitor isn't known, though being female it could be one of many said to haunt the Palace, including Henry's third and fifth wives, Jane Seymour and Catherine Howard respectively. Queen Catherine was the second to die on the block and her pleading cries are still heard in what has become known as The Haunted Gallery.

It is claimed that a tunnel once existed between the cellars of The Kings Arms and the Palace, though evidence is no more than hearsay. Unlikely as it is, the imagination has little trouble finding uses for such a passage in almost 400 years of the pub's existence.

Food, as well as drink, is a cut above the average at The Kings Arms – the newly opened restaurant and bar has both an à la carte and a table d'hote menu. The wide selection of bar snacks is of exceptional quality, featuring hot stuffed jacket potatoes with a choice of 15 fillings, hot country bread and butter and a special selection of cheeses.

right as far as the ivy covered arch, which you should pass through. The path then takes you along through fragrant rose gardens, which take up much of the seven acre Tiltyard, once used for jousting tournaments. Pass through the next gate on the right, turn left and take the next path to the right. This leads to the world famous maze, the entrance to which is concealed on the left. (NB Closed from 1st November to 1st March.) The maze was originally planted in 1714, at the end of Queen Anne's reign. Once you have successfully negotiated the maze, turn sharp left and leave the park through the majestic Lion Gate, the stone pillars of which bear the monogram of Queen Anne.

Immediately left outside the gate is **The Kings Arms**, with its battery of hand-drawn favourites such as Godards Black Horse (affectionately known as GBH) and Stan Smiths Old Brewery Bitter.

From The Kings Arms cross the road and head into Bushy Park through the gates next to the Greyhound Hotel (not forgetting the gates close at 16.00) and head back up to the Diana Fountain and car park.

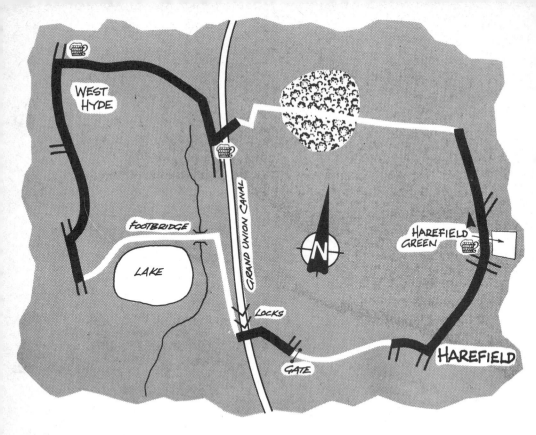

5   Harefield

APPROXIMATELY 4 Miles

The District

Harefield is the oldest parish in what today is the London Borough of Hillingdon. It has an unassuming beauty typical of many English country towns with its valley setting and string of irregularly shaped lakes lying by the river surrounded by wooded uplands. Harefield was accounted for in the Domesday survey where it was assessed as consisting of two mills, meadow for a plough, pasture for the village cattle, pannage for 1200 hogs and four fish ponds containing 1000 eels. The total value was calculated at £12!

The estates are now in the possession of the Newdegate family and have been since they were acquired in 1675.

Harefield Place, the manor house, has known many famous visitors, including the time in 1602 when Queen Elizabeth I dropped in for a long weekend causing everyone to be on their best behaviour. In the midst of this great social whirl was the staging of a new play brought down from London – 'Othello' by a certain William Shakespeare. It is thought most probable that the man himself came down to direct the play. The house was burnt down in 1660. The fire was started by a well-known wit, Sir Charles Smedley, whilst smoking in bed (some people will stop at nothing for a laugh). The house was rebuilt but was demolished at the end of the 19th century and a 'modern' mansion now occupies the site.

The Grand Union Canal which runs through Harefield was the original source of much of the town's income as it linked Harefield to the markets of London.

Another notable feature of Harefield is its picturesque flint, brick and stone parish church, dating back to the 12th century. It is filled with monuments and brasses commemorating past members of the Newdegate family.

How to Get There

By road take the Harefield/Rickmansworth Road south from Rickmansworth (approx 2½ miles).

By rail to Rickmansworth or Ruislip.

By bus the 128 runs regularly between Rickmansworth and Ruislip, or Green Line numbers 347 and 348.

The Harefield Walk

Facing the village green outside **The Kings Arms**, proceed left along Rickmansworth Road. Turn left down Hill End Road past the now famous Harefield Hospital, pioneer in the field of heart transplants. After a short walk you pass the entrance to Whiteheath Farm on your right. A little further up on the left is a public footpath sign. Follow this path between the hospital grounds and Harefield Squash and Sports Centre.

This narrow footpath leads down through a small but picturesque private wood, which gets very steep in places. The path is narrow and for most of its length guarded on either side by iron fencing. Apparently the quiet beauty of the path is a front for a series of unexplained disturbances. Dogs have been known to relinquish a lifetime's subservience and turn all but white haired in their struggle to leave the wood. Other four-legged beings have been known to

The Inns

The Kings Arms, Harefield

The Kings Arms sits by the crossroads in the centre of Harefield opposite the village green. Parts of this black and white half-timbered building are thought to date back to the 15th century. Most of the building however is 17th century.

An old smithy used to stand next to it and the stables out at the back are a testament to the days when the pub was a coaching inn. Nowadays, the smithy's site is occupied by a restaurant featuring a distinctive hammer-beam roof. The locals are friendly and seem to enjoy relating the area's history and legend. All in all it's a comfortable local pub with a large open log fire and attractive low beamed ceilings.

The restaurant offers a three course meal for a fiver. Bar snacks include a variety of hot meals as well as ploughman's, sandwiches and rolls. The forecourt has ample room for parking and as the pub faces on to the busy main road it is easily accessible by car.

The Fisheries, Harefield

Beautifully situated on the Grand Union Canal, The Fisheries also stand by the ancient fishing grounds of the River Colne. These waters have been popular with anglers since Saxon times and a

►

become uncharacteristically placid. There have been reports of wierd apparitions, accompanied by doleful voices and strange sounds. There has been no credible explanation for all this although various 'tall stories' have originated in the bars of local pubs.

There is undoubtedly a connection with the marshy hollow lying at the bottom of the footpath as the water, which used to be much deeper, was rumoured to be inhabited by a water fairy known as The Glaistig. Legend has it that she is part seductive woman and part goat – a fact which she attempts to hide beneath a flowing green dress. After having lured men to dance with her, she feeds vampire-like on their blood. Oddly enough she has also been known to save children from drowning and to have shown kindness to old people! Local folklore is further heightened by the potential power of the local wild primroses which, if eaten, enable one to see fairies. Some farmers hereabouts report that cows have been herded for milking by an invisible presence – one can only presume that they (the farmers) have been on the primroses again.

Anyway to get back to the walk . . . at the end of the footpath, you should follow the dirt track, then turn left along the road. At the end of Summerhouse Lane bear right around the bell tower and continue past the various factory gates to a sharp bend to the right. This is a particularly dangerous spot for pedestrians. Over the canal stands **The Fisheries** which is reached via the little bridge close to the locks and weir, a place which is again steeped in ancient legend. The pub occupies a particularly beautiful location and it is well worth pausing for a while to imbibe the serene and tranquil air (and the beer).

From the Fisheries continue up the road past the car park and away from the canal. After less than half a mile you come across **The Royal Oak** which faces on to the main A412. This is the village of West Hyde, composed of a small cluster of houses around the pub. The brick and timber frame building is the haunt of a quiet, friendly but unusually anonymous ghost. Untroublesome as he is, his popularity is somewhat threatened by his annoying habit of leaving the bolts off doors when going out at night. Unlike many pub ghosts he's thought to be teetotal, the level in the rum bottles being undisturbed. (Rum being the favourite tipple of by far the majority of after hours phantoms.)

From The Royal Oak follow the sign left for Denham. This road runs parallel to the A412, the latter thankfully bearing the brunt of the heavy traffic. Follow it to the end where it meets the A412. Ignore the first green footpath sign, as this would take you back to The Fisheries, continue to the next footpath sign (Footpath number 1. Canal $\frac{1}{2}$ mile) and follow the track round to the left away from the gravel chip bays. Hundreds of ducks find sanctuary on and around these waters, giving amusing displays of courtship at the appropriate time of the year. The gravel roadway curls around the picturesque lake to Rickmansworth Sailing Club.

Before the road turns towards the clubhouse, there is a narrow metal footbridge running over towards the plant hire depot by the river which will bring you out again by the Grand Union Canal. Turn right along the towpath. The River Colne runs off down the weir to the right at the bridge. Further up is a lock next to which stands an attractive half-timber thatched cottage. There is a grand old building next to the lock, dated 1870, which now functions as Black Jacks Mill Restaurant. You should swing left over the bridge here and at the road bear right. On the corner, a little further up, is an iron gate and stile. Climb the stile and make your way diagonally across the field at about 45° to the canal. A colourful parade of canal boats are often moored along the bank here.

Head for a large tree in the corner where you'll see two concrete posts marked with white arrows showing the direction of the footpath up through the trees. Once through the trees, skirt the bracken to the left along the easily identifiable track. There is a good view at this point back over the shimmering lakes. Continue straight on at the stile, eventually arriving at a gate. This brings us into Merle Avenue leading down to Rickmansworth Road. Here turn left along Harefield's main shopping street to eventually arrive at the green and The Kings Arms.

proliferation of eels here was referred to in the Domesday Book.

According to legend a small monastic settlement originally occupied the site. The ghost of one of this brethren is thought by locals to return periodically, apparently the pub is his favourite haunting ground. The inn probably started life as a coaching stop, as it has stables out the back. These proved useful in later years to house the canal horses that pulled the early barges. The pub is completely surrounded by water and has a large car park at the back.

The Royal Oak, Rickmansworth

For the best beers on this walk call in at The Royal Oak. The Winter Royal, Trophy and SPA are all brewed locally at Marlow and are hand-drawn. West Hyde is a small place consisting of very few houses and the pub — which was first built as a coaching inn in the 18th century, though it has seen much alteration since.

The lunches, served in the restaurant, are very popular as they are reasonably priced and generally show a wide variety including steaks, omelettes, chicken, gammon and trout. Alternative quick snacks include pizza, beefburger, hotdog, and steak and kidney pie and the usual sandwiches and rolls.

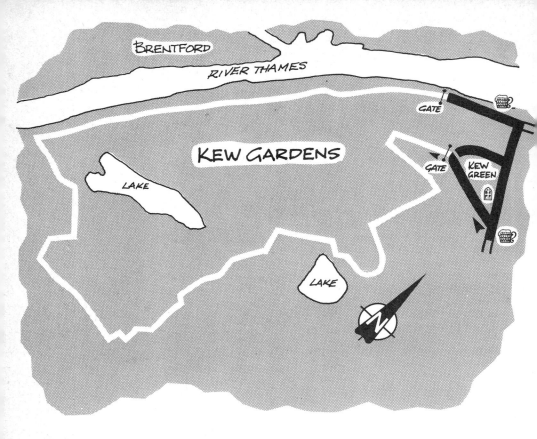

6   Kew

APPROXIMATELY 4 Miles

The District

The name Kew has undergone various transformations – the original spelling 'kaiho' referring to the proximity of Kew to the quay and the river. Kew has a large village green dominated by the parish church of St Anne's, with the impressive gates of the botanical gardens to one side and the main road and the village pond to the other. This was originally a backwater of the Thames where it is said Henry VIII would moor his barge before galloping off to Richmond Palace.

The village is reached by road over Kew Bridge where, in 1760, a messenger broke the news of the King's death to his heir Prince George Frederick and presumably prevented him from fal-

ling (or leaping?) into the river. On the riverside is a Georgian house containing the Kew Herbarium, open only to specialists, it harbours specimens of over seven million dried plants.

Kew Gardens were handed over to the nation in 1841. Originally a private obsession of Lord Capel's, a man bewitched by strange and exotic plants, the land was leased out to the Royal family when he died. Kew became increasingly popular in the 18th century as a fashionable place for rendezvous. The gardens were opened in the summer months for one day a week, entrance being restricted to persons 'genteely dressed'. Eventually Queen Charlotte, wife of George III was forced to seek a more secluded retreat and the Queen's Cottage was built as a place where she could picnic in peace. The grounds remain the quietest area today and it is possible to see a wide variety of birds here, often at close quarters. Other notable buildings and landmarks include Kew Palace, built in 1631 for a Dutch merchant and taken over as a permanent place of residence for George III and his 15 children; the Pagoda, a ten-storey octagonal building and the Orangery which is now an exhibition area.

The Queen's Garden, behind Kew Palace, was opened to the public in 1969 by Elizabeth II, and is laid out in 17th century fashion with a parterre, a sunken garden and a gazebo (a roofed structure, open on all sides).

How to Get There
By road Kew lies on the A307 which can be reached from the A205 South Circular Road.
By rail to Kew Bridge from Waterloo or Kew Gardens from Broad Street.
By tube to Kew Gardens.
By bus numbers 27, 65 and 90B.

The Kew Walk
The starting point for this walk is the famous **Coach and Horses Hotel**. The pub fronts on to Kew Road in a corner of the green facing out towards the Botanical Gardens. It may be reached most easily by public transport, via Kew Bridge Station and Kew Bridge itself. From the front of the station strike out over the bridge down towards the Coach and Horses on the left side of the Green. Alternatively, parking space is available either around the Green (depending on the time of year) or in the car park of the Gardens, which is well signposted. From the front of The Coach and Horses cross Kew Road and walk down the side of the Green towards the architectural mass of The Parish Church of St Annes. The church has close connections with the Royal Family and is indeed known as a Royal Church. The Painters Gainsborough and Zoffany are buried in the churchyard.

Proceed from the church towards the huge wrought and gilt main gates of Kew Gardens, at the far end of the Green. The gardens are open daily from 10.00

The Inns

The Coach and Horses Hotel, Kew Green
The Coach and Horses dates back to the 16th century when it was a natural stop off point for journeys short and long. There are some original old stables at the back and it is known that royalty has visited the pub in the past. The wooden panelling, low ceilings and exposed beams in the one large bar help maintain a genial atmosphere. There is a separate luncheon restaurant with a full a la carte menu and good selection of wines. There is also an extensive snack menu — specialising in various home-made pies.

All the beers are hand-drawn, including Youngs Ordinary Bitter, Special Bitter and Winter Warmer. There is also London lager, and the standard bottled beers and spirits. A large garden with tables and umbrellas lies at the back where children may be left if necessary.

Rose and Crown, Kew Green
The Rose and Crown stands on the river side of Kew Green. The origins of the pub lie somewhere in the early 1800s. The inside is wooden panelled and cosy and its most loyal customer has frequented the house for seventy years.

(except Christmas Day and New Year's Day) until 16.00 in winter and 20.00 in summer. For opening times of the various glasshouses and museums check at the gates. Admission to the gardens is a mere 10p, which I'm sure you'll later agree is the best tenpenceworth in London. The gardens cover more than 300 acres and support an incredible 45,000 species of plant.

Once through the turnstile, walk straight ahead along Broad Walk passing Aroid House (belonging to the Lily Family). Take the next path left around to the front of what is known as The Orangery – here you'll find an orientation exhibition and a detailed guide can be bought for 75p.

Out of the Bookshop turn left staying on the same path. Cross over a path and take the next right fork after the gateway round to the Succulent House. From here you can see the Cambridge Cottage Garden (where the Duke of Cambridge once lived) and the iris and bulb gardens. At the end of the Succulent House, walk straight on between the giant tufts of the 'tall grasses' either side of the path. On the left is in fact the 'Grass Garden' where a multitude of grasses and bamboos are cultivated. The houses behind the Grass Garden are known as the T-Range (from the original shape) – watch out for the one way system, essential in the summer. To the right is the old Ice House which pre-dates the gardens and is barely visible now beneath the ivy. Take a left at the crossroads by the Ice House and stay on this path to where the Temple of Aeolus stands atop an artificial mound. On your left at this point is the Rose Pergola, and to its left the Rock Gardens, all of which are worth a visit.

The Temple of Aeolus is one of a number of strange and peculiarly out of place constructions dotted around the gardens. These are generally the 'follies' of Sir William Chambers, an architect with an eye for the bizarre and include the 163 ft Pagoda (which contains nothing more than a staircase), the Ruined Arch and Temples of Bellona and Arethusa.

Take the path to the right before the Cumberland Gate and follow it round past the drinking fountain and museum (see doorway for details of opening times). At this point you are confronted by the most stunning view in the gardens – looking out across the enormous pond with its fountain you can see the Queen Beasts, above which towers the glass Palm House, its giant foliage outlined against the sky. Skirt the lake to the right following the path past the Circle to the Palm House, where you should climb the spiral staircases and walk amidst the treetop foliage.

Leave the Palm House via the same door and turn left to resume the walk. Follow the semi-circle of the Rose Garden and take the second pathway off to the right. This leads through the Japanese cherries to King William's Temple. Walk around and past this along the path leading directly away from the Temple. This pathway is surrounded by mixed shrubs. Ahead is the second of the giant glasshouses – The Temperate House, the largest ornamental glasshouse in the world. Enter the house from this end and hope to reach the other side before it gets dark. Alternatively, follow the path round to the right and call in at the Australian House. Take the path directly away from the Temperate House and turn first left towards the Pagoda and refreshment pavillion.

Retrace your steps along this same path after refreshment and a visit to the Pagoda. Stay on this path (Oak Avenue) to the end and then continue in a straight line on to the grass and along the clearly defined avenue of trees. It is important to continue in as straight a line as possible. When you encounter a crossways path, turn right, passing on the right, the giant Redwoods from California. Take the next turning on the right. On the way down this path you'll notice to the right an avenue of trees named Cedar Vista which gives a clear view back down to the Pagoda. At this point turn left and strike out over the grass up Cedar Vista away from the Pagoda. The next path encountered is the end of Cedar Vista, straight ahead is an artificial lake. Turn left and stay with this path – bearing right at both intersections on the bends.

The area to the left are the grounds of Queen Charlotte's Cottage and if you wish to visit them you should take the path to the left at the drinking fountain and then retrace your steps to rejoin the walk. Otherwise continue to the end of the path and turn right to follow the riverside path.

When you come to some giant oak trees, leave the path and continue over the grass along what is called Riverside Avenue. Follow the Avenue until you reach a gate on the left where you leave the gardens (Brentford Gate) and join the river path across the car park. Take care, as the banks are steep and often muddy.

The large red brick structure to your right is Kew Palace, built in 1631. Follow the river path until you reach a sign pointing right to The Royal Botanical Gardens Main Gate. Follow this direction out to the Green and turn left. Walk up this side of the Green until you reach the welcome sign of the **Rose and Crown**. There are actually three pubs here, giving either a choice or a crawl. After the Rose and Crown is The Kings Arms – also a Courage house. Across Kew Road facing that section of the common is The Antelope, an eye-catching black and white building.

Hand-drawn Directors Bitter is on tap, along with Tavern, JC, lagers and draught Guinness. Various hot and cold snacks are available at lunchtime, though hot food isn't 'on' in the evenings. There is a garden at the back and verandah with tables at the front.

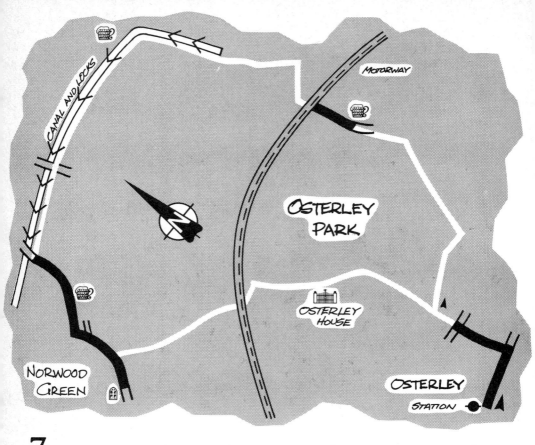

7   Osterley Park

APPROXIMATELY 4¾ Miles

The District

Taking a walk around Osterley Park and its surrounds is like biting into some historical layer cake which will only occasionally set your teeth on edge. There is no chance to tell yourself on setting out from the station that you are headed for some rustic idyll as the jets scream their way to Heathrow and you step out into the Great West Road.

But once round the corner, you are in a district about which you can be faintly nostalgic if you have a taste for the suburbs. Thornbury Road is a quiet shopping street where getting the groceries was possibly once a social event and not a chore. Just past the railway bridge is a secondhand bookshop that looks worth a

browse before entering the park itself.

Locals say that the great houses of Osterley and Syon Parks were built as acts of rivalry to see who could reach the greater heights of opulence. Certainly there was no lack of wealth, as the original manor, now probably the stable block, was built by Sir Thomas Gresham, one of the most prosperous merchants of his age and founder of the Royal Exchange.

A chronicler of the time tells how Elizabeth I remarked that she would prefer one forecourt of the house to be divided by a wall. Overnight, workmen were brought in and the wall erected – all of which led witty courtiers to observe that Sir Thomas "could so soon change a building as he had built a ' Change and that a house was easier divided than united". Such a fun-loving bunch.

Later owners, the Child family, used the money made in banking to build themselves the main house, a monument to 18th century classicism. It was initially designed by Sir William Chambers and furnished by Robert Adam and it is Adam's interior work (in the Chambers!) and furniture designs that make the house almost unique. The stable block, Adam's semi-circular garden house, the Doric Temple and the ornamental lakes make the grounds of the house well worth a look around.

But, if the house is worth giving yourself plenty of time for, there is much more to see before you return from a walk, which at times, is more like a guided tour of transport history. When you leave the grounds, you hit one of those barren stretches of roadway that only motorway planners seem capable of designing; so grit your teeth as you pass under the M4, cushioning yourself with the thought that without such sterility, the trains would be unbearably packed.

Reaching the Grand Union Canal where it joins the River Brent is like stepping through a time warp though unfortunately there is little left of the industrial traffic that brought the canal system into existence. Along the canal are the half sunken remains of several working barges – symbols, of our mismanaged transport policies. At the bottom lock are ponds, now becoming choked with organic slime. They once fed the locks with water, to compensate for the frequent opening and closing. On the same bank as the towpath is a high wall enclosing St Bernard's Hospital. Rumour has it that the ghosts of two nuns haunt the spot where, one foggy night they fell into

The Inns

The Hare and Hounds, Windmill Lane, Osterley

This attractive mock Tudor building dates from 1904 and stands on the spot where local farm workers once slaked their thirst during harvesting. It originally had four bars and a skittle alley now all replaced by a horseshoe bar though enough of the leaded light windows and open hearth period grates remain to give the room a comfortable lived-in atmosphere.

Mr Darko Luger has three Fullers Bitters on handpumps, Extra Special, Ordinary Best and London Pride, plus Hock (a mild). Keg draughts are Guinness, Harp and Kronenburg and Strongbow cider. There's a choice of wine in bottles and by the glass and a substantial range of spirits and Fullers bottled beers. Hot and cold snacks are served.

The large garden is especially well suited for children, away from the main road and with a slide, a seesaw and swings. Summer nights sometimes see parties in the garden featuring Caribbean steel bands. Pub games are darts, fruit machines and the dreaded Space Invaders.

the canal and drowned. Watch out for the cyclists who like to sprint on this section and who would doubtless have done for the sisters, with or without fog.

Further along is the point where the road crosses the canal and the canal crosses the railway. Now your transport lesson is really motoring – I mean steaming – perhaps cruising. Take your pick.

At the end of this section, you find yourself walking back through suburban landscape and the kind of inter-war architecture – notable only for its restrained variety. It ends at Tentelow Lane which still has the feel of village life hovering somewhere between the 14th century church, the pub and, on the right hand side of the road, the curious small building marked "Free School". Back into Osterley Park again, on the run-in to the house and grounds, you should see plenty of reminders that you are, for all the jets, motorways, railways and canals, in a pocket of farming country and animals will get killed if you leave gates open.

How to Get There
By road follow the A4 Great West Road out of London which passes to the south of Osterley Park.
By tube to Osterley Park.
By bus numbers 111 and 120 (regular), 110, 91 and 116 (irregular), and 320 and 704 (Green Line).

The Osterley Park Walk
As may have been apparent, the introduction was rather more linear than usual and so it's advisable, when walking, to read the introduction and the walk instructions in conjunction, for maximum information and enjoyment.

Take the Piccadilly line, Heathrow Central branch, to Osterley Park Station. On leaving the station, turn left along the Great West Road. At the first set of traffic lights, with a Mobil garage on your left, turn up left Thornbury Road. Walk past the shops and across the railway bridge to the T-junction. The main drive into Osterley Park is ahead on the other side of the road. Go through the gates, past the gate-house to the first set of white gates 250 yards on. On the right, immediately before these is a kissing-gate. Follow the fenced path beyond it, to a second gate where the path makes a dog-leg round the perimeter of the park. The path is clearly defined by fencing until you come to a brick wall where it emerges on to a green in front of another park entrance. Walk past the twin white gate-houses without re-entering the park itself and make for the road. On the far side is **The Hare and Hounds.**

Turn right out of the pub and walk towards the motorway which crosses the road. Continue under the M4 and the road bends left. The footpath on this side of the road ends at Warren Farm playing Fields. Turn right down a narrow path running between the high link fences separating the playing fields and neighbouring field. At the bottom is a railway line. Turn left and continue to walk along the outside of the playing field perimeter, until you come to a level crossing which leads to a stile. Cross this and walk straight on to a second stile 50 yards away which leads on to the canal bank.

Take the path leading to the first set of locks on your left and cross these by

means of a narrow walkway on the upper lock gate.

Turn right and walk across the footbridge where the River Brent joins the canal.

Turn left at the end of the bridge and walk 75 yards up Green Lane until you see **The Fox** on your right. When you leave the pub, retrace your steps to the canal lock and continue to walk up the path, without crossing the canal, past five more locks. At the bridge, the canal crosses the railway and the road crosses the canal. Continue under the road bridge along the canal towpath past another lock to the next white bridge. Walk under it and turn sharp right to join the road and cross the canal.

Fifty yards down the road, take the right fork along Melbury Avenue until you come to a junction with Minterne Avenue, where you turn left. This road meets Tentelow Lane and you turn right along it and cross it. 200 yards up Tentelow Lane on the left is **The Plough**. With your thirst drenched, take a narrow footpath that starts between the pub and its outhouses. The path crosses a residential street and leads straight back into Osterley Park.

Follow the path as it bears slightly left across the field towards a roadbridge over the motorway, clearly visible. Cross the motorway by this bridge and follow the road round to twin gate-houses which you walk between. This drive leads to the main house and its stable block. As you leave the front entrance of the house, walk towards the ornamental lake which is on the right, and take the path running between two stretches of water. This drive leads back to the first gate you entered. From here, retrace your steps to the Underground station.

The Fox, Green Lane, Hanwell

The Fox is near enough London's waterways to have once been a waterman's pub. The building is thought to date from the first half of the 19th century. A solid Victorian pub with overhanging eaves and ornate doorway, it dominates a row of artisans' cottages further down the lane.

Inside, the bar is one room with a dining area to the rear. The walls are in dark wood panelling and the ceiling has exposed 'rafters'. Courage Directors and Best Bitter are on handpump and the kegs are Tavern, Bitter, Guinness, Harp Special and Kronenburg. There is a wine list, full Courage range of bottled beers, spirits and sherries.

The Fox's main boast is its lunchtime menu, Mondays to Fridays, 12.00-14.00. There's a full menu with fresh vegetables at reasonable rates and a range of bar snacks, sandwiches, rolls and home-made pasties.

The only pub game is darts and there is taped background music. Children can be catered for in the garden which has a lawn, benches and tables.

The Plough, Tentelow Lane, Southall

The Plough is more than 600 years old and is listed. Possibly, it was built to house workmen building the church which stands opposite. It has withstood the ravages of time better than many and landlord Peter Wilson still has one of the original oak bricks used in its interior walls. Its stables suggest a link with coach travel.

A ghost reputedly walks outside but will not come in (a teetotaller?) despite the friendly atmosphere and the good beer. Fullers Extra Special, London Pride, Ordinary and Chiswick cask conditioned are on handpumps. The kegs are Harp and Guinness and there is a range of bottled and canned beers. Wine is available by the glass. There is a range of bar snacks and hot and cold meals, with a daily 'home-cooked' special.

Children are welcome in the garden which has paving stones, tables and umbrellas.

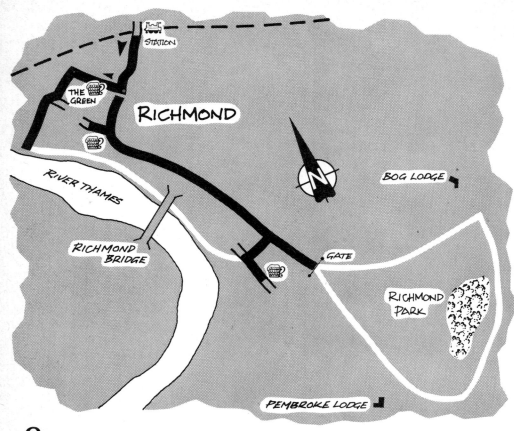

8   Richmond

The District

Richmond may be tainted by the brashness of 20th century building development but on the whole it has retained a charm and elegance that dates back to the days when it was first made a Royal Manor. In the 19th century the novelist Nancy Mitford saw Richmond as "a sort of fairyland, a piece of old Arcadia, a holiday spot for ladies and gentlemen" and despite its proximity to the 'big smoke', this description still seems remarkably accurate today.

A favourite with royalty (the present Queen is still 'Lord' of the manor) the area was originally known as Schene (hence East Sheen) and housed the royal palace, but when Richard II's wife Anne died there he cursed it and had it demolished. Henry VII eventually commissioned the building of a magnificent palace covering some ten acres and renamed it Richmond. The Tudors basked in their luxuriant lifestyle at Richmond and enjoyed regular jousting tournaments and pageants on Richmond Green. Wardrobe Court, a long row of buildings, and Gate House are the only parts of the palace that remain standing.

Richmond is the proud possessor of what has been deemed "the most beautiful urban green in England" where, on summer evenings, the constant crack of the cricket bat can be heard. It is surrounded by all manner of architectural riches, including Maids of Honour Row, built by George I as lodgings for the court's ladies-in-waiting. These ladies lent their name to a particularly delicious cheesecake (still on sale in Richmond) the original recipe of which is rumoured to have fetched £1,000.

The park was first enclosed, despite opposition from local landowners, by Charles I in 1637. Its most famous inhabitants today are the red and fallow deer which roam freely over its 2,000 acres and Princess Alexandra and Angus Ogilvy, who have occupied Thatched Lodge Cottage since their marriage in 1963. In the middle of the park are the Pen Ponds, artificially created in the 18th century and now choc-a-bloc with carp, eels, roach, perch and pike. As much of the park is scrub and coarse woodland it gives rise to many notoriously shy and furtive residents, such as foxes, badgers, weasels, and grey squirrels.

How to Get There

By road Richmond can be reached by taking the A3 and then the A308 or the A205 South Circular Road from central London.
By rail to Richmond from Waterloo and Broad Street.
By tube to Richmond.
By bus numbers 27, 37, 65, 90 and 290 (regular), 33, 71, 73 and 265 (irregular) and 714 and 716 (Green Line).

The Richmond Walk

If you travel by train, turn left from the station and cross the road at the zebra crossing. Continue down until the road forks. Turn right at this point down Duke Street and head straight for **The Cobwebs** on the left-hand side. The walk proper starts from The Cobwebs on Duke Street between the High Street

The Inns

The Cobwebs, Richmond

Established in 1601, The Cobwebs has close links with the famous Richmond Theatre, which is just around the corner. The name conjures up images of a somewhat murky interior, though the days when it was threatened with the loss of its license, unless the ceiling was cleaned, are long past. Old theatre bills, many signed, adorn the walls, attesting to the patronage of visiting actors and actresses. A former Cobwebs barmaid, found fame by becoming the first woman to sail single-handed round the world — resulting in the ordeal of meeting Eamonn Andrews on *This Is Your Life*. Cottage pie, pizza and practically anything with chips, go down well with the hand-drawn Stag and London Bitters Watneys Special and Ben Truman are alternatives but I would recommend giving the draught Guinness the 'once over' first.

Rose of York, Richmond

Once the stables of Nightingale Hall, the Rose of York is the only Samuel Smiths house in London. The terrace, which in summer is bordered by white roses, looks down over green pasture, to the and the green. Having sampled the Stag or London bitters continue down Duke Street to stylish Richmond Green. Cross the road and follow the footpath which runs diagonally across the Green. The expanse of grass is surrounded by a beautiful tree-lined square, containing a mixture of Georgian, Queen Anne and Victorian buildings. To the right there are also modern houses, which, though fairly inconspicuous do not contribute to its elegant character. As cricket matches take place here in the summer it might be advisable to walk round the edge.

Having crossed the green, go into Old Palace Lane in the corner and follow it round to the river. To your left is a good view of Asgill House, a Palladian style villa built around 1758, for Sir Charles Asgill who became Lord Mayor. The stretch of bank by Twickenham Bridge is a mooring for various barges and river boats and, at low water, it is possible to walk along part of it on the shale of the river bed, keeping an eye open for any priceless remnants from the royal past of Richmond, which might be left uncovered by the ebbing tides. This attractive riverscape also takes in many swans and the weeping willows of the eyot opposite.

Continue down to Richmond Bridge – a feature of Thames life since 1777, it was constructed in Portland stone to replace the old horse-ferry. A low archway takes you under the bridge to Richmond Landing Stage and a refreshment area. There is also a pizza restaurant open all year from 18.00 until midnight. River trips are possible for most of the year from nearby Richmond Canoe Club. Rejoin the river path and follow it to its end, on Petersham Road. Turn right at the road and you should see the enticing sign of Samuel Smiths' **Rose of York.**

When you leave the pub retrace your steps to the first turning right – Nightingale Lane, signposted to Petersham Hotel. Now suitably fortified for the steep 1:6 climb, stride uphill to Wick House, a past residence of Sir Joshua Reynolds who used it mainly for entertaining, between 1772 and 1792. Turn right and head for the gates of Richmond Park, which should now be clearly visible.

Inside the gates follow the road which forks right and leads to the car park, and gates of Pembroke Lodge. It is open to the public and a short walk around the gardens is recommended. From the car park take the next path to the left, past Oak Lodge, and into the extensive woods of solid English oak. Over to the right are Pen Ponds. The path becomes less distinguishable, but try and stay on it, keeping to the fence and bearing to the left at the fork. Then bear right away from the fence as it curves left and stay on this path until you reach the road. There are usually large numbers of deer in this area, staring intently as you pass by, which can be quite an unnerving experience. Take the road back to Richmond Gate. If you are feeling really energetic, buy a map from the gate-keeper in order to be able to explore the park more fully. Go right outside the gates, cross the zebra crossing, continue past the ornate RSPCA fountain, heading in the direction of Wick House. Once on Richmond Hill it is easy to understand why the view is so well known, in particular the famous and much painted bend in the river. It is claimed that from the viewing platform here Windsor Castle can be seen on a clear day, as well as at least parts of six counties.

Stay on Richmond Hill, walk past the Terrace Gardens on the left, and a little further down, on the right, the fantastic Old Vicarage School appears like a giant castle in white icing. You can tell you are nearing the town centre as there is a sudden proliferation of wine bars, restaurants and antique shops. At the

junction with the main street, cross to the left, and just past the post office is **The Old Ship.**

From The Old Ship go straight up the bustling main street – George Street, which is directly opposite. Duke Street runs off to the left further along, and the station is over the bridge on the right.

famous bend in the river, featured in the paintings of Reynolds and Turner. Inside, the large bar has been recently refurbished entirely in English oak. The award of 'Pub of the Year 1980', seems well justified. Apart from the spirits, the drinks are all Samuel Smiths, including hand-drawn Old Brewery Bitter, keg Sovereign and several draught lagers. Food at the Rose of York is a speciality, as it is all home-cooked and prepared. A typical menu includes soups, pâté, roast turkey, oysters, poached trout, pickwick pie and various salads – and that's not the complete picture. Friendly staff, open fires, the smell of English oak, good food, and Old Brewery Bitter – what more could you ask for?

The Old Ship, Richmond
This former 17th century coaching inn has undergone a total transformation and is now a mock steamship! In fact, this has turned out none too badly and you can almost feel the floor moving in the back bar – although I suppose this could be due to the potency of the Winter Warmer. If Winter Warmer isn't on, there's Ordinary and Special Bitter, both hand-drawn; Youngs lager, or draught Guinness. Included in the home-cooked snack menu, are bubble and squeak, shepherd's pie, and scotch eggs.

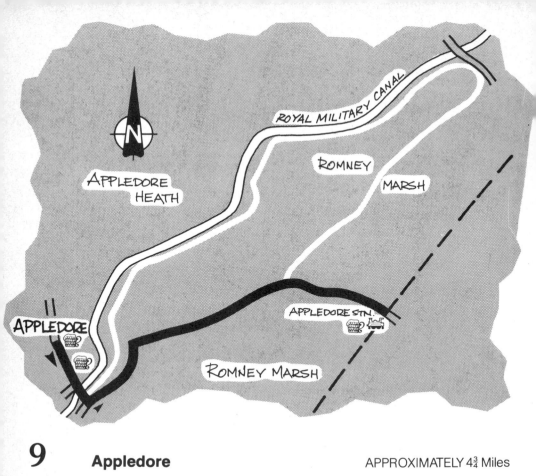

9   **Appledore**

APPROXIMATELY 4¾ Miles

The District

One of the most amazing things about Appledore is the fact that it once stood on a spit of land jutting out over the mudflats of the old English Channel. Where the oddly atmospheric landscape of Romney Marsh begins on the southern side of the Royal Military Canal, there was once a maze of muddy shallows and saltings, at low tide, which became a windlashed yet navigable creek at high tide. This coastal access worked two ways; it brought the village trade but also made it a stopover point on the main invasion route from the continent.

The former inhabitants of what is now a quiet and relaxed Kent village, mercifully free of modern traffic, witnessed the arri-

val of Julius Caesar at the time of tidal lagoons and swamps, when the roaming Roman built walls nearby to hold back the sea. In 892, a Danish invasion fleet of 250 long ships rowed up the Rother Estuary, hove to at Alpudre (meaning 'at the apple tree') and built an earthwork as a prelude to ravaging the countryside: it took King Alfred and his men 5 years to dislodge them. In 1380 it was the turn of the French to disrupt village social life when they set fire to the church and everything else that would burn, then a year later it was the local men themselves who shattered the peace by joining Wat Tyler's peasant rebellion. In 1450 the men of Appledore again took up arms, this time in the name of Jack Cade, another peasant leader. The village population diminished in the 17th and 18th centuries, as the seaway silted up and left Appledore stranded.

The Royal Military (or Shorncliff and Rye) Canal, 'which describes a 30 mile arc round Romney Marsh', was dug in 1804 to prevent invasion by Napoleon. Unique in being built for military purposes, it was designed both as a means of communication for troops and as a barrier to progress across what was, and still is, very flat land. Barely elevated above sea level, it zig-zags every 500 yards or so and this meant that cannons could be placed at each bend to command an extensive line of fire . . . really, the idea of it was to buy time to rally defences. In 1807, an act was passed bringing the canal into commercial operation and till the railway arrived in 1851 it provided a regular barge and passenger service while serving the additional purpose of helping to drain the surrounding marshes. In 1877 it was leased for one shilling per annum to the Jurats of the Level of Romney Marsh and fell into disuse till it was re-fortified for use against Hitler in the Second World War. Again it never saw action but you can still see pillboxes on the canal's landward side.

"The world, according to the best geographers, is divided into Europe, Asia, Africa, America and Romney Marsh" or so wrote Barham in his *Ingoldsby Legends.* Lombard put it differently and announced derogatorily of the Marsh that, "a man would rather finde goode grasse under foote than holesome Aire above the head". Romney Marsh is famous for its 200,000 sheep — descendants of the breed that almost caused the collapse of English agriculture when huge numbers were success-

The Inns

The Red Lion, Appledore

The Red Lion stands at the southern end of Appledore's quiet main street, opposite a garden with an old Howitzer gun from the war Memorial at Cranbrook. The pub was built in the Thirties on the site of a 17th century coaching inn, whose picture you can see on the wall. In those days, there was one coach a day and now local transport consists of one bus a week. That's progress for you.

The building itself is brickbuilt and 'neo-Georgian' and inside there's one bar with decorations which include a gnu skull, a ditching spade used to 'unearth' the canal, pig ring pliers, a hop fork, a thatching stick, manhandling shears and an old beer funnel.

Beers include hand-drawn Courages Best and Directors and snacks come hot and cold, including chilli con carne and scampi. In summer, there are tables outside.

The Railway Inn, Appledore

Six miles along the track from Tenterden, and six miles from Rye in the opposite direction, stands Appledore Station and next to it, The Railway Inn. The present pub was built around 1900 when the old one started subsiding into the nearby

45

fully exported to the American prairies; its giant frogs, 5″ long and the largest in Europe – descendants of a breed loosed by a much-travelled zoologist – and its 'owlers' or smugglers, a breed of men who swopped local wool for lace, tobacco and spirits and 'tuwit-tawoos' in clandestine recognition. Their exploits inspired Kipling:– ''If you wake at midnight and hear a horse's feet/ Don't go drawing back the blinds or looking in the street/ Them that ask no questions isn't told a lie/ Watch the wall, my darling, while the gentlemen go by/ ''.

Nearby Tenterden is the epitome of a graceful Kentish Town. Thought to be William Caxton's birthplace, it has a tapering high street lined with Georgian shops and weatherboarded houses. The Kent and Sussex Railway offers veteran steam engines and a steep run with fantastic views between April and December and Tenterden and Sussex. St Mildred's tower offers a steep climb and just as fantastic views, if you manage to reach the top under your own steam.

The walk is as flat as the proverbial pancake, stretching as it does all the way from Appledore to Higham Farm, then back along the bank of the Royal Military Canal. Your altitude will average a steady 3 metres above sea level and gumboots should be worn for full enjoyment.

How to Get There

By road take the B2080 south-east from Tenterden, Appledore is approx 5 miles along the road.
By rail direct to Appledore.

The Appledore Walk

Turn left from **The Red Lion** into Appledore's wide, pleasant main (and almost only) street and go into the 13th Century church of SS Peter and Paul which is almost next door. The arch of the tower still bears the scorch marks left by the unruly French raider who ransacked and raided the village on an uninvited visit in the 14th century and left it ablaze and gory. Below your feet lies the sole surviving portion of Sir Philip Chute who was Henry VIII's standard bearer. Buried in the church in 1567, poor Sir Philip's body was displaced and jettisoned by uncaring workmen who wanted to make space for the Munk family vault in 1817. Only his jawbone was left behind (no doubt, it had dropped off in astonishment) and this was 'reverrently re-interred' at a later date – 'sic transit gloria mundi' as the church guide so aptly puts it. Then there's former curate Robert Combe who chose unconventional burial 'with unfastened coffin and coffin deep only', not far beneath your feet and not locked in either. Further in this morbid vein, look in the churchyard and you should find the grave of Sally Wimble aged 10 and a butcher's boy who fought at Waterloo. If by now you feel the need of a little light relief, cast your eye over the rules for campanologists at the back of the building, which should (w)ring a few smiles from you.

To continue, go left from the church gate and pass 'The Studio' on your right along the narrow road. Going out of town, cross the bridge and thereby the canal, too; eyes right for the waterside pillbox. Swing left after the bridge with the canal now on *your left* and, beyond it, the church. To your right is 'Appledores Answer' which begs an obvious question or two; the line of hedge is Lausania, the sheds are former aircraft hangers and the huge 'crazy golf course' is a garden centre. Follow the road which bends left with the canal, then right without it. Though normally quiet, the road can be busy so wend a fairly wary way past white weatherboarded houses and gardens. Look out for makeshift chicken coops in orchards and a flock of goatish looking Jacob's sheep.

On your right you'll pass Rheewall Cottage and Brick on Edge and flat fields

which may be golden with corn in summer but which can be unremittingly flat in bleak mid-winter. The landscape here has the peculiar atmosphere of Romney Marsh; it is shaped by trees and hedges and dominated by the sky. 600 yards or so past Brick on Edge, just where the road swings right towards Blackmore Farm, you'll find a stony track to the left marked 'public footpath'.

Detour. If you wish to visit **The Railway Inn** (and why not?), keep going past Blackmore Farm along this lovely rural lane with its views over verdant meadows populated by woolly specks. The Railway is indeed by the railway – a (part-time) station in such a small place being a rare sight nowadays. To get back (in case your judgement is impaired by overconsumption) turn left out of the pub, flutter between Rheewell Papillons(!) and Blackmore Farm to find the stony track to the right just before the road bends left. *End of detour.*

Cross the bridge to go through the metal gate which leads to a vast plateau of open pasture land uncluttered by fences . . . this is because it's cluttered with numerous irrigation ditches. At one time (up to medieval times), this land was completely covered by the sea at high tide and it has taken centuries of human toil to tame it and drain it: Appledore used to be on the coast which is now 8 miles away. During the war this area was a minefield and if you mine in it now you'll discover many old sea shells from the old sea shore. Anyway, it used to be a lot more dangerous to pass this way.

With the steep-sided irrigation ditch on your left follow the grassy track. (You must keep this ditch constantly to your left till you get near the Royal Military Canal). The ill-defined path takes you

river. The original Railway was built at the same time as the railway and the railway was built at the instigation of the Duke of Wellington in 1851.

The present Railway has white rendered walls with etched glass from the old inn. Its single bar contains no less than 3 open fires and houses a collection of railway paraphernalia. The hand-pumps here turn out Fremlins Bitter, Youngers No 3 and Shepherd Neame and, on keg, a number of lagers, bitters and milds are available. If that isn't enough, hot food is on offer every day up to 30 minutes before closing time and this includes home-made cottage pies and sandwiches made with fresh bread from the local bakery. Outside there are $1\frac{1}{2}$ acres of grass, where you can play bat and trap, the old Kent game which is an early ancestor of cricket, or watch Morris dancing, a less strenuous option.

The Swan Hotel, Appledore

The Swan has been a pub since the 18th century. It offers cask conditioned beers and lager and a full menu of hot and cold snacks or 'à la carte' if you prefer. The hotel part of it has five letting rooms and children are allowed in, outside the bar area. As an antidote to the effects of the juke box in the public bar, classical music is played in the saloon.

through a metal gate and into a field with a long low wooden hut in it. Rabbits abound around here. When the fields get too wet, sluice gates are opened and water is released into the canal. The land here may be·flat, but it's fascinating; by no means the monotonous stretch it appears to be on the map.

Through two more metal gates with the ditch still to the left, watch out for the furrowed brows of the hillocks to the left, where ugly pylons stride. Hereabouts the mud is heavy and clinging as you stagger along the edge of a potato field. After this, when the track re-appears, you'll probably think it's a mirage.

With the ever darker and danker ditch still left, keep on past an old stone bridge and a brambled wooden gate. You may see a gaggle of white domestic geese here in the fields, which are also a stopover point for migrating Canadian geese on their annual wild goose chase across the Atlantic. After another over-grown bridge on the left and an old gate which is being dragged down by brambles, turn left with the ditch, then right with it towards the road ahead. Choose your path through the field here and you'll come to a gate in its corner. Watch out for trains on the horizon which can be very near round here! Watch out also for 5″ frogs.

Pass under powerlines with a house to your right; then, turn left over a bridge by a sluice gate and through a metal gate. This is where you ditch the ditch. To your right there's a patch of rippling wind-swept water.

In the corner of the field by the road, there's a series of gates and a concrete bridge, which lead you to the road across more ditch. Turn left at the road and fol-low it to the canal, where you turn left along the public footpath side, the near-side bank. This affords you a better view than the other (National Trust bank!) one would. See the introduction for the his-tory of the canal and look around you for fleeting specimens of contemporary natural history. On the wing, in summer,

you can see kingfishers, green sandpip-ers and lesser spotted woodpeckers; in winter, there are lapwings, field fare and red poll.

On the other side of the bank are pillboxes commanding lengthy lines of fire from bends in the canal – they are placed on the landward side of the water to hold up invasion from the southern coast. Keep along the bank, closing any gate you may encounter, until you reach the road beyond the pumping house. Turn right at the road, then go right over the bridge and past 'The Old Watch House' by the village sign. In the village, either roar into The Red Lion and ask politely for a pint or swan into **The Swan** and state your case before the bar.

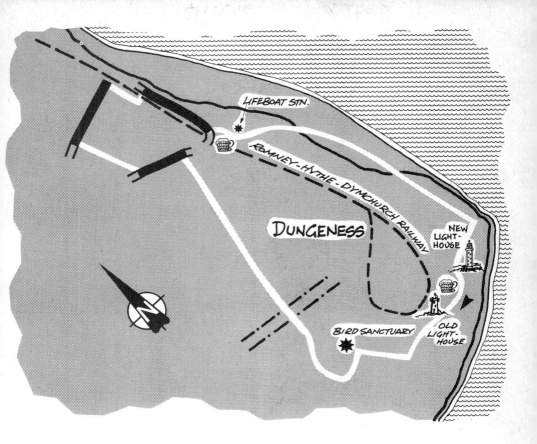

10   **Dungeness**

The District

There is something faintly alien and extra-terrestrial about the Dungeness promontory. Nothing on this stretch of coast is like anywhere else. It is a land that noticably changes all the time. In the great floods of 1288 the River Rother burst its banks and re-routed itself to flow into the sea at Rye. Old Winchelsea was swept away, the port of New Romney, the original outlet where boats had previously tied up to the church wall, was left high and dry a mile from the sea, and the shingle bank of Denge Beach and the Ness was slowly built up by the conflicting forces of the river and tides. The steep-sided shingle bank is still constantly building, and advances nine feet

into the sea every year. Consequently, a new lighthouse was built in 1961 to replace the 1904 model, which, by then, was so far from the retreating sea that the new power station would have prevented a full sweep of the light.

The Ness, the most southerly part of Kent only 26 miles from Cap Gris Nez (Cape Grey Nose), is one of the most dangerous points in the English Channel, for, due to the steepness of the shingle bank, a lot of channel shipping passes within a pebble's throw of the land. In certain lights, the throb of the engines, the smooth passing of the ships and maybe even the blast of a foghorn can all add to the 'other worldly' atmosphere of this spot.

➤

Dungeness Power Station is an excellent example of good simple design and 'lends distinction and interest to its flat country setting'. This is true in good weather; but given a stiff breeze, lashing rain or spooky sea-mist, this technological hot-house for energy, with its pylons striding aggressively across the scrubby and pebbly hinterland, can dominate this essentially primitive landscape. Windsocks stand like sentries to monitor any radioactive leakage in the air and it's both comforting and disturbing to be told that the only time any was registered, was after the Harrisburg nuclear disaster in the United States.

It's perhaps by comparison with the power station that all the houses on the Ness look so rudimentary and temporary. What is ironic is that it is not difficult to imagine Dungeness as a location for a film about life *after* a nuclear disaster. Add to all this the usually adverse weather (if it isn't very windy for ten days together, then it's a record) and its lonely, even desolate, end-of-the-road feeling and you have an area of unique character and consequently, great interest.

Much of the Ness' life is unsurprisingly connected with the sea. The uncommercialised beach (such a relief) is the home and workplace of the fishermen who trawl and drift in their luggers and fresh fish can be bought here every day. It's a popular beach with sea-anglers who catch many cod and bass, especially near the power station outfall. In days gone by, it was a thriving smuggling centre (and maybe still is); the isolation, the thousands of waterchannels on Walland Marsh and the scrub of Denge Beach created ideal conditions for it. Dr Syn was a clergyman and a smuggler who used to follow both vocation and trade in the area. Sadly, he was only a character in a book but he brings us to the final mention in this introduction . . .

An engine of the 15 inch gauge New Romney-Hythe-Dymchurch Railway is named after him. Reputedly the smallest public railway in the world, it has a good collection of nine steam engines. They are miniature replicas of actual full-size steam engines and can pull twelve or more laden coaches up to 20 mph. The extension to Dungeness only operates between Easter and September.

The walk goes from The Britannia to The Pilot via the Bird Observatory and Denge Beach. It then returns along the real beach. The walk is flat but the stretch back along the beach on the pebbles can be tiring.

How to Get There
By road take the A259 south-west from Hythe, turn left on to the B2075 and then left again on to an unclassified road for Dungeness (approx 16 miles).
By rail take a train to Sandling and then change on to the Romney, Hythe and Dymchurch line for Dungeness. ✲
By bus there is no direct bus service, but the 95, 553, 554 and the 555 from Hythe go nearby.

The Dungeness Walk
Just before you get to the old lighthouse and the nuclear power station, you find **The Britannia** – the walk starts here. You must remember that there was a time, not very long ago (at least before 1965, when the power station was finished), that Dungeness was a very remote and unpestered part of the world. In those good old days, The Britannia could easily waive the rules with no fear of opposition. Nowadays 'last orders' and 'drinking-up time' mean what they say. So leave legally – you can always come back.

Walk through the car park, back to the road and in front of you is an old Pullman car, slightly disguised as a house. It's the house of one of The Britannia's bar-staff and a visiting American once offered between £7,000 and £10,000 for it, to ship it back stateside and, presumably, impress his friends. The offer was declined. Turn right, heading along the road towards the old lighthouse and the power station. As you walk, you pass more rolling stock converted to dwellings. This is only natural since people in this area have been known to live in the fishing boats – beach luggers – hauled up on to the beach and have also used upturned boat hulls as roofs for their ramshackle DIY homes. Even nowadays, the number of temporary-looking shack-houses easily outnumbers any real 'houses' on the Ness.

You pass Trinity House's round house by the old black-painted lighthouse, which is visitable and climbable in the summer. Go straight on here, past the 'Private Road – No Entry' sign; you don't go to the power station, only towards it. At the triangle, go right and then soon, right again, along a tarmac road with the power station's concrete fence on your left. The power station (a type 'A') was finished in 1965 and was the fifth nuclear power station built by and for the Central Electricity Generating Board. It has an unparalleled safety record which may be part of the reason why the locals don't mind having a nuclear power plant as a next-door neighbour. Although it's not unpleasing to the eye, I'm not sure I'd like to live in its shadow or indeed within 50 miles of it.

You're now aiming for a row of coast-guards' cottages surrounded by a grassy rampart of pebbles. Where the road cuts through this rampart, climb up to your left and walk round the top. The house on the right-hand end of the row is a Bird Observatory. Acting as a focus for the 12,000 acre bird reserve on the Lydd-Dungeness promontory, the Observatory has recorded more than 200 species of native and passing birds in the last ten years and rings 6,000 birds every year. Walking round the rampart, from where you get good views of the power station, you soon arrive at some corrugated sheds: here, you go left across the grassy causeway over the depression. On the far side, fork right along a grassy track towards the buildings in the distance.

This track leads you through pebbly scrub with gorse and brambles and across what looks like a disused railway line, evidenced by the recognisable fence-posts. Turning half left after this, you cross what looks like another disused railway line, evidenced by the sleepers. Oddly, the O/S map, usually so reliable, only marks one line. From here, you head off along a broad grassy track through the bushes which soon give way to gorse, teasel and heather, with pebble dunes on your left. You may notice thousands of holes – the area is, appar-

The Inns

The Britannia, Dungeness

The previous incarnation of The Britannia, an old wooden Britannia, was burnt down in 1951 and the present Britannia was converted from some mid-50s army barracks. It's a one-storey, pink painted, pebbledash building with 18 inch brick walls and a concrete roof. In fact, there used to be a Bofors gun on the roof. Open fires in both bars contribute to the very friendly atmosphere of what is, on the outside, a pub rather like a coal bunker. Outside is a horse-cart used long ago to bring the beer across the beach. The wide wheels prevented it from sinking into the pebbles, though what happened to the horses' hooves I don't know. It's a lifeboating pub and has a set of photos of past coxswains.

It's a Courage pub and Harry Loader, your landlord, stocks Best Bitter, Mild, Kronenburg and Hofmeister lagers and draught Guinness. Food includes sausage, egg pie, pasty, bacon, burger, beef cutlet, chicken, cod, plaice and scampi or any combination of them with or without chips. There are also salads, ploughmans, sandwiches and tea or coffee. The food is good and very good value. In fact, the same can be said for the whole pub.

The Pilot, Near Dungeness

There once was a Pilot which was simply the upturned hull of a boat on stilts with makeshift walls. The present Pilot is a 50s building near the Lifeboat Station with a real roof and brick walls! Warm and friendly it has a children's room and two bars. It's a Courage pub.

ently, 'covered with foxes', so eyes skinned for them. This stretch of land is called Denge Beach and you may hear bangs and thumps from the west; this is the Army, happy as sand-boys, moving shells from one place to another by howitzer.

Aim for the large building ahead and when you get there, leave this row of cottages (the end one has a cartwheel on its front wall) on your left and walk in front of its garages. You reach the road where you turn left and soon you pass battlemented Homestead (an Englishman's home is . . .), Pebbles (self-explanatory) on your left and Stonefield (also self-explanatory) and Pluto on your right. This last house is so named because it was from Dungeness that the Pluto oil pipeline went across the English Channel to supply the allied invasion force in France after D-Day.

Just after the telegraph lines cross the road, head off half left across the grassy, pebbly scrubland. There is no particular path across this broomy, mossy tract, but after a short while, you meet a tarmaced concrete road, where you turn right. As you walk towards the bridge, you can see where they've extracted pebbles for concrete and, rather more surprisingly, cosmetics. Is make-up a form of cement?

Follow the road towards the coast and just before the bridge, drop down to the right to walk along the miniature railway line. When the trains are running, you may well be overtaken by one, so watch out and remember that, in the long term, it's not a terribly good idea to tie your annoying and whining offspring across the tracks — the trains don't move fast enough to inflict much more than bruises and scratches. When there is a derelict building on your right, turn left along the path between the bungalows. Turn right along the road in front of the bungalows and their gardens with their various gnomes, lifebelts, ponds, lions, etc. Soon you arrive at **The Pilot**.

From here, there are two ways of returning to the Ness. Between Easter and September you should be able to catch a miniature train back to Dungeness from behind **The Pilot**; or, if you are feeling more energetic, leave the pub by the door into the car park and, facing the sea, turn right towards the RNLI. Skirt round the front of pink and green Frantrige and walk, in front of Beachcroft with its 'walled' lawns and semi-circular flower bed, to the Lifeboat Station. There has been a lifeboat here since 1826 and it is called out between 18 and 20 times a year, though, before Dover was given a new high-speed lifeboat, there were many more call-outs. The Lifeboat Station is open and can be visited.

Walk down the lifeboat ramp to the sea and turn right along the pebblebank. This part of the walk is nothing less than gruelling, so take your time, stopping to rest and watch the anglers as they stare out to sea, willing the cod and bass on to their hooks. Soon you reach the fishing boats — beach luggers — which are unselfconsciously and photogenically pulled up on to the shingle bank, where they sit in rows.

As you begin to round the point, turn inland and head across an area, where they scrape for pebbles, towards the new, November 1961, lighthouse. Here you meet the road and you turn left to get back to The Britannia, where you can shake the pebbles out of your shoes.

✱ Summer only.

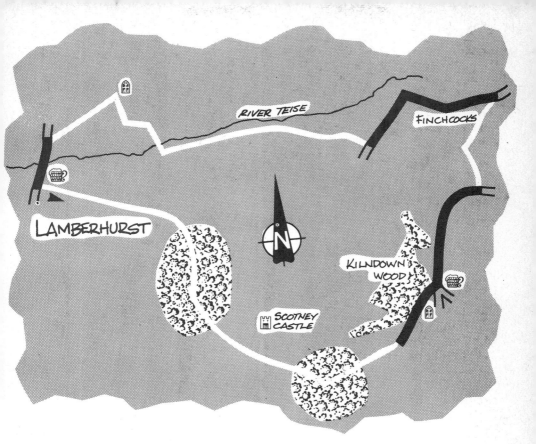

11 Lamberhurst

The District

Tunbridge Wells grew up round the 'chalybeate' springs first discovered by Lord North in 1606 and came to rival Bath as a spa in Regency times. Such social acolytes as Dr Johnson, David Garrick, 'Prinny' (the Prince of Wales) and his friend Beau Nash appeared to enjoy the doubtless tonic but tart-tasting water of the Wells, which was supposed to be consumed in daily doses of 18 pints as a treatment for anaemia and most other disorders, imaginary and real. The Pantiles, a colonnaded promenade with a raised musicians gallery, Decimus Burton's Calverly Crescent and the 17th century church, dedicated to Charles I and one of two such in England, are all worth visiting in the town before you go for one of your many pints of iron-bearing spring water.

On your way to Lamberhurst from the place which became Royal Tunbridge Wells in 1909, you will go past Bayham Abbey, whose 'atmospheric' (sic) ruins are open to the skies and the public all year round. The early 13th century walls stand in Sussex and are the remains of the monastic site plundered by Wolsey in order that he might finance colleges at Ipswich and Oxford.

Lamberhurst is a fine Kentish village once famous for its iron works and now the centre of a hop growing district. It stands by the River Teise on ground which has always been susceptible to

➤

53

flooding and used to be on the main coach route to the coast. When in Lamberhurst, you should visit the alpine garden of Scotney Castle which is famous for its azaleas and rhodedendrons and the Owl House, a small tile-hung and half-timbered, 16th century building and former haunt of owlers (smugglers). The Owl house has lovely gardens, too.

Since the village lies in a hop-growing area, you would think that the fields around here had always been involved in producing the buds which flavour beer; this is, however, not the case. While clay tablets of 2,600 BC may record that beer was prescribed for 'medicinal purposes' by Sumerian pharmacists, it is true that beer had still not reached these shores 4,000 years later – it was not until the early 16th century that beer was first imported to England from Holland.

To grow good hops, poles must be kept well apart so that the bines don't mingle as they grow upwards towards the sun; bines don't grow round their poles. Hops ripen in late August and September and are then picked and taken to the oast house kilns. During the drying period, ventilation is strictly controlled and the circular cowl of the oast house can be rotated according to the direction of the wind. After drying, the hops will retain only 10 percent of their original moisture and in this condition they are packed in sacks and sent all over, including to Holland! If you wonder what the difference is between ale and beer the Herbal of Gerard explains it in inimitable fashion . . . "for the hops rather make it (beer) a physicall drinke to keepe the bodie in health than as an ordinary drinke for the quenching of our thirst (ale)".

From Lamberhurst the walk crosses undulating country on its way past Scotney Castle to the Globe and Rainbow at Kilndown, a village which was the site of an ironmaking kiln in the 18th century. The wriggling River Teise accompanies you on much of the homeward route through what is probably the best rambling country in 'The Garden of England'. The walk is pretty even-paced.

How to Get There
By road take the A21 south-east from Tonbridge, Lamberhurst is on this road (approx $10\frac{1}{2}$ miles).
By rail to Tunbridge Wells or Frant.
By bus the 260 from Tunbridge Wells or the 256 from Frant.

The Lamberhurst Walk
For a start, check in to **The Chequers Inn** check out to the left for your next move and turn left into the car park behind the pub. On your way, you will see a section of railings on display which testifies to the fact that Lamberhurst belongs to an area once famous for its iron work. These railings were commissioned from the village as a surround for St Paul's and this particular stretch came home to rust in its Wealden place of origin. As for the rest of the railings rejected by Wren's cathedral; they were sent to Canada on a ship which sunk depositing 200 tons of prime Kentish iron on the bottom of the Atlantic. The Gloucester Forge, the village's last and well-reputed foundry, ceased operation in 1765 some years after providing the cathedral with its 200 tons of metal work at a cost of £11,000 . . . today Kent still has iron in the soil but this serves only as a vitamin source for local fruits, cereals and hops.

Leave by the gate at the back of the car park which leads into a sports ground. Skirting the square, head across the cricket pitch and through the gap to the left of two trees, marked by the warmly welcoming notice provided by Helyas Football Club. Walk along between the football pitches unless someone passes to you in which case you can dribble down the wing on your way to a stile in the right-hand corner of the field. Cross this and you're on your third sport though an anxious golfer may shout 'fore' as you proceed across the golf course.

Starting with the hedge on your right, go straight across the fairway to another marked stile – in a hawthorn hedge. Continue in the same direction to a third stile which you climb to leave the golf course. Next, head half-right to a stile to the left of the further oak tree. This stile takes you onto a concrete track and another opposite takes you off. By the corner of the wood, there's another stile beside a gate . . . adjust your gait to climb it with style and go steeply up the right-hand edge of this field with the wood to your right. Catch your breath, then hold it in admiration for the view of the old-established and sedate farmlands of the Weald behind you.

In the top corner of the field, there's a large kissing-gate. Breeze through this and along the marked Public Footpath towards Kilndown. This takes you along the top edge of the field, over a stile and then, using the wedge-shaped marker posts for guidance, along the right-hand side of the next field with the wood on your right. Continue till you reach the stile in the corner and your entrance to the wood, 70 yards or so to the right of the house. Take the slightly smaller path straight into the wood and to the next marker post by a little pond, both of which you leave to your left.

At the road go straight across, up a bank, past a National Trust sign and through a metal gate into a field where you head leftish downhill. This old estate field has trees that could and have grown tall and broad in the unconfined conditions. Aim for a white gate just on the far

The Inns

The Chequers Inn, Lamberhurst

Not quite as old as the hills, The Chequers was built between 1380 and 1400 as a cidery and bakery . . . then it became a beery (brewery) as well. Before the dissolution it was owned by local abbies including Bayham and St Augustine's in Canterbury. Later it became a coaching inn and a major stop for continental travellers on the route between London and the South Coast. The pub is mentioned in the Torrington Diaries of 1788.

The exterior is now 'mock' Tudor and inside you can be guaranteed the support of solid oak beams and the warmth of an inglenook fire place in winter.

Two real ales are available from hand-pumps (Whitbread Fremlins) and there are special malt whiskies and vintage ports to warm the cockles of your heart. More cash can be exchanged for bar snacks, both hot and cold, and, if that's not enough, you can enjoy 'haute cuisine' in a 'continental restaurant' on the premises. Out the back, there is a simple grassy garden looking out over the river where kids are welcome.

The Globe and Rainbow Inn, Kilndown

The Globe and Rainbow is a 'free house'

side of a small bridge which straddles a silvery stream. Go through this gate and the rather less stately metal model which follows, then pursue the track to a second small bridge and a third gate (the second white one). At the fork go straight on upwards almost parallel with the road nearby on your right. Next comes a third white gate and Kilnwood Wood.

Along a shaded old driveway, you soon reach a T-junction where you go left along the marked track towards Kilndown. Ignore the inviting turns to the left as you follow the clay track which climbs past a large-bricked and white-gated cottage on your left. Keep straight on towards a large fir tree with a broken kissing-gate and a five bar gate beneath. Walk along this path through trees and, at the fork, leave the marker to your left, i.e. go straight along the narrow path which takes you to the road.

To your right as you emerge is an oast house (wedge-shaped) but turn left and pass Vine Cottage and Highdown on your way down the lane to Christ Church, where you'll find a large lych-gate with stone seats, a cobbled pathway and ranks of yews which flank the large building of 1841. Scraping your shoes on the porch scrapers of this austere, Victorian Gothic Revivalist's painstaking realisation, you'll be impressed to know that this church was chosen as the scene of a wedding in the Dick Emery Show.

Head further down the lane to **The Globe and Rainbow**. Out the back, at night, there's the spectacle of a floodlit paddock. During the day there's an eight mile view boasting countryside unspoilt by telegraph poles or houses . . . all the way to Goudhurst.

Turn right out of the pub along the tree-lined road where there's soon a view to the left over the rolling Kent countryside between you and Lamberhurst. The view ahead stretches to Goudhurst poised on its hill top. The road drops just before Riseden and, when you reach the letter box set in the wall of the lane to the left, turn left along the stony track by a misshapenly charming house. There's a

hop field to your left and then the track goes through farm buildings, past another oast house and a complex pulley-device used in the peculiar rituals of local farming.

Swing left by a garage and at the T-junction, go right downhill to a wooden gate. With a large depression on your right and a gate on your left, go straight towards the three visible chimneys of early 18th century Finchcocks. Walk across in front of its grand stage-set facade and at the corner of the field go right for 70 yards or so to the stile by the gate. Finchcocks was built for Edward Bathurst in 1725 in the then popular Baroque style; the statue over the door is Queen Anne. Till quite recently, the building was used as a ballet school and it is about to be opened to the public. Once over the stile, turn left along the lane to find a private sign by Finchcocks side – luckily, we don't go as far as Scotneys Farm, so keep going, passing the sight of a cluster of oast house cowls and a hop field to your right . . .

Just after the bridge over a stream and just at the beginning of the avenue of tall trees, go right through a five bar wooden farmgate into a field along the route of the public footpath. After this, head just left of straight across to a lichen-covered gate.

As you go through this, there are farm buildings to your left on the hill above.

Follow the track which follows the contours left around the hill until you turn right through a gate into a hop field recognisable by its wirework and wooden support system. Hop, skip and jump along its left-hand edge (how else?), to and through a gate and on and beyond to meet the River Teise, where you head upstream (left) along the bank. It's a steep-sided stream, so don't dangle children or other possessions over the edge even in jest. Following the bank, you must climb over a fence cum stile before you arrive near a shed, where you climb a stile and a fence between it and the river to remain the bank's faithful follower. The banks wind and meander faithfully following the river and veer right at one point where your path bears off, up and left – don't panic, galactic hikers, it's only a temporary hitch, you rejoin the bank soon, having climbed a stile on the way. The river is still on your right and the church now beyond it.

Find the bridge by a huge oak tree and you find your way over the river. From here, aim straight for the church and a second bridge in the meadow leading to it. Was the river diverted at one time? Enter the churchyard through a kissing-gate where you'll see lots of sheep shuffle, snuffle and chomp like lost souls among the gravestones . . . now you know why each grave is fenced off. Views from the churchyard are soothing and restful, just as they should be. Walk to the right round the church which has windows of the 14th and a tower of the 15th century. There's a yew, with a 25 foot girth (not a 'ewe') and tree experts may wish to estimate its age.

Leave the precincts by the small wooden gate by the large wooden gate in a corner. The tarmac road encountered takes you from here under Court Lodge and above the golf course to the road. Turn left to pass The George and Dragon, which may be a stopover point on your way back to The Chequers, mate.

which stands beside a village cricket ground and overlooks a breathtaking view of the Weald. Built in 1714 to serve as a coaching inn, it saw service in the past as an administrative building, which included the rent office of Lord Beresford. The Globe remained Crown property till 1957.

Room number 1 upstairs is haunted by a ghost called Fred, supposed to be an ex-landlord who fatally shot himself early in the 19th century. The building itself is part 18th century, part Victorian with clay peg tiles and a high-pitched roof.

There are two bars, an inglenook and all the exposed beams you could wish for. Beers from the wood include Youngs Ordinary and Special, Fullers London Pride and Arkles 3bs and there are 11 top pressure beers! Being a famous cricketing club, there is accommodation for 18 and a wide range of snacks and a 'main menu' restaurant to keep all these people happy. Home of the Kent Crawlers Walkers Club, the Globe has a huge garden, trad jazz nights and a friendly atmosphere. There are no space invaders or juke boxes; these are strictly forbidden! Kids however, are welcome.

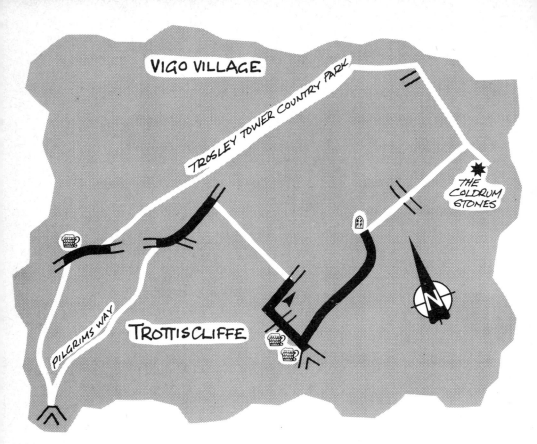

12   **Trottiscliffe**   APPROXIMATELY 5½ Miles

The District

Despite its origins as the cliff owned by a man called Trott, Trottiscliffe belies its written appearance by being pronounced 'Trosley' or even 'Troslif'. Trottiscliffe is a quiet and pretty Kentish village, off today's beaten track but not far from the ancient trackways marked now as the North Downs and Pilgrim Ways. Its most famous inhabitant, Graham Sutherland the artist, chose to live and paint here in a main street with weatherboarded country houses and roadside oasts. The village church is dedicated to Ss Peter and Paul and was built on a tract of attractive land offered by Offa, King of Mercia, to the See of Rochester after the battle of Otford. This was some time ago.

The Pilgrims Way, which makes up part of the walk, has been trodden since the New Stone Age when its position by the chalk hills offered a way of bypassing the difficulties of the plains roads with their mud, bogs and dangerous wild animals. In the Middle Ages, pilgrims passed along its length on their way to and from the shrine of Becket at Canterbury Cathedral; some were even going as far as Palestine . . .

The main point of a pilgrimage was (so to speak) to gain early remission from Hell. In an era of morbid apprehension, the Church operated a system of indulgences, the accumulation of which kept their congregations busy and the priests in power. Absolution could provide a person with freedom from guilt but, and this was the snag, not from punishment in Purgatory. The great advantage of a penance made with bare feet was that it *did* take the place of perdition ... planning for the future, a penitent could ensure that he would have enough points (indulgences) to gain an absolute discharge from eternal damnation. Often convicted criminals undertook pilgrimage in sackcloth and ashes, their feet bound with iron fetters, since this was their only way of paying the price of crime – wellingtons will suffice for you.

A refinement of the system enabled the unhealthy and the wealthy to pay someone to travel in their stead and it was also possible to set aside a (tidy) sum to have your soul pilgrimaged for after death. By the late medieval period, pardonners appeared on the scene selling pilgrims pardons which couldn't have helped much, since most pardonners were complete charlatans. Healing was another motive for making the trip to Canterbury and, no doubt, these journeys were the only opportunity for poor people to take a holiday and see the world. Roughly speaking, pilgrimages and their popularity mirror the growth, the flowering and the degeneration of the Church in the Middle Ages.

The abbey of St Mary's at nearby West Malling was where the four knights who murdered Becket first sought shelter on their way back to London after their terrible deed. When they had been given food and drink, had said grace and were just about to eat, an invisible hand dashed their food to the floor and sent them forth in terror.

The walk goes from Trottiscliffe's two pubs to the eponymous inn of Vigo Village. From there, it follows the North Downs ridge through Trosley Tower Country Park to the amazing Coldrum Stones, which are part of the neolithic necropolis to be found on both sides of the Medway Valley. From this National Trust site it is not a long way back to the original point of departure. This is a fairly easy walk with varied views of the North Kent countryside along the way.

How to Get There
By road take the A25 east from Sevenoaks, turn left onto the A227 at

▶

The Inns

The George, Trottiscliffe
The George has been plying its trade beside Trottiscliffe village green since it was built with ships' timbers in 1500. In 1700 this old coaching inn was taken over by Whitbreads, which makes Whitbreads older than I thought. Recently the chimney fell down and with its collapse came the discovery of a priest's hole, an old mud-walking shoe, a corn dolly and an old boot.

This pub has a Kent peg roof and a warm and welcoming interior with brass everywhere, hop hung beams, low doors and an inglenook fireplace. Its Trophy, Tankard and Whitbread Best are all on keg and those of you who favour draught Guinness will not go thirsty. There are meals of all sorts and children can be kept in a side room.

The Plough, Trottiscliffe
The Plough stands in the middle of the village and in general is quieter than The George. In case you don't recognise it, there's an old plough on the roof and it is a fairly old building with white walls.

Inside there's a comfortable lounge with a blazing fire in winter and horse brasses galore. In the public bar you can test your Latin against a set of jokey

▶

Borough Green and then right onto an unclassified road for Trottiscliffe (approx 10 miles).
By rail to Borough Green and Wrotham.
By bus the 58 runs regularly from Borough Green and Wrotham.

The Trottiscliffe Walk

After a pint at **The George**, turn left up Taylors Lane leaving the small village green behind you. This way you soon reach **The Plough** where further nutrition can be obtained. Trotting in a straight line (still, I hope) up the lane, you come across the spot where white doves live contentedly alongside mallards, mandarins and muscovies by a quiet roadside pond. Soon after this, turn right up Green Lane past elegant Trottiscliffe House and the selection of ramshackle wooden huts which command the adjacent allotments.

At the end of the lane, there's a path to the right of the houses, which leads to a gate beyond which you can see the church. Don't go straight on! After this gate, turn immediately left and head for the hills, namely the North Downs. Your path now goes straight (by fields) towards the trees on the escarpment ahead. To your right, as you go, is the church which nestles among trees in a well-sheltered dip and, beyond it, a line of boxlike houses on the near brow. Cross one stile after another and you come to a metal gate on the edge of the wood.

Go through and turn left along the upper lane of two. Look up and you should see squirrels scurrying across and along the ivy-draped branches above – below you is a large villa built in an incongruous 'hacienda' style. At the road, turn right up Vigo Hill, then left within 120 yards to proceed along the path beside, and just before, a well camouflaged thatched cottage.

This lane, the Pilgrims Way, takes you behind the secretive cottage and to your left you can enjoy the view its windows provide over lush well tended Kentish farmland and Mereworth Woods. The fact that London is only 35 miles away is hard to believe as you peaceably plod along. Not unusually, this landscape changes with the seasons; in summer it pushes up acres of corn, in winter its muddy furrows are naked to the wind – all year round however there is the massive presence of the North Downs which rise so steeply to your right.

Like the pilgrims before you, keep on the straight and narrow path, muddy though it often is. This may help you to understand 'the mire and slough' of Chaucer's Tales, not to mention the 'slough of despond' of Bunyan; but let's not exaggerate. If you're very observant you may spot graffiti left by the medieval pardon seekers; small crosses cut deep in the roadside stones, biblical initials etc.

When you reach the track by the trees at the end of the path just before the road, make a hairpin turn to the right and head upwards into the wood leaving the telegraph pole to your right. A sunken path takes you up among the trees where it's only sensible to take a break to stop and listen to the medley of the forest birds. The acoustics are first class and enable you to appreciate the warbling songbirds chorus, the pigeons' repetitive doo-wop and the steady beat supplied by the antics of the ant-eating green woodpecker. Anyway, you need the rest. Enough of all that as you inspect the cross-sections of the roots protruding from the path's crumbling chalky banks.

At the choice of paths, fork left and upwards into the wood with its mixture of deciduous and evergreen trees. Someone has very aptly scrawled 'The Secret Garden' on the entranceway to the long and high walled garden which appears on your right and this was most certainly not the old pilgrims. As you peer through the rusting wrought iron gates, I should tell you that this was once the garden of Trosley Towers, an 18th century house commissioned by Waterlow, a local millionaire who is to be excused his self-indulgence on two other counts . . . a private, rhododendron-lined drive to Meopham Station and a private racecourse built in this vicinity. The Towers was knocked down at the start of World War II, being too obvious a landmark for German bombers on their way to batter London. The garden today wears a coat of ivy and a cloak of mystery, I could almost swear I could see the outlines of a house . . .

Soon you come across a second set of gates to your right and the beginnings (and remains) of that private driveway to the station. Keep following the track, past a house and to the road.

At the road, turn right and cross to **The Vigo**. Originally The Higher Drovers Inn, a toll house set by a forest crossroads, this pub has seen centuries come and go and adapted to each set of customers that history has brought. It stopped taking tolls as late as 1905 and has since relied exclusively on the quality of its beers and hospitality for income.

Turn left out of The Vigo and left again down a lane which is inclined at 1:6. As you wend your way down, on the right above you is the old abandoned officer's mess from the second World War which appears to be straight out of a Waugh novel; indeed many of the men from the mess were not unwilling to pass the odd hour or two in The Vigo as an antidote to the rigours of military training. The bridge ahead was built to get the men across to the training ground. I was told that due to the excessive harshness of the training scheme, there was an average of one suicide a day in the war years, but then I was also told that the woods are packed with dumps of unexploded ammunition and wartime gin bottles. Beyond the bridge down the hill lies the 'Lower Drovers Inn/Pilgrims House', a former pilgrim's inn and now a private residence.

Just before the elegant army bridge, turn left up the bank then right towards the horse stiles near the bridge. Listening carefully for the patter of tiny hooves, go through these and follow the wide and airy central avenue of the signposted

crests and your manual dexterity on the video machines and bar billiard table.

Hand-drawn Fremlins Bitter and keg Tankard and Mild are just what is needed to go with the toasted sandwiches on sale here and in summer you can sit out in the garden.

The Vigo, Vigo

In 1471, The Upper Drovers was built to act as tollhouse and alehouse at the country crossroads here. Some time later, a sailor from the village saved the life of Sir George Rook (the admiral commanding the fleet in the Peninsular Wars) at the siege of Vigo. Amply rewarded with doubloons, the sailor came back to the village, bought the pub and renamed it after the battle. Subsequently, the village came to be called after the pub, an unusual switch of events. More recently, while repairs were being carried out on the roof, the priest's hole, where local boys were hidden from the Tilbury press gangs, was discovered.

Mrs Lilian Ashwell has held the licence of the Vigo for over 50 years and has ensured that the two bars have retained all their old style. On the walls are idyllic pictures of the countryside, hops are hung everywhere, paraffin heaters provide warmth in winter to supplement that of the inglenook fireplace and generally there's a charming rough and ready quality to the place. The beers are excellent — hand-drawn Youngs, Canterbury and Bass and keg McEwans (the latter considered behind the bar 'all arms and legs' — work this out for yourself). The snacks consist solely of peanuts and Scotch eggs but you can play the ancient Sussex game of Dadlums and throw 'cheeses' at skittles while you munch and crunch on those. The Vigo is highly recommended, a dying breed of pub.

North Downs Way as it runs through Trosley Tower Country Park. As the path splits in two, a fair way along, fork right on the broader offspring . . . keep to the right-hand edge of the ridge. To your left you will see a large raised platform . . . which must have been used in military training . . .

Just as the path is beginning to seem endless, it swings you left and up to a wooden gate . . . At this point Ryarsh is down to your right and Vigo Village (named after the pub!) invisible on the other side of the hill. Slip through the kissing-gate by the wooden gate and turn right on a track which slants down through the trees. You will probably feel shock at the brightness of daylight as you emerge at length onto The Pilgrims Way (now a road) from between two houses. Two or three strides to the right, then turn left along the Longbarrow footpath with its views to the left of The Mallings, East and West, Snodland itself and the Medway Gap.

When the path ends, continue in the same direction along a track with well-rounded fields, bisected to the left by a private road. You'll find the Longbarrow, called the Coldrum Stones, halfway round the bend and over a stile.

These sarsen stones mark the burial place of 22 people whose heads were 'long', whose bodies were short and who lived about 2,000 BC. Studies have revealed that they suffered badly from rheumatism which is thought to be due to their 'constant squatting'. The massive stone slabs (dolmens) which litter the site (some upright, others fallen) still stand guard after 4,000 years of service over the graves of 'sleeping British chieftains'. It is almost certain that human sacrifice once took place on this spot, since their pagan religion demanded rather 'unBritishly' that chiefs were not buried alone, that is, without their wives and slaves. An ancient skeleton uncovered here among the monoliths was taken away for Christian burial by the rector of Meopham, which resulted in the 'wagg-

ish' local vicar writing to ask him "what he meant by stealing his oldest parishioner". One last word or two on this numinous graveyard; none of the large stones here is of a kind to be found locally and the likelihood is that they were carried here by glaciers and left strewn around, with the disappearance of the substance of the Ice Age.

Go left from the stile and retrace your steps past the private road, now to your right. Go back to where the Longbarrow path trailed off. Instead of getting back on it, go left with the track into the field, where you should only use the stile if you think it is good form. Follow the left edge of the field and dip with the path into the woods to come out into a grassy lane with quirky wooden huts on either side and scuttling pheasants. On your left, a paddock; on your right, the darkened brow of The Downs.

At the road cross to the stile and follow the path to the church which is probably of Saxon origin. As you thread your way between well-manured fields, a golden weather vane appears above the trees which form an umbrella over the quiet churchyard. Beyond the next stile, turn right between 'Whitakers' and the old granary opposite (now a garage) to get to the church of Ss Peter and Paul. The church is also home to local archaeological finds (including the bones of the 'long headed, short-bodied race') and a museum of local events; a photo of an old Trosley wedding instantly evokes the past. The massive pulpit came from Westminster Abbey which partly explains why it's so enormous.

Turn left out of the churchyard and walk down to the road, where you turn right along Church Lane. Soon there's a pavement on the right and after that a primary school appears on the left. Turn left along School Lane and come back to Taylors Lane, where you must turn left for The George and right for The Plough . . . either choice leading you to a good country pub.

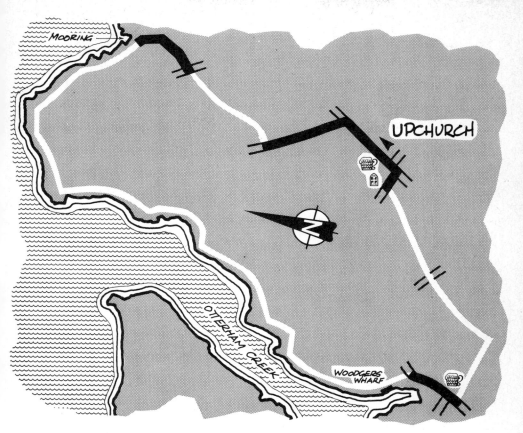

13 Upchurch

APPROXIMATELY 4¾ Miles

The District

You'd be forgiven for thinking that 'Men of Kent' and 'Kentish Men' were and are one and the same; you'd be wrong, they're not. Just what the distinction is, and why it should be, seems clouded in mystery, but what is certain, is that the River Medway is the natural boundary that has always separated 'Men of Kent' in the east from 'Kentish Men' in the west.

Flowing through a countryside of apples, pears, cherries and innumerable hopfields, it arrives at the small conurbation of the Medway towns, with the cathedral city of Rochester as the most important and oldest. Looking quite different from how we imagine 'Dickensian'

to be, it has a few remaining landmarks which feature in his work – Jasper's Gate, the Corn Exchange clock and The Bull Hotel (the Blue Boar in *Great Expectations*). Indeed, there's a museum of Dickensiana in Eastgate House which includes the summerhouse from nearby Gad's Hill Place where he wrote the unfinished *Mystery of Edwin Drood*.

Dickens spent some of his childhood in Chatham where his father worked in the Naval Pay Office – in fact, Chatham almost breathes Navy and shipping. The world famous Dockyard was established by Henry VIII and many famous ships were built and launched here, most notably Nelson's 'Victory' in 1765. Surprisingly, the Naval Depot dates back only as

➤

far as 1890. The Medway then passes Gillingham, which has a good military museum in the Royal Engineers' barracks, then Upchurch and Lower Halstow on its way to the Isle of Sheppey where it meets the Thames Estuary and the realization that it is only a tributary of that greater river. Sheppey means 'sheep island' in Anglo Saxon and its reclaimed pastures have nourished sheep for 1000 years or more.

With the main Medway channel beyond marshes, creeks, saltings and sandbanks, Upchurch and Lower Halstow lie in a corner of much mud, mud which has always been part of the area's lifeblood, for mud means pottery and bricks. Remains of Roman villas and fragments of their pottery show that the Romans knew and exploited this good thing when they saw it. The Jutes weren't blind to it either and they set up their first pottery at Upchurch and there have been brickworks here ever since. Tons of bricks from here were used by English builders down the ages and inspection of local churches (often the oldest buildings) show how early church architects put them to use. A good example is Lower Halstow's lovely 13th century church. An odd tale of this creekside church is that its plain (and non-brick) font was cracked by the booms of practising anti-aircraft gunners, to reveal a perfect Norman font (again non-brick) inside.

In Tudor times, hulks of disused ships, often later used as prison-ships, were beached on the mudflats near Upchurch and the vicar of Upchurch was also vicar of the hulks. One such vicar was Edmund Drake who had left Devon to escape religious troubles. He probably taught his son the basic skills of seamanship on the Medway with its mudflats and quirky tides. His son obviously learned well, for he went on to become one of the best and most famous sailors of all. He was Sir Francis Drake.

The walk follows lanes out of Upchurch, goes through fields to Ham Green and arrives at the Medway Estuary by a small mooring. It follows the sea wall all the way to Woodgers Wharf and returns through fields and orchards to Upchurch. The walk is longish but is never anything like difficult.

How to Get There

By road take the A2 east from Gillingham and then turn left onto unclassified road after Rainham (approx 5 miles).
By rail to Rainham.
By bus catch the 327 from Rainham.

The Upchurch Walk

Turn left out of **The Crown** and walk along The Street past One Step Behind, an antique and junk shop, and go straight on past The Poles on your left and then past a field of young trees. Now you realize why The Poles is so named. Continue along The Street between orchards and then turn left along Poot Lane. You pass Red Brick Cottage with its 'daring' plant pot – can this house really have been built in 1893? Further on, there's a yellow cottage with a lovely garden containing silver birch, prairie grass and a variety of shrub firs. As you walk on along Poot Lane (great name), look out for lapwings with their distinctive crests, strutting about in the reedy field to your left. This is their home and they like it here.

Just after Upchurch Poultry Farm, turn right, opposite aptly named Sea Croft and Misty Marsh, along a public footpath marked FP3. This path runs between a field and an overgrown hedge and soon passes derelict Nissen huts on the right. These are the first of other signs of military presence here – there were many anti-aircraft batteries along the Thames and Medway estuaries, as the rivers provided the safest approaches to London for the Luftwaffe. The path follows the fence as it swings right to a stile, with old gun emplacements on the right.

Aim for the footpath-sign slightly to the right ahead and then walk along between fences to a fence/stile. After a short and narrow avenue of ivy-clad oaks, you climb another fence/stile into an orchard. Walk along its left-hand edge to a stile into a field with its 'Dogs Must be Kept on a Lead' notice. Walk again along the left-hand edge and, at the beginning of the metal railings, climb over where it's marked and continue in the same direction, now on a track with the fence on your right. Passing a shed, you go through a gate and walk straight on to a stile by the white gate, patrolled and guarded by noisy chickens.

Turn right onto the lane and then left across the front of Ham Green Farm down the lane marked as a public footpath. The lane runs between an old barn with a corrugated iron roof and a bountiful garden. Then it's orchards again to left and right. In winter, these orchards and the marshy land beyond can be a temporary home for harriers, both hen and marsh, and if you're lucky you may spot a sparrowhawk. The hedgerows along the lane are full of smaller birds' nests – easily visible, in winter, in the bare branches, but don't investigate in spring and summer. You pass, on your left, a green house and then greenhouses (what clever writing) and ignoring a public footpath going off right, you arrive at a small sheltered mooring.

Climb the stile to the left of the gate made of an old mast, and follow the path along the sea wall. Turn left where you have to, to avoid walking into the water, and now you can give full rein to the ornithologist in you. There are birds galore – marsh birds, river birds, sea birds and field birds. Waders, divers,

The Inns

The Crown, Upchurch

At the centre of the village, The Crown has always been a pub. It adjoins the churchyard and until 50 or 60 years ago post mortems and burial preparations were carried out in a separate bar and then the bodies were passed out of the window into the churchyard for burial. Perhaps this accounts for footsteps in the bar that can be heard from below in the cellar. When Mr Cockhill rushes up to 'serve the customer', there is no-one there.

A plainish, but friendly pub, it has an open fire in the public bar, an 80 year old grandfather clock and a collection of 100 year old porcelain beer pumps.

Courage beers include Best Bitter, Tavern, Light Mild and two lagers. Sandwiches are the only pub grub available.

The Three Sisters, Otterham Quay

Almost surrounded by orchards and hop-fields, it is near a large and modern brick factory. Built on higher ground than a previous incarnation, The Lord Hanley, the pub is named after the three Hubbard sisters, unwed and philanthropic daughters of an Upchurch vicar. They ran a soup kitchen from the back of the pub, way back in 1664 and are buried in Upchurch graveyard. Outside the pub, by the right-hand front corner, is the Three Sisters Stone, which apparently goes vertically down 40 ft or more. It's a similar stone to those at Stonehenge and Kit's Coty House near Maidstone. It's extremely hard and it's a mystery how it got there.

The inside of the pub is no less interesting and has a distinctive nautical flavour. The bars' decorations include ships' plaques, a diver's helmet and a gyroscope compass and there's an dippers and, of course, thousands of oystercatchers and gulls. Soon, there's a hedge on your right; turn right, through the gap in it and follow the path back to the water's edge. You arrive at a stile, which you cross, and you continue – in fact for quite a long way now, you will be walking on the sea wall. To your right are low-lying islands, inhabited only by birds, and ahead is the Isle of Grain's Kingsnorth Power Station with its huge chimney. Of course, you'll probably have seen it, when you got out of your car, but I thought I'd mention it.

Just after a stagnant-looking pond on your left, you come to an ex-stile with a mostly obliterated 'Private' sign. Several locals told me that everybody uses the path and that it's OK to do so. So walk on with impunity and without guilt. Where the sea wall swings left, there's the first of a few raggedy flags and to your right, in the water, there's a peculiar barge with a caravan (!) on it, though whether it's always there, I don't know: the home of a nautical gypsy? Peering out above the trees on the hill way up to your left, is the double spire of Upchurch church (which is double in itself) and now you're walking towards Gillingham.

The sea wall swings left again, back towards Upchurch, and now you can see Motney Hill Sewage Works. Later, you'll be walking closer to it and, depending on the wind-direction, you'll be holding your nose. You cross another ex-stile with a tattered flag nearby and onto a third ex-stile and a third flag. As you trudge on, watch for the cormorants which skim the wavelets searching for food. At the fourth flag, there's actually a proper stile and, having crossed it, you walk on towards the Sewage Works. Not quite soon enough, you arrive at and cross a stile where, to your right there are dirty old barges tied up together.

Go through the gateway, turn left and then immediately right. This track takes you round the back of what is Woodgers Wharf. At the T-junction by the fence which protects the coasters and the wharf equipment, go left along the track. It swings inland and you can see Otterham Quay down to your right. The track then swings right and left to meet the road by a row of cottages with greenhouses behind. Turn right along the road. As it bends to the right downhill, walk on the pavement under the high wall as there's often heavy traffic (in both senses) along here. Just after the 'Beware of the dog – it bites anything' notice you arrive at **The Three Sisters**, just opposite the brickfields. In the past, of course, bricks were simply baked mud and in the days before the sea walls, this area, being a tidal estuary, was rich in mud. The mud was collected by 'muddies' in the same way that, on building sites, it is 'brickies' who construct things with the bricks. Many of the local churches are made with bricks from the brickfields hereabouts.

Leave the pub by the door onto the road and turn left and then left again, to walk along the wide track along the wall of the pub leading to Upchurch church. Go straight on, passing the 'No Through Road – Footpath only' notice and continue past the cottages and farm buildings on your right. Beyond the farm, go left at the 'Private Road – No Footpath' sign and follow the track which follows the line of telegraph poles. It leads you down and then up, and soon brings you out onto Wallbridge Lane, where you turn right.

You turn almost immediately left down the marked public footpath on the far side of the second detached house called Guigne-Noire. My French dictionary tells me that this means either 'black ill-luck' or 'black sweet cherry'. I favour the latter for fairly obvious reasons. At any rate, at the end of this ambivalently named house, the path swings rightish through an old orchard. There's not much space for overtaking on this path and you should watch out for low-flying apples. The path joins a track and continues in the same direction until it eventually emerges into a housing estate, which you walk straight through to meet the road. Turn right here and pausing to visit the lovely church with its unique double spire (unless you are a philistine), turn left back to The Crown.

aquarium, a parakeet, lots of copper and brassware and a collection of key rings.

It's a Courage pub and serves the usual Courage beers. There are also 9 whiskies, 5 brandies and lots of liqueurs. Food is of the pies/pizzas/sausage rolls variety with sandwiches of course. In summer, kids might like the tree house, slide and swings in the garden of lawn and flowerbeds.

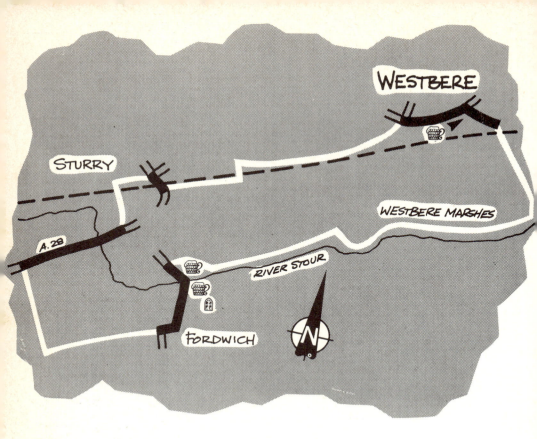

14 Westbere

APPROXIMATELY 4¾ Miles

The District

"It is the bounden duty of every English-speaking man and woman to visit Canterbury at least twice in their lives." Archbishop Frederick Temple (1821-1902).

There can be few places anywhere with so much to see in so small an area as Canterbury, the city which has been the metropolitical centre of the Church of England since AD 602 (yes, metropolitical). Once you escape from the lengthy Canterbury tailbacks and the hordes of ice-cream eating schoolkids and camera-toting tourists to the cool and calm of the cathedral, you'll discover that a visit here has much more to do with beauty than duty, 'bounden' or otherwise.

The Cathedral Church of Christ, Canterbury, to give it its full due, has survived shooting, looting, the Dissolution, air pollution and the Blitz with style and emerged from each historical setback with a new addition to its 'distinctive blend' of architecture. The present structure was instigated by Lanfranc, the first Norman archbishop, and inspired by William of Sens and William the Englishman. You should take time to inspect the premises thoroughly, including the stained glass windows, The Tomb of the Black Prince and the Bell Harry Tower above all else.

The cathedral was the setting of the notorious murder which not only sparked off works by T S Eliot, Tennyson and

Anouilh but also the medieval boom in pilgrimage: this murder was axiomatic in the struggle for power between Church and State. Thomas Becket, former chancellor of the Realm and warrior prelate in the French wars, returned to Canterbury from exile in 1170 and resumed his position at the head of the Church. It was a role he embraced with austerity (hair shirt, lice-ridden body, the usual stuff) as he continued to make the outspoken attacks on Henry II, which were to prove his downfall. "Of the caitiffs who eat my bread, are there none to rid me of this low-born priest?", was the King's (perhaps rhetorical) question, which sent 4 knights to 'the metropolitical centre of the Church of England' to make its leader an ex-archbishop and the Becket cult a going concern: Canterbury grew fat on the stream of penitents and incurables who thronged to the shrine in the cathedral. Henry II came, too, an act of contrition which began for him at St Dunstan's where he shed his shoes and finery, and ended at Becket's shrine where he had himself scourged. Many of Canterbury's archbishops met a violent end, including St Alphege who was carried off by Danes in 1012 and beaten to death with beef bones during a rowdy Viking feast at Greenwich . . . Robert Runcie beware.

St Augustine's was always Christ Church's great rival in the monastic pecking order but manouevered less successfully at the time of the Dissolution, which it failed to avoid. Augustine arrived in Canterbury in AD 597 and built an abbey outside the walls of King Aethelbert's city. One of the most important ecclesiastical sites in England, St Augustine's grounds contain a pillar which may (or may not) be a phallic symbol of significance in the rites of Athelbert's former religion and therefore an early church organ . . . (or indeed not). Sadly, it has just been announced that St Augustines is to close to the public due to the Conservative's cuts.

Everything is within walking distance in Canterbury and what follows is a list of a few sites and sights within the city boundaries. St Martin's is the oldest church still holding services in England. St Dunstan's vaults contain the head of Thomas More, who lost it when he could

The Inns

Ye Olde Yewe Tree, Westbere

With walls of the purest medieval cow dung and riverbank mud all held together by lime and horse hair and held up by ancient ships timbers, there is no doubt about Ye Olde Yewe Tree's early 14th century origins. Built in the days before architects, there are beams all around and not a nail in sight inside, this is because the oak beams are held together by expert wood pegging.

The bar itself is festooned with hops and dominated by a long ash table which came from a monastery 300 years ago. The panelling is Victorian and there are old English beams to match the old English game of Ring the Bull which can be and is played on what looks like an oversize dart board.

Queen Anne (probably Anne of Cleves) once spent the night here and Dick Turpin is supposed to have escaped the long (but not long enough) arm of the law through an upstairs window. A knife to be found sticking in the sill until 20 years ago was thrown at his disappearing form . . . so the story goes. If ghosts exist then many regulars have seen two friendly souls here, who come through the door (way) after customers and sit each in their own place in the bar. One is not and would not sanction Henry VIII's divorce from Anne Boleyn. Other churches to see are St Pancras and St Mildred's. The King's School is the oldest school in England with druidic origins and Kent University on Tyler Hill (of more recent vintage) annually unleashes 800 talented graduates on the world. The Westgate is a large medieval traffic hazard which doubles as a museum where you can enjoy the sight of fetters, manacles, gyves and a compact, condemned cell, as well as a rooftop view over the city. Westgate Gardens offer a peaceful stroll by the river. The Weavers with its ducking stool, Greyfriars (entry by Stour Street), The Dane John, the Castle Keep, the St Laurence cricket ground, the ancient city walls and the Roman remains under the Longmarket so dramatically uncovered by the Luftwaffe are all of great interest, too.

Cantwarbyrig has developed richly since it was the huddle of Belgic huts by the River Stour discovered during the Caeserian operations of 54 BC and later converted into the Roman regional centre of Durovernum. Make no bones about it . . . it is your duty to visit Canterbury, at least once.

The walk itself runs from the lovely village of Westbere by lakes, marsh and riverside to Fordwich. After an inn-depth exploration of a second lovely village you then wend your way back through Sturry and by railway line to Ye Olde Yewe. The going is easy.

How to Get There
By road take the A28 north-east from Canterbury, Westbere is on the road after Sturry (approx 3½ miles).
By rail to Sturry.
By bus the 608, 609, 610, 628 and 629 all operate between Sturry and Westbere.

The Westbere Walk
By Westbere's pub, there's a yew tree whose roots go back to before the time of the Domesday Book. The tree is over a thousand years old and has, amongst other tricky historic moments, survived the Pogrom against its race initiated by King Richard who was trying to restrict the number of long bows which might be twanged against him.

Turn right out of **Ye Olde Yewe Tree** and make your way down Walnut Tree Lane, leaving Bushy Hill Road and a telephone box to your left. Before you pass a row of modern bungalows, you'll see an ancient lichen-covered barn on your way down to the railway crossing. Here you encounter your first pair of British Rail kissing-gates, surely a contradiction in terms. Stop, look and listen before crossing; at the other side there's a sign saying 'Armed trespassers will be prosecuted' – for poachers!

Take the main path straight ahead and turn left along the waterside track with Westbere Lake to your right as you continue. Partly created by mining subsidence, the lakes here were hollowed out for their gravel which is used to make cement. This has led to an ecological boom in the area and the establishment of a bird sanctuary. If you peer beyond the Norfolk rushes (used in thatching) you may see Canada geese, black-headed geese and flocks of other water fowl.

Follow the path past algae-filled pools on the one side and the gently lapping lake on the other – try not to fall into either. When you reach the bank of the 'brown' River Stour, turn right and head upstream. All around you will see silent and furtive strangers loitering with umbrellas and binoculars . . . don't worry they're only trout fishermen and ornithologists.

Beyond the river to your left is Trenly Park Wood. It's odd to think that much of this area lay under sea in the not so distant past and, in fact, that Julius Caesar sailed up the river in 54 BC. The Stour itself was once much bigger and a thriving commercial channel before the silt built up in the river mouth at Sandwich. Separate elements of the river flow disparately further upstream (including through Canterbury) but by the time it reaches Fordwich it is the navigable Great Stour, which is what you see beside you. There are rat holes above the water-line and the embankment is lined with alders, the odd pleasure boat and warning signs concerning the dangers of the local mud. Pass Fordwich Boat Club and turn left at the road to pause a while by the bridge.

Fordwich used to be a 'limb' of the Cinque Port of Sandwich and served as a landing place for the Caen stone which was used to build both St Augustine's Abbey and Canterbury Cathedral. The old wharfs here have witnessed many protracted quarrels between the two monastic factions over landing dues and tolls levied on goods for the surrounding area. One particularly bitter wrangle over landing rights between the Prior of Christchurch (the cathedral order) and the Abbot of St Augustine's ended with the former paying the latter an annual rent of one red rose for land at Fordwich . . . This was in 1285.

Fordwich, though small, enjoyed royal privilege in return for contributing ships to the Royal Navy. The corporate status of the village, however, diminished gradually with the silting up of the mouth of the Stour and suddenly with the passing of Victorian legislation. The construction of a railway line between Canterbury and Whitstable in 1830 finally put paid to Fordwich's import trade and marked the end of a beautifully profitable friendship with the cathedral city. To this day, Fordwich still pays Ship Money to the Cinque Port of Sandwich now decimalised to the symbolic sum of 17p.

After another bridge, you come to **The George and Dragon** and if you round the corner you will reach **The Fordwich Arms** near the Old Village Shop and the church of St Mary the Virgin. The Arms stands opposite the smallest town hall in England which has a courtroom upstairs and a lockup on the ground floor. Hanging over the 'grey' river here you can see the

an old woman, the other is an old man with a wide-brimmed hat, former publican Dickie Davies (of all names) who could not bear to leave the place.

The beers are excellent and gravity fed; Shepherd Neame, Whitbreads, Canterbury Ale and Theakstones. Grolsch lager can be healthily combined with 'non preservative' hamburgers, ploughman's or blacksmith's lunch. Out the back is a garden with a pair of nightingales and a view over the lakes; oh, and the matting (very durable) came from Betteshanger Colliery. You should be warned that you may be pressganged into a game of darts by the locals: this is a free house you can not afford to miss!

The George and Dragon Hotel, Fordwich

The George and Dragon once had the right to collect the tolls on the stone bridge which crosses the nearby Stour, a river which is noted for its trout, a specimen of which can be seen on the mayorial coat of arms of Fordwich. The George is a rambling building with low-pitched rooms and winding passages typical of many Fordwich houses. Where there's now fishing at the foot of the flower garden, Caeser may have once landed his legendary legionaries . . . times have changed.

The hotel offers a selection of real ales from old pumps as well as the pick of 48 wines. Children are welcomed. To eat there are bar snacks, hot/cold buffet lunches or meals in the à la carte restaurant.

old cucking (or ducking) stool once used to deal with nagging wives much to the amusement, no doubt, of local men. Fordwich has quite a history of horrific civic and religious retribution; notions of justice such as the drowning of thieves and separate quite distinct punishments for women seem savage today. For instance, a woman found guilty of 'quarrelling or slander' was made to carry 'a certain mortar' the length of the village preceded by a pipe-playing jester, whose mocking services she had to pay for with a penny. What 'a certain mortar' was, I don't know.

In St Mary's you can buy an excellent (and thick) book called 'Fordwich . . . the lost Port' (approx £1) and a booklet to tell you all about the church itself which dates from Saxon times. 'The Fordwich Stone' and 'The Penitent's Chair' are of special interest and should you meet a 'hatless, booted and cloaked figure by the churchyard gate, then it's more than likely that this is Colonel Short. Col Short died in 1716 and is the local ghost. A

staunch loyalist, he quarrelled over politics with John Nicholls the local vicar . . . ironically, there's little difference between them now since they lie buried a few feet apart under the chancel here.

Go back to the road and turn left up the High Street of this lovely village. Veer right with the road after Primrose Villa and then, as the road swings left, keep straight on by the track to the right of rebuilt Fordwich House and its imposing (-ish) gateway. Behind the house is a path which cuts across the fields, take it. To the left are trim lines of apple trees and, everywhere above, power lines.

At the far end of the field, the path winds a little left through a brambley trough, then right over a small bridge and a stile to emerge through a thorn thicket onto a golf course. Here watch for Blue Spots before your eyes, or coming straight at your head, even as you drive yourself straight across two fairways till you reach a fence: Remember, golf is the sport with the highest mortality rate. Find the stile almost under the power lines, cross it and its near neighbour, then turn right towards the distant road to go over scrub and heathland.

Soon you must go over a broken stile and into a wood and rapidly swing left to emerge into broad daylight and to the unwholesome sight of the municipal rubbish dump. In a wind its hard to tell squawking seagulls from the fluttering plastic bags which catch on the trees. Follow on between the trees and the fence on the left which is the only thing at present between you and the scrap heap.

Climb a small fence next to the dump to arrive on a marshy common where you continue across a small wooden bridge and through a gate into the field by the road. Leave this by the metal gate opposite 'Ferryfield Farm' and turn right along the pavement. This takes you past a wealth of glasshouses and a garage for beetles – that's what it says!

Pass over two bridges of two distinct sizes, each with 'a lovely peep of the blue Stour' and you're truly in Sturry, a name which derives from Estuari. After the second bridge, turn left up Milner Lane; there are, you will observe, no lack of 'no fishing' notices here as you pass by houses roofed with Kent pegs and Milner

Court, King's School's little brother. Walk along the path through the churchyard – the building has a 15th century tower and Norman foundations – to the far side. Now turn perversely left up the road marked 'OUT ONLY' and soon you pass an old oast house to your left on the way to more (and more sightly) BR kissing-gates. The enterprising school you've just passed converted its old tithe barn into indoor tennis courts.

Once more, be careful as you cross lines with this walk. On the far side, turn immediately right on a path beside the railway which takes you past Sturry Station's platforms on its way to the road.

Cross the road, turn right across the crossing and keep going to Field Way, into which you turn left. There's a path to the right of the white gate ahead – it's slightly overgrown, so you could slip along by the cricket field – which you follow past the cricket clubhouse and leave to the right just behind the football clubhouse, a neat way of avoiding the sunken bath. Go over a metal stile to the miniature railway circuit which often operates during summer.

By the danger sign, turn left through the gap in the hedge and, being on the wrong side of the tracks once more, cross carefully by the stile and the kissing-gate, which, lo and behold, you can't miss. This is where the kissing-gates have to stop as you turn right to follow the lane by the line till it runs out in a hay field near Westbere. On your way, an evergreen hedge on the far side tries to conceal the evergrey industrial landscape of the local cement industry, the very one which uses the gravel from the lakes. It's interesting to watch the work processes for a while – there's nothing like watching others work, especially the delicate craft of concrete manufacture.

As stated, the path suddenly stops and you're in a field. Strike off half right for a white house and leave by the path to its right. At the road, turn right and follow lengthy Westbere Lane back to Ye Olde Yewe (ye can't escape yerself, you see). If it's summer make sure you sit in the garden with its wonderful view over the lakes and its resident nightingales . . . which may even serenade you, if you're lucky and they're on song.

The Fordwich Arms, Fordwich

The Fordwich Arms stands by the side of the River Stour opposite Englands oldest town hall. Today's building replaces the previous pub which burned down in the 1920s. Unkindly described as 'Brewer's Tudor' in the local guide, its brick and ivy façade blends in reasonably with its ancient surroundings.

Inside, there's an oak-panelled dining room and an open plan bar with real ale available from handpumps. For more solid nourishment, you can turn to a good menu of home cooking and bar snacks. Beside the river there's a patio with tables and umbrellas and a soothing outlook over the Stour. Be careful to take off muddy gumboots since this pub has been known to turn away the less sartorially elegant.

15 Ditchling

APPROXIMATELY 4 Miles

The District

Ditchling is a typically gracious Sussex village in the shadow of the 'blunt, bow-headed, whale-backed Downs', as Kipling called them. Ditchling has a main street of 16th and 17th century half-timbered buildings interspersed with Georgian houses and antique shops. The village is affluent and very 'English' and some inhabitants still wear Inverness capes or drive well-polished Morris 1000s (or do both) as they go about their Saturday shopping. As if to confirm all this 'Englishness', Emmet, the eccentric inventor, and Gracie Fields, the eccentric singer, lived here as did a famous English smuggler called Cond.

Standing in the High Street, you can look beyond the village to Ditchling Beacon, which is 813 feet tall, a statistic which makes it the fourth highest point on the South Downs and the third highest in Sussex. Cut deep in the slope nearby is an ancient artificial trench known as the Slype; 'deeper than a man is tall', it formed a concealed trackway down to the forest of the Weald. The question is, who did it conceal from what?

Stoolball, an old Sussex game, is still played on summer evenings, in Ditchling. The ball is bowled underarm to a batsman with a large, 'table-tennis' bat defending a 'stool', one-foot square and mounted on a stake 47″ from the ground. The batsman can be given out 'body before wicket', which emphasises that the game is not quite cricket. On the village common is a post crowned by a rooster, dated 1734. This replaced the gibbet used to hang a Jewish peddlar who cut the throats of the host, the hostess and the maid of The Royal Oak Inn and whose bones were left hanging till they fell to pieces as a warning to ill-intentioned passers-by. The old gibbet was said to cure toothache and consequently was steadily whittled away to nothing by locals with dental problems, leaving only crude and painful treatment available to them.

Nearby Brighton is just the place for passing time pleasurably. The famous resort has three miles of promenades, a dolphinarium, a little Madame Tussauds, popcorn, piers and picture postcards, sea, sun, sand and shingles, electric railways, arcades and bingo, mods and rockers . . . the list is endless. Brighton has been on holiday since the Prince Regent arrived in 1783 and mixed motifs with the Royal Pavilion. You can't help enjoying Sussex by the sea . . . (don't you) wish you were here.

The walk begins in Ditchling High Street and follows footpaths to the heights of Ditchling Beacon before returning via 'pastoral' Westmeston. The view from the top of the Beacon, which you must pay for with a stiff climb, is fantastic but be warned that its slopes are suitable only for the healthy consenting adult, tough kids and hale and hearty grandparents.

How to Get There
By road take the A23 north from Brighton, turn right onto the A273 and then right onto the B2122. Ditchling is on this road (approx 8 miles).
By rail to Hassocks.
By bus take the 124, 136 or 173 from Hassocks.

The Ditchling Walk
Quench your thirst in **The Sandrock**, then cross the road and go up Church Lane and the first building on the left has TS 1799 carved into its stonework. 'So what,' you may all say, as you turn left into the churchyard to get to a place of worship which was originally built during the boom in European churchbuilding of

The Inns

The Sandrock, Ditchling
The Sandrock was built early this century and owes its name to the cellars cut deep in the Sandrock below. The previous Sandrock was a brewery and pub, not to mention a haunt of smugglers, who cut a tunnel from the cellars to the graveyard as part of their surreptitious subterranean network. There were once gravel pits out the back of the building and a stone wall from that era is protected by a preservation order.

Inside there are two bars with two open fires, a curved oakwood bar, post-Victorian panelling, a collection of old maps and old regulars, too. The Sandrock is plain, pleasant and friendly.

To drink, there's a choice of hand-drawn Stag, keg Watneys, Ben Truman

the 13th century. St Margaret's (of Antioch) is constructed of Caen stone from Normandy and local chalk and flint. Its nave stands on the site of a Saxon church from the time when Dicelinga (as it was called) was a Royal Vill of Alfred The Great. The Saxon church itself stood on an ancient Pagan knoll. The green in front of it was once a farmyard and running underneath the whole area are the tunnels which proved so handy for smugglers. Oh yes . . . the porch entrance is round the far side, opposite The White Horse.

Leave by the wooden gate which gives on to West Street and turn left. The Elizabethan house, to your right before you turn, is Wings Place, a golden handshake from Henry VIII to Anne of Cleves, who managed to keep her head throughout her marriage to the fun-loving monarch and the building after its dissolution. It was built by Henry Poole whose monument stands in Abergavenny Chapel in the church. Anne of Cleves herself probably never set dainty foot inside it; she had plenty of other houses. Cross the road to get to **The White Horse** which shares its premises with a dental surgery. Choose your own preferred treatment. Underneath West Street are more of the smugglers' tunnels which honeycomb the foundations of this old Sussex village.

Go right, on leaving The White Horse and then south down South Street past Ditchling Press (the old workhouse) and the Jointure where Sir Frank Brangwyn lived and painted — 'jointure' means 'dowry'. As South St goes right and Beacon Road evolves on the left, bisect the angle of the two roads to find the public footpath which begins by the bench dedicated to the aesthetic philosopher Arthur Howell. The path runs between a wooden fence and a hedge offering glimpses of back gardens, washing lines and a bird fancier's flight of fancies.

In a circular lawn at the centre of a circle of houses, there's a friendly lamppost which illuminates your further progress and points out the whereabouts of the footpath to the Beacon (to the right of 'Flats 21-28' between hedges). After a plank bridge and a stile of sorts, turn left and follow the left-hand hedge as you head for the Downs which you can see rising beyond the fields ahead. Cross the stile by the overgrown thorn tree and keep to the path which curves left and crosses a second plank bridge into a field with a frisky white pony. Head along with the road to your left and go past a stile in the corner of the field. Now, find the stile in the far right-hand corner of the wedge-shaped field and, if you don't get muddy here, you never will. Pass under the trees across stile number three to find a further stile on the far side of the copse. Aim to the right of the now visible barn passing the hens, geese and tups conversing round a mobile chicken shack on your way to a further stile. To your right is a pond as you look to find the continuation of your path on the other side of the track between two corrugated outhouses and into the trees. The path winds you through the wood to a stile. From this, aim for the wooden gate by the lane in the far right-hand corner of the field. Now, the beacon is to the left on the towering escarpment ahead and there are signs of ancient agriculture all over its steep, strength-sapping slopes.

Turn left along the lane (aptly named Narrow Road) and then right at the crossroads, direction 'The Beacon'. 40 yards or so on, there's a public footpath sign to the right of the road. Follow it and the going gets stiff up a clay track — slippery, when wet. As you grittily climb, marvel (through clenched teeth) at the view on the right over the fertile farmlands in the lea of the downs — take frequent pauses, wipe your brow, think of the good you're doing yourself.

What you see below was once the forest of Anderida, the hostile haunt of many dangerous denizens and presented to Osferth by Alfred. When the path branches by the sign for The Nature Reserve, go right up its steeper limb . . . he wrote sadistically. Behind, below, the view over flat lands and the prosperity its tractability has brought. Ahead, above, a stile and the pain of uphill progress — after the stile keep going up. The more you get up, the more the wind does, too, and by this time your cheeks should be rosy to deep purple . . . hold on to your hat.

Near the ridge top, branch up left for the summit and you should find a stile near at hand ahead. You're part of the skyline as you turn left enjoying your topographical overview, the colourful animated map below to your left and, to your right, high hay fields. Heigh ho, it *was* worth the climb. Find your own way to the broader path by the fence and the prevailing wind should propel you gently along it. As panoramas go, this view runs a long way.

Soon you get to a triangulation point which marks the highest spot on the South Downs – 813 feet. Near this bracing spot you will also find a direction finder pointing out the highest geological protruberances visible around you but, sadly, from here you look in vain for the sea. Iron Age earthworks are detectable on the heights here as was a beacon lit in Elizabethan times to warn people of the Spanish Armada so unsportingly sailing up the English Channel. It was re-lit to celebrate Elizabeth II's jubilee and, no doubt, will be again in days to come.

Your path goes on past a car park and across the road over the summit. Go through the well-hung gate on the far side of the road and to the right there's a view over rolling and close-contoured upland farmscape. Follow the fence on your left, ignoring the stile, till you descend where the old sunken path loops downwards and backwards at a point where the hill is scarred and chalky. Below are sheep fields and the now sagging terraces of the ancient field system. The slope of the hill here is just right for sitting on . . . on a clear day, you can see forever. (Half left, Ditchling and Keymer; beyond them Burgess Hill.)

Still you can't sit here forever. To continue, go down through a double gate saying 'Pedigree Accredited Cattle' (no offence intended) and turn right past a lone and sickly rose hip bush towards Westmeston. A field to the left warns you against bulls in a time-honoured fashion, as you head for the right-hand side of double gates and along a chalky off-white track behind it and between trees. But first take a look back at the ethereal

and Mild and Draught Guinness and, to eat, there's a good menu which includes scampi and pizza. There's a garden with swings and slides and inside you can play with a shove ha'penny set and a pack of cards.

The White Horse, Ditchling
Opposite the village church and next door to Wings Place which once belonged to Anne of Cleves, the White Horse is a 16th century coaching inn with peg tiles and white rendered walls. Deep cellars underneath the building are linked by passages to Wings Place and the church and these were extensively used at one time by the village smugglers.

The White Horse has one bar with a coal fire, sabres on the wall, carthorse traces and brasses, stirrups, shears, hand cuffs, foreign coins and tartan wallpaper, a reminder of a previous Scottish landlord. It also has a games room with three pool tables.

Strong Country Bitter and Pompey Royal are both delivered by hand-pump, while Mild, Trophy, Tankard and Guinness are all available on keg. The malt whisky comes in 25 different varieties. Hot snacks are 'comprehensive' and include ploughman's, fisherman's lunches, pizza and macaroni cheese. Children are allowed in the beer garden in summer.

river of clouds flowing just above the hill top where you were.

Past Westmeston Farm and a row of new but old and old but new cottages, you come to the road. Across it and right is Westmeston Church, comprising a mixture of early English and Norman styles. It dates from the 11th century and has somehow lost the paintings of the Cluniac monks which used to cover its interior walls. The question is 'how?'

Back at the road turn right for Henfield (in big letters!) and leave the telephone box behind to the left. Just past the bus stop on the left-hand side, the path goes up the bank past 'Lily Bank'. Keep straight along this for a stile; be careful, it's loose. With Westmeston Place and its hidden priest's hole to the right, head straight for the next stile past the kind of horse you could easily lead to water and just as easily make drink, judging by his/her affability. Now follow the right-hand edge of the field to the next stile, not far off. The following stile is half left by a plank bridge and within sight of old ploughs by a pretty dew pond and outhouse. To continue, find the next stile in the far right-hand corner of a field which is damp and squelches underfoot – you can even hear undersoil moisture. From here, it's 50 yards half right to a stile and then a little left of straight across for the stile with the broken tread. Step warily and then, half left towards Ditchling and a further stile. From this one, it's $\frac{3}{8}$ right (yes $\frac{3}{8}$) to the next and a small bridge and a backyard alley.

Thus, in time, you emerge opposite 'Shirley Croft', a house, not a girl, in a suburban backwater with well-shaped hedges, well modulated birdsong and the constant background buzz of lawnmowers. Hiccup politely right across the road to find the public footpath between 'Odd Acre' and the hedge to its right. Pass a white gate, a kissing one and a stile on your way to the road.

Cross the road towards the football pitches and turn left. Turn right with the sign for Public Conveniences (which is disturbingly like a public footpath sign) through a gate, past a car park and behind a pavilion, where sporting teams are served with sporting teas. Follow the left-hand hedge to the tennis courts, looking back occasionally at the Downs to see if you can spot the 'V' of trees planted for Queen Victoria's jubilee. It's rumoured that the game of 'stoolball' is played in these grounds on summer evenings.

Turn left after the courts and go along a potholed lane passing 'Lattenbells' on your right. At the next lane either cross and go to the left of 'Pardons' through a kissing-gate or go right up East End Lane. The former course of action will bring you face to face with a gazebo and a half-eaten fish on a stick – this is built into a wall on your right before a second kissing-gate. At the road, turn right and go where haywains waggons have gone before, squeezing narrowly and messily between the close-set houses which used to be there (and are now demolished) on their way to market. Turn right up the High Street to pass the old bank (a 16th century former tenement) on your way to the Sandrock.

Take the latter route up East End Lane and you will go by 'Walnut Tree Cottage' with its cat slide roof (denoting 16th century origins) and its well with wheel and chain and 'Dymocks' whose family owners (of the same name) are 'hereditary challengers for the crown' and have been at each coronation since Richard II's . . . this sounds dangerous! Forge Cottage is of interest, too, along this beautiful lane. When you reach the top, turn down left for the Sandrock, where they have measures and potions to revive the weary walker, that you should have become by this point.

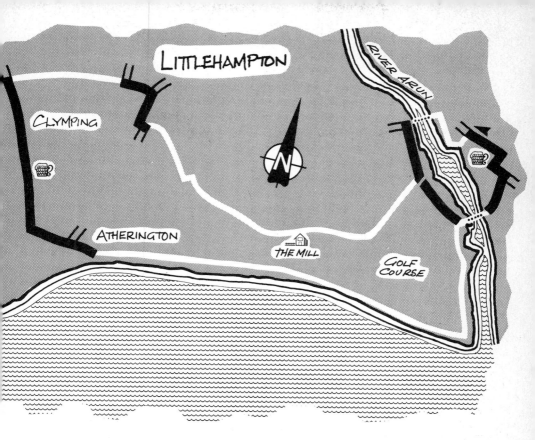

16   **Littlehampton**   APPROXIMATELY 4¾ Miles

The District

Sea air and salt water were the twin virtues extolled by a Dr Russell in a book in 1750. His book was widely read and soon reached the bedside table of the Prince of Wales, later to become George IV. Enthused, he espoused the cause and led the trend that, with his royal example, swept the country. Led by Brighton, the Sussex coastline put itself fairly and squarely on the domestic tourist map. The resorts here, that sprang up, or were developed, all faced south and therefore had maximum sunshine: indeed nowadays there's a friendly rivalry between them about which has the most sunshine hours annually – not exactly the sort of thing the town council-

lors can influence in committee. Their various beaches of sand, pebbles and a mixture of the two provide, and have provided, good safe bathing and sailing and successful angling.

A scaled down version of Brighton, and a mile from the village of Bersted, 'dear little Bognor' as Queen Victoria affectionately called it, was designed by Sir Richard Hotham, an ex-Southwark ex-hatter in the 1790s. Although sometimes looked on with favour by aristocracy and royalty, it was a modest seaside resort built for the middle classes and this was, amongst other reasons, probably why it was the model for Jane Austen's Sanditon. The 'Regis', about which all snobbish Bognorites were

▶

undoubtedly very smug, was added after George V's convalescence at nearby Aldwick in 1928-9. Though it's as well for any contemporary town snobs, if they remain, to remember that this King was once heard to dismiss their own town with the short and sweet epithet, "Bugger Bognor". So Princess Anne and her father are only the latest in a long line of swearing royals. Less favoured now by VIP visitors, Bognor has had to move slightly downmarket and had to allow the construction of Billy Butlin's first holiday camp and the less sedate forms of entertainment that catered to the new class of customer. And in the long run Bognor has benefited from this more balanced trade.

Skirting round inland of Littlehampton, you come to Arundel, an old town climbing to the top of its hill and overlooked by the cathedral, a vast, but not great, 1870s building and the castle, seat of the Dukes of Norfolk. The keep and gateway date from the Normans but most of the rest is Victorian — it was restored in the 1890s. Most of the interior is in the heavily impressive mock baronial style then in vogue and, when Queen Victoria stayed here, her bed and its matching furniture was made specially for the visit. The art collection is impressive and includes paintings by Van Dyck, Reynolds and Gainsborough, there's also an exhibition of ceremonial robes. All worth a visit.

To head seaward again, you follow the fast flowing River Arun, the largest Sussex river, downstream to the ancient Port of Arundel, Littlehampton. Even allowing for the fact that the Arun's exit into the sea was re-cut in 1600, 1626, 1628, 1657, 1715 and finally in 1730, Littlehampton has been a useful little port down the ages. After the inevitable Roman settlement, the Normans saw its value as a port and most of the Caen stone brought from Normandy for their fine churches was imported here. French prisoners from the battle of Crècy were brought here and, 40 years later, so were 80 captured French ships. They contained 20,000 tons of wine which must

have kept the small port going for about a century. Nowadays, Littlehampton still has at least one ship per day, though with less exciting cargo (sand-ballast, timber, stone and pumice) and its boatyards remain as central to the life of the town as tourism.

Developed by the Victorians, the resort became popular with artists and writers. Constable painted its windmill (long gone), Byron lived happily here and a nice story tells of how Samuel Taylor Coleridge was walking along the beach one day and heard Greek being spoken. Investigating, he discovered Rev Harry Francis Cary, translator of Dante, reading Homer to his son. The men became friends and Coleridge used his literary clout to advertise the works of the Italian writer.

Littlehampton has miles of safe (in fact the safest on the Sussex coast) sandy beaches on both sides of the Arun, offers good sailing, with two sailing clubs, is renowned for its fresh and sea water angling and has a golf course. And you'll have to decide for yourselves whether William Blake, who lived in nearby Felpham for 3 years, was right when he wrote,

"The Sussex men are noted fools
And weak in their brain-pan"

— an amusing if dubious jibe from a usually most visionary poet.

How to Get There
By road Littlehampton lies on the A259 coast road between Bognor Regis and Worthing.
By rail to Littlehampton.

The Littlehampton Walk
Start from **The White Hart** and, on leaving, turn right out of the pub and then

right again along Surrey Street. At Argyll 'Hall, fork right along River Road, following it along through the No Entry signs and past the riverside warehouses and workshops. Soon you arrive at **The Arun View Inn**, just after the footbridge. After your drink, cross the footbridge. (This bridge should be completed in March 1981, but if it is not, due to bad weather, bad management, lack of interest and/or money, there's a free bus service every 20 minutes to take you to the far side of the river.)

When you have crossed the rather brown River Arun, turn left at the telephone box along the straight road, marked as public footpaths to Clymping and West Beach. Amongst the bizarre names on this short stretch of road are on your right, 'Seanormous' – a modestly sized house, not really very close to the sea, and 'Kandy Park' – a mobile-home site and, on your left, the Canadian Village. There may be good reasons for these names, but they elude me. Amongst the yacht building firms are Osborne's, who also make lifeboats.

At the entrance to Littlehampton Golf Course at the end, take the public footpath to the right round the side of Kandy Park. As you walk out from the protection of its slatted fence, watch out for drivers to your right (you'll see what I mean). You walk straight on along the raised path along the edge of a scrubby wood and a rather stagnant-looking stream.

As you wander along this easy, but sometimes muddy path, your ears will be assailed by a variety of noises depending on the wind direction and general weather conditions. Closest to you, there's the twittering of the birds in the trees and furthest away there's the roaring of the surf to your left and the whine of traffic to your right.

In between, there's the 'puck' of no 4 irons on the plastic of golfers' balls and the squealing and grunting of pigs. The first of the pig fields on the walk is on your right.

The path re-enters the strip of wood – now more brambly and thorny than wooded – giving you glimpses of the golf-course and, after a while you reach the Mill, where there are more rooting porkers on your right. The Mill used to be a windmill, grinding out flour, but now it's

The Inns

The White Hart, Littlehampton

The White Hart is the main pub of the walk and after it was built in 1761, was one of the main coaching inns on the Shoreham to Portsmouth route. In its history, its name has changed from a creature of the air – The Swan, to a creature of the water – The Dolphin, to a creature of the land. All of these creatures are quite special – so is the pub.

Large and attractive bay windows were added in 1935 to both bars, giving light and space. Yet the pub is full of some of the most interesting 'things' I have seen in my research. Assiduously collected over 25 years by Rex Huggins, they are predominantly nautical. A list is not possible but here's a couple of tempters: a letter requesting one of the swords above the bar, as an ornament for Nelson's cabin in 'The Victory' and a copy of his last letter to Lady Emma Hamilton, written from his flagship on 19th October 1805. Really, you have to see for yourself. This pub is friendly, inviting and recommended.

It's a Watneys house with Special Bitter, Special Mild, Ben Truman, Guinness and two lagers. There's a full lunch on offer during the week, and hot and cold bar snacks on weekends and in the evenings.

►

a rather expensive private school, grinding rich children, through the educational mill of 'O' and 'A' levels. The path continues in the same direction, behind the buildings – they're on your left – and on through the trees. You pass caravans, student accommodation possibly, as the path runs along the middle of the by now thinner strip of woodland, soon with pig fields on both sides.

When you reach the end of the wood, head off roughly in the direction the sign points, aiming for the nearest thorn-tree on the bank of the drainage channel. At this tree, turn left along the bank and cross the concrete bridge onto the other bank. Now turning left along the water's edge, follow the channel to a shed mostly hidden by trees and, where the channel swings left, you continue along the edge of the field. At the corner, go along beside the white building to a track leading to Clymping camp. Turn right. The track soon bends left and then right (ignore the public footpath sign here) and, after it's been joined by a track from the right, runs between a half-timbered and brick barn and a lovely thatched house on your right and impressive Kents Farm House on your left.

Here turn left along the lane, passing an 1862 house, large modern farm buildings and a horrible, foul, stagnant, rubbish-filled pond – all on your right. Where the lane bends to the right, go straight on and, at the school, go straight on again, now along a straight tarmac path, past the school's football pitch and between fields.

The path swings left under large pine trees and leads you out between houses onto Clymping Street at Spring Cottage. Turn left, wondering just how they managed to get the hut into the tree in Spring Cottage's garden, and follow The Street down, past the Ark, to **The Black Horse.**

Having led yourself to The Black Horse and made yourself a drink (or something like that) turn left out of the pub and continue down The Street. You pass the entrance of Bailiffscourt Hotel, an edifice oddly built, to say the least. It was built to look like a monastery by Lord Moyne, who was the British Ambassador to Egypt at the time of the discovery of Tutankhamun's tomb – a fairly useless piece of information. Whole different sections of the 'monastery' were brought from other buildings all over the place and then, somehow, fitted together like a jigsaw and the result, surprisingly, is very harmonious.

The Street leads down to Atherington, a hamlet that's a victim of the advancing sea. All that remain now are Atherington Cottages and a few derelict farm buildings; the rest of the hamlet has gone, destroyed largely by the pebbles, and the surf that pushed them inland. You'll see that the sea wall has been strengthened now with large concrete blocks, so maybe Atherington could arise, Phoenix-like, in the car park. Some hope.

At the pebbly, groyned beach turn left and really there's only one walk-instruction now, until you reach the mouth of the Arun – walk along the beach to the mouth of the Arun. After the Mill, in its copse of tall fir trees, you can choose whether to walk on the beach, watching out for various waders and the ubiquitous oystercatchers, or on the dunes, watching out, in warm weather for the nudists who have been known to strip off in the seclusion of these sandy hillocks. This choice really depends on whether your ornithological bent outweighs your voyeuristic bent. But, in the same way that you would not pester the birds, don't pester the nudists.

When you reach the mouth of the Arun, you have no alternative but to turn inland up to the Moorings. Follow the little road up to the Golf Clubhouse on your left. In summer, you can catch a passenger ferry across the river here (10p adults, children less) and, on the far bank, turn left along Pier Road. You pass the Littlehampton Harbour Board building and various timber yards, until you reach a T-junction where you go left back to The White Hart.

In winter when the ferry doesn't run, walk on past the Golf Clubhouse to where the road dips down and to the left away from the river. Here take the tarmac path that forks to the right and follow it past an astonishing collection of widely-differing houseboats, of all ages and types. Endora isn't perhaps the most desirable of residences, but the old MTBs, narrow boats, houseboats and barges are entertaining and somewhat different from housing estates in Surbiton. The path emerges onto a road, which hopefully you should recognize. Follow it to the T-junction at the end where, either you catch your free bus back to Littlehampton, or you walk across the footbridge. On the far bank you simply walk back along River Road to Surrey Street and The White Hart.

The Arun View Inn, Littlehampton

Just next to the old roadbridge and its new footbridge replacement, The Arun View has two bars, The Fisherman's and The River, and the latter has been modernised with picture windows to overlook, as does the adjoining terrace, the Arun with its bobbing swans and boats. The pub has a mildly nautical flavour with its pictures of boats, and ships' wheels, lights and crests.

On handpump are Whitbread's Pompey Royal and Strong's Bitter with Pompey Extra, as a winter warmer. Other drinks are standard, and so is the hot and cold bar food.

The Black Horse, Clymping

Records from 1630 show that The Black-Horse was a village pub then, and that the building was originally, as is evident from its white-painted exterior, three cottages. It's a friendly and go-ahead pub with one large bar and a restaurant with a 7-day a week à la carte menu. When the Watneys' architects redesigned the interior, they managed to keep some of the old atmosphere with exposed brick walls, two open fires (one has a lovely duck's nest grate) and old seating. Alan Becker, the landlord, has added old ornaments (including a stag's head) and a piano, which anyone can play, if they're good enough and nobody objects.

Amongst the Watneys' standards are Tamplins (from Sussex) and Stag on handpump and naturally, as there's a restaurant, there's a good selection of wines available. Bar snacks are varied, home-made, and recommended.

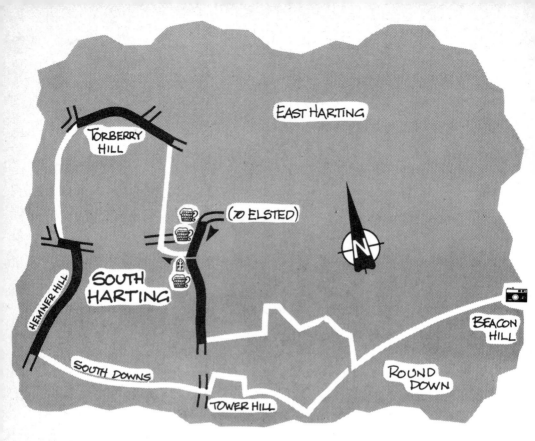

17   South Harting

APPROXIMATELY 6 Miles

The District

'Sweetest of the Downland villages,' South Harting is one of the three Hartings which stand in beautiful countryside beside the South Downs. Distinguished from the others by its 'harmonious mixture of red brick Georgian houses and older stone dwellings', the village is dominated by the green copper spire of the church of Ss Mary and Gabriel . . . not, however on Whit Monday.

Every Whit Monday, the streets of South Harting are taken over for the Feast of the Old Club. The Old Club was formed as a friendly society in the early 19th century in order to protect the working men (and their families) of the village from the worst vicissitudes of their impoverished and insecure existence at a time of low wages, high prices and incurable illness . . . (sounds familiar!). The Club provided paid up members with pensions, medical care and funeral costs. In these relatively affluent times, its function has changed and on Whit Monday club members assemble outside the village pubs between 9.00 and 10.00 in the morning, where a roll is called. After a traditional church service, a procession is held through the streets of the village and this is led by two 'stewards' holding six foot staves. Next in line are two men carrying red, white and blue flags, then bandsmen and finally the members themselves, two abreast wearing red, white and blue rosettes and bearing peeled hazel wands. This bizarre procession proceeds to the strains of 'The Red, White and Blue' and 'Sussex by the Sea' and to the village square where a beech tree is 'encircled', before the ceremony finishes back at the church once more. It is most likely that all this is a modern continuation of the ancient tree cult from the days when the local economy was almost entirely dependant on the products of its forests . . . the occasion symbolises the vigorous life of the woods being brought into the village itself. After this fertility rite, the feast and a dance are held for members and their guests.

Though the village blacksmith is still kept busy at his anvil, most of the old trades of the Hartings have long since gone: all the 'snobs' (the old travelling cobblers) have disappeared and the grometmakers, too. The gromet industry came to South Harting in 1925 at the instigation of one Alfred Barnes. Gromets were meticulously prepared strips of cotton (from $\frac{1}{4}''$ to $\frac{3}{4}''$), meticulously sewn round metal rods and used as washers in boilers; their function was not unimportant since they were necessary to prevent explosions. Large ocean liners had as many as 100,000 gromets, a figure which matches the number the women of South Harting's cottage industry could turn out each week at the height of the Second World War, when the peak of production was reached. After the war, the business slumped and advances in machine-making produced new solutions to the problems of gromet manufacture and unemployment for local women.

Elsted, a near neighbour of the Hartings, has a fine, reconstructed Saxon church and a real, old country pub: The Three Horseshoes. Uppark, owned by

The Inns

The White Hart Inn, South Harting

The White Hart is a beautiful old pub dating back to 1682 when it was built as a coaching inn on the 'back road' between Portsmouth and London and originally known as 'The Old Buck'. There are three bars, a sunken dining room and a function room round the back. The rooms are spacious with a 'wealth' of beams and five magnificent log burning fires, as good as you will find anywhere . . . you can sit in the nook of one of them. A connecting door dates from the pub's first opening hour.

The interior walls of the building are decorated with old farm implements (a turf cutter, a silage knife, a rickknife, a malt shovel, gin traps etc.) and old prints and photos, including a particularly entertaining portrait of Victorian regulars. There is a ghost, too, which is heard but not seen – with the noise of drinking and footsteps in the bar but no apparition.

Elegant Mr Read, the landlord, dispenses hand-drawn Friary Meux and Burtons, keg DD and Mild providing you pay him to do so, and everything you could want to eat, too, including garlic bread and salads. Bar billiards can be played in one bar and out the back there is half an acre of walled garden. This pub is particularly recommended.

◀

the National Trust, was built in its commanding position on a crest in the Downs after a new pump, capable of getting the necessary water supply up there, had been invented. The foursquare house was built for Lord Grey in the 1680s by the same William Talman who built Chatsworth Palace and is now a museum of 18th century furnishings and therefore aswim with flock wallpaper. Uppark has its place in history and is thought to have been the hiding-place of Monmouth and his fellow plotters. When Nelson was offered the house after his success in the Napoleonic wars, he declined it on the grounds that his horses would be quickly worn out by the steepness of the front drive. Famous occupants include Emma Hart, whom Greville befriended, Romney painted, Horatio loved and Sir William Hamilton married, otherwise Lady Hamilton who was shown the door in 1871, Sir Harry Featherstonehaugh, who married his head dairy maid in his seventies and a young H G Wells, whose mother kept house. Judge Jeffries had none of Nelson's reservations about the property and tried desperately to get his hands on Uppark during his last years of favour but, before he could do so, he was sent to the Tower. Queen Anne is not dead at Uppark . . . it's really worth a visit.

The walk goes from South Harting past Torberry Hill, up Henner Hill, then along the South Downs Way at a height of 500 feet above sea level. The highspot is 793 feet (give or take an inch or two) Beacon Hill, which offers fantastic views over the Fold Country before you head down into the village. The walk is quite steep but not difficult; the paths may be muddy at times.

How to Get There

By road take the A286 north from Chichester and then turn left onto the B2141, South Harting is on the road (approx 11 miles).
By rail to Petersfield.
By bus take the 261 or the 262 from Petersfield.

The South Harting Walk

Starting from **The Ship**, walk up the main street towards the tall church steeple of the village. On your way, you will pass the old village pump hopefully across the road to your left and **The White Hart Inn** on your right. The White Hart has five magnificent, logburning fires, three separate bars and a friendly atmosphere, don't miss it. Anthony Trollope used to live in the village (1880-82) and probably drunk here, too.

Leaving the inn, turn right and then take the lane to the right of the church. Before doing so, a visit to Ss Mary and Gabriel's could not lead you far wrong. The 14th century church is interesting not just for its size and grace or the corkscrew wooden staircase leading to the bell tower but also for the exhibition of local history it houses. The war memorial in its yard was carved by Eric Gill and you should look for the stocks and whipping post nearby. The building is known as 'The Cathedral of the Downs' (a title inherited from the now defunct church at Treyford) and its copper steeple is a landmark for miles around as you will soon see for yourselves. As you proceed along the lane, you have to turn right just before the farmyard to follow the marked public footpath. This promptly swings left and on to a farm lane, where you turn right and make for the road.

Go, straight across the road and saunter through a kissing-gate to follow a long straight path between fields. At this point, you are nearly surrounded by a loop of hills — behind you is the village spire and, to your right across the fields, the old buildings of Harting Manor House. Press on to find the stile at the end of the straight; pause to look back, then hop it and go left up the lane.

As you turn a corner and the road drops, you can see West Harting below you and an oast house cowl on the horizon. At the T-junction, turn left past The Old Inn on the corner and 'Stick No Bills', too. Above you, to the left is wooded Torberry Hill whose Iron Age fortifications (wooden palisades and deep dug ditches) once served as a refuge for women, children and beasts when their menfolk were off beating up the neighbouring barbarians as was their custom. To your right is a curious tin building and beyond it open fields. So far, this has all been very flat . . . so far . . . but ahead is the high beech-covered South Downs escarpment.

Go past the 'well endowed' garden of Dell Cottage, cosy under its hill, and then keep straight on at a country crossroads which tries to lure you to Quebec and Goose Green. Soon after the crossing, there is a footpath up the left-hand bank of the road which you must follow as it winds round the bottom of the hill just above the road. If you are feeling hyperactive, disperse some energy be climbing the steep slope to your left and inspecting what little remains of the ancient fort – there are wild plum and apple trees dating from early cultivation. If you do, do not forget to come back to this path.

The shaded path comes to a full stop by the road and opposite the lane to Hucks Holt Farm. A full stop for it, but a comma for you; keep going up this lane with South Harting steeple to your left as you coast past Leigh House on your right. This metalled road is the easy way to get up the South Downs and you should have time to spot pheasant shooting local aristocrats in winter here. In

The Coach and Horses, South Harting

The Coach and Horses, at the foot of the South Downs Escarpment, was built in 1906 on the site of an old beer house, whose garages once stabled the extra horses needed to get coaches and the gentry up the hill to Uppark. It is a down to earth pub with a snug bar and a particularly warm welcome for hikers and walkers. In the main bar, there's a coal fire, a large table to sit round and plenty of good beer, including local Ballard's Best.

Other beers are Badgers Best and Fullers ESB (hand-drawn), draught Bass, keg Tartan and Chieftain Mild. There is home-made soup, and toasted sandwiches to warm your heart's cockles and an airy garden in summer to cool them down again. The Coach and Horses once handled 80 walkers recreating a pilgrimage from Arundel so they should be able to deal with you . . . and there is a children's room.

The Three Horsehoes, Elsted

The Three Horseshoes has been serving beer since 1606 and 'in the family' since 1900. Before the 17th century, it was a farmstead on the large West Dean Estate.

Behind the bar of this old country pub is an invoice dated 1918, when whisky and gin cost 40 shillings a gallon as the document proves. It cost Winifred Tullett's father £20 to 'come in' to the business at the turn of the century.

On the walls of the low ceilinged rooms are old pictures of country scenes and you can enjoy Friary Meux Best Bitter from the wood in a lovely garden with a view of the Devils Jumps and of the remains of Didling Church. The only pump on the bar is for lager and the only snacks are bread and cheese with chutney, crisps and peanuts.

The Ship, South Harting

Built one or two years after The White Hart up the street, The Ship has two friendly and lively bars. The village pubs summer Henner Hill is a walkover for ramblers and a chopping centre for woodpeckers.

Before the summit there is a small quarry to your right and then a house called 'Downlands' on the left. By this house, turn left along the South Downs Way at a cruising height of 482 feet above sea level as you continue along a clay track with kale fields left and dark hills right. The tower ahead is on Tower Hill, which is altogether logical, if unimaginative. Oh yes, a word of warning – the track here can be very muddy in winter necessitating a trudge through the sludge; so, don't forget your wellingtons.

South Harting appears left below you (which it is) as you stride along this 'mere ripple' of a hill, relatively speaking, of course, since it came into existence as an echo of the huge geological rumble which threw up the European Alps, namely the Alpine orogeny. The North and South Downs were once one piece but countless centuries of erosion have scooped out their soft centre, which is lucky for local people.

Don't be side tracked, keep to the main track which dips as you get near Tower Hill. The tower was built to commemorate the foundation of a colony at Vandalia in America. Under Tower Hill, there is a junction of tracks at which point you turn right for the nearby road. This you immediately cross before continuing leftish along the South Downs Way on the far side of the tarmac. The tower has meanwhile disappeared above you, hidden by hillside. Uppark, a home of Lady Hamilton among others, lies further beyond it.

The track rises in the direction of Beacon Hill, unmistakably tall at 793 feet. This old beacon was part of the 18th century semaphore route between Portsmouth and London and must have relayed the news of Nelson's victory at Trafalgar. Below to the left is the road, which your path eventually crosses to reach a chalky pathway leading to South Harting Downs car park.

Head to the left of the car park and through a gate. Below you is a magnificent spread of the Sussex Weald, 'a feast for the eyes'. You can now see how you have 'looped the loop' (already mentioned); below you, under the hill, is Downs Place. 600 yards or so from the car park now the top of Round Down, there's a public footpath (signposted) down to the left, initially leading through gorse bushes. This is how to get back to South Harting but first, if you like, continue to the Beacon ahead. Model gliders (remote controlled) share the turbulent air space around here with hovering sharp-eyed kestrels. Did you know that if a kestrel could read, it would be able to read a newspaper 100 yards away? You do now.

Back at the path, go down between the gorse bushes on a slope which loses height rapidly as you head for South Harting in full view of ancient earthworks and modern fields. These are the words of a 19th century Harting labourer describing 'a day in the life!':

"Out in the morning at 4 o'clock. Mouthful of bread and cheese and a pint of ale. Then off to the harvest field. Reaping and mowing till 8. Then morning breakfast and small beer. Breakfast – a piece of fat pork as thick as your hat (a broad-rimmed wideawake) is wide. Then work till 10 o'clock: then a mouthful of bread and cheese and a pint of strong beer – 'farnooner' (forenooner) we called it. Work till 12. Then at dinner in the farm-house; sometimes a leg of mutton, sometimes a piece of ham and plum pudding. Then work till 5; then a 'nunch' and a quart of ale. Nunch was cheese, 'twas skimmed cheese though. Then work till sunset: then home and have supper and a pint of ale. I never knew a man drunk in a harvest field in my life. Could drink 6 quarts, and believe that a man could drink 2 gallons in a day."

The steep path goes down past a vague stile — where there's a fork keep left — and a second before the embankment which borders the road. Go straight across the road to pick up the sunken track to the left of a graceful old metal gate. The track swings left, then right and bristles and hums with natural life. To the left is a view of an old thatched cottage, barn to match and a gipsy caravan for good measure.

At the junction of tracks, go left and left again, to go past the thatched cottage which is actually called Hampshire Farm, I think. Leave it to the left and follow the right-hand edge of the field. Above you on the ridge you can see horsemen and women galloping in outline across the skyline. Past the token stile in a generously contoured field, you'll come to a double stile and finally, another by the road.

Go right after this and **The Coach and Horses** is round a couple of bends if you keep to the road. On your way, you'll pass an old millhouse by Engine Farm (in the bowels of which you can still hear rushing water) and a couple of thatched cottages. The pub itself is on the left in the shadow of the church steeple and is the only place in the village where you can get Ballard's Best, the local brew from Rogate.

Leaving The Coach and Horses, turn left for The White Hart, The Ship and (by car) **The Three Horseshoes** and the Saxon Church at Elsted. One from three is a difficult choice here . . . and I have no idea which is best.

have played a large part in the history of South Harting and are annually included in the festivities of the Old Club Feast, when beech boughs are placed above their doorways and huge amounts of beer are consumed.

The Ship has bench seating, log fires and lots of horse brasses. Sitting here, you can wonder whether Nelson ever warmed his hands at the inglenook on his way to meeting Lady Hamilton at Uppark.

Available for the drinking are hand-drawn Stag, keg Ben Truman, Watneys Bitter and Special and Tamplins, too. Draught Guinness and Special liquer coffees are also on hand to satisfy your thirst. Pints of prawns, jacket potatoes, knickerbocker glories, home-made steak and kidney pies are there for the eating and you can, in summer, take them into a garden with a lawn and a climbing frame. As you go in you will notice yourself clambering over a flood step . . . in the past gum-booted regulars have been seen drinking nonchalantly with water lapping gently round their ankles.

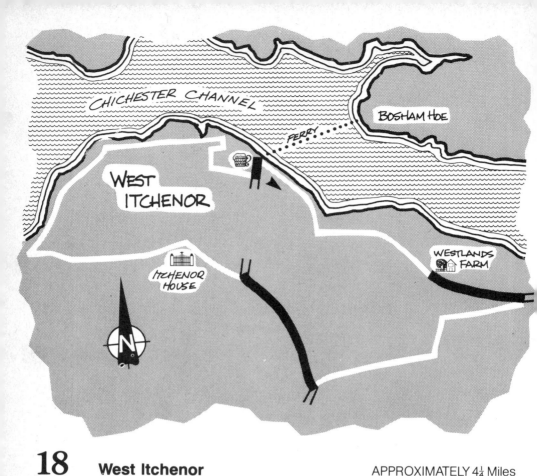

18 **West Itchenor**   APPROXIMATELY 4¼ Miles

The District

The most popular sailing village in Chichester Harbour, West Itchenor lies at the end of a road all of its own and is thus well protected from through traffic and far from the madding crowds of Bognor. 'That enchanting village of romantic isolation' or 'the secluded motor boating centre', as early explorers termed it, is part of an area of Outstanding Natural Beauty and makes an ideal spot for a quiet amble round the southern coast.

The word 'Itchenor' comes from the old English 'ora', meaning 'landing spot' or 'hard' and the name 'Icca', whose bearer must have been chief of the area. If you wonder why the village should additionally be called West when there is no occidental counterpart, this is because there used to be an Itchenor East whose existence was noted in the Domesday Book: all records of that village cease after the Great Plague.

In AD 43 the Romans under Claudius sailed by Itchenor on their way up the Chichester Channel to establish their Second Garrison at Fishbourne Palace. This region came in handy as a springboard for the invasions of the Isle of Wight and the wild West of England . . . indeed today, many local hedges still follow the line of Roman roads. From a later time, the 1500 year old border between the territories of the South and West Saxons which runs through the harbour is still observed but is now considered to mark the boundary between Sussex and Hants.

Charles II used to keep his Royal Yacht, 'Fubs', at anchor off Itchenor Hard. The name, 'Fubs', which is a far cry from 'Britannia', was also his pet name for his mistress, Louise, the Duchess of Portsmouth. In between clandestine assignments, 'Fubs' was also employed to ship the Grand Prior of France to Dieppe 'post haste', after the Gallic priest had heinously offended His Royal Highness.

Today, Itchenor has no shops, no post office and a preponderance of older citizens, who are gradually being replaced by young and (socially) mobile couples. Usually quiet, it comes alive at weekends and in summer with trippers and sailing types. Being a setting off point for Cherbourg, twelve nautical hours away, it has its own Customs and Excise Post. One last word of advice . . . be careful not to make the mistake I did of calling the local sailing club, a 'yacht club', as this offends local 'yachters'.

Take the ferry from Itchenor to Bosham (pronounced Bozzum) Hoe and you need only walk a mile to the village itself to see the Church of the Holy Trinity, founded by Dicul, an Irish monk. The church was publicised in the Bayeux Tapestry for being the nearest recognisable landmark to the point from which Harold sailed on his ill-advised trip to Normandy, pre-1066. The remains of Canute's daughter were dug up here in 1865, lending credence to the belief (espoused by the local tourist authority) that this was where the 'sadistic Danish oceanographer' enjoyed his finest hour. Retire to The Anchor Bleu above the harbour to enjoy the sight, on the foreshore, of tourists' misparked cars being sub-

►

The Inns

The Ship Inn, West Itchenor

The present Ship Inn was built on the site of the old Ship Inn, and a stone's throw from the sea. In the days when boat building was a thriving concern and coal from Newcastle was landed in the inn's yard on its way to Chichester, there were two pubs in the village. A ship's bell was used to call workers back to work. A tunnel from under The Ship extends 2 miles to Redlands Farm and this was used in the illicit trade which flourished on the southern coast, smuggling. The inn sign was painted by Charles Dixon in 1932.

Inside there are pictures, prints and models of ships, ropes spliced and whipped naval fashion by the bar, tassles for ships bells, a boat hook and a mace-like gyroscopic barometer. Derek Woods is an ex-naval commander and everything is kept ship-shape. The bar has a coal fire, a 'salty' atmosphere and a spotty dog called Domino, who was rescued by Chichester Dog Society and now presides genially over the place.

Hand-drawn Stag and Tauplins, Keg Ben Truman and Special, or Draught Guinness are there to deal with your thirst. In winter, the bar snacks are home-made and, in summer, cold buffet salads are served. There's a restaurant where children are admitted and the summer season sees tables outside.

merged by incoming tides, just as Canute once was . . . how quaint! People never learn. Seven generations of the interrelated Haines and Rogers families have manned the ferries which leave Itchenor for Bosham on the even hour between 1000 and 1800, Sats, Suns and Bank Holidays and every weekday from mid-July to mid-Sept, 50p-ish. If, it rains during your visit to the area, blame St Wilfred, who arrived at the spot during a drought which had lasted for 3 years. Wilfred converted Ethelwald, the local king, to christianity, an act which caused the heavens to open immediately. Ever since, it has rained frequently.

The walk goes from The Ship Inn, Itchenor, round the sheltered headland to Westlands Farm, from which point it loops back across corn fields and via Itchenor Park before following a blustery stretch of coastline back to The Ship. The area is flat and the going is easy.

How to Get There

By road take the A285 south-west from Chichester, then proceed along the B2179 before turning right on to an unclassfied road at Skipton Green for West Itchenor (approx $6\frac{1}{2}$ miles).
By rail to Chichester.
By bus take the 252 or 253 from Chichester.

The West Itchenor Walk

Fill your holds with liquid cargo at **The Ship Inn** before turning left down the main street for the sea which is but a stone's throw away . . . on arrival, you'll discover the many stones that must have been flung as proof of this contention. On your way along the cobbled pavement which leads to the quayside you'll pass, among others, pink Twitten Cottage which was built around 1700. Once thatched and weatherboarded for protection against gales and the sea, it was restored in 1877 and roofed with Sussex pegs. A 'twitten' is a path 'twixt houses.

By the Sussex Police Marine Section and the Harbour Office which overlook the hard, turn right but not before breathing in the view and a few lungfuls of fresh sea air. As your eyes follow the ferry route across to Bosham Hoe beyond bobbing yachts and boats, your ears will not be able to avoid the constant sound of clinking halyards in the everblowing breeze. In Saxon times, Danish raiders in a 'long ship' stole up the channel by dawn and ransacked Bosham, taking with them, as they left the church bell. The men of Itchenor put to sea, sank the 'long ship' and killed the Danes. However they could not salvage the bell which fell to the bottom of the channel and has since tolled for no-one, at all.

Having turned right, walk along the shingly path by the sloping sea wall with its many drainage outlets on your right. To your left is the glutinous estuary mud, so beloved of ducks and waders that they decorate its surface at low tide with the elaborate and erratic patterns their webbed feet leave behind. The inlet, being no river, is tidal and famous for its Brent geese in wintertime and otherwise for wigeons, ring plovers, redshanks and flocks of other bewinged and usually shrieking specimens. At a time of fiscal shortage in the past, the King's taxmen tried to assess this channel as a river for (higher) tax purposes, an attempt which was firmly rebuffed by locals.

When you reach the vast wooden wharf of the Sailing Club (NB most specifically *not* a yacht club!), there's a swimming pool and a pump to keep it functioning. Continuing along the path by the creek, there's a house with petrified lions in the garden and a host of jetties jutting over muddy back waters. Oh yes and still the noise of metal wire on masts. Boats are all around, motionless or making headway up the channel, boats of every size, shape and hue . . . and name, Orion, Free Flyer, the inevitable JR and

Snoopies by the fleet of small dinghies.

The path raises itself and bends right past a wooden hut and there's a wall left and a hedge right as you continue up a narrow lane. Turn left at the end of the lane to make your way past the black lampposts of 'Harbour House'. Turn right along the public footpath by 'The Spinney' and 'Mallard Creek' to continue by trees and fields to a stile. Beyond, walk the grassy stretch between cornfields admiring a tiny, distant Chichester Cathedral at the end of the creek. This is supposed to look particularly beautiful on a moonlit night.

In the far corner of the field, pass through the metal gate and go on past a small round pond with a boat, in a bird-filled farmyard. Continue up Westlands Farm's Drive and there's a vast chicken field on your left which looks like a tiny Stalag 17. Here you can watch the inmates holding hen parties all day long. Add clucking to clinking and you have an idea of the sounds which fill the air.

Beyond cottages 2 and 3, turn right at the end of the farm road and through the second gate (not the white one). Now follow the signposted path along the right-hand edge of the field past invisible yapping dogs, which are behind the

hedge on the right. Provocative scuffling noises will only encourage them.

The field is vast and you must, at one point, dodge right then back left to by-pass a stream. In the far corner of the field, turn left. Then with the hedge on your right, make for the other corner, from which you can follow the public footpath signs to West Itchenor. Don't cross the plank bridge and stile to your left. With flat fields on either side, the footpath is an unclogged channel through a sea of corn and it leads you just to the right of a now redundant stile. Soon you must go over a stile, a foot-bridge and bend to the left of an obvi-ously exclusive lane (since it is so heavily fortified!). At the road, go right down Itchenor's wide, long and interesting main street.

The old canopy of elms which shel-tered the road until comparatively recently has now gone under to the Dutch disease and left a line of stumps in memoriam. As you keep along the well-kept grassy verge you pass thatched 'Itchenor Gate' and 'Fishery' with its once explosive 'nameplate'. The street is a hotch-potch of eccentric architecture; 'Little Court' seems to have a moat and garden pillars, 'One Pear Tree' is most exactly named and a touch of the 'neo-Normans' is provided by 'The Oast'. After 'The Old House Farm', the road slopes left and you arrive at the lych-gate of the church of St Nicholas founded by one Hugh Esturmy.

Dedicated to the patron saint of child-ren and seafarers, it was built over 800 years ago. Before the implementation of sea walls and good drainage, the church stood on an island connected to the vil-lage by a bridge, a state of affairs which naturally resulted in very sparse con-gregations at leap services. In 1820 due to an 'extraordinarily high tide', which came over the sea wall, the service was cancelled and the local ferryman was seen conducting his service inland, row-ing his boat over the nearby hedges. The glass in the windows is mostly recent and depicts the four seasons in a homely way. Beyond the church is a line of lovely, tall poplars.

Going right from the gate of the church, follow the road till it curves right. Here, go straight on through the white

▶

gates in to Itchenor Park. Before you reach the house itself, bend right 'with the tradesmen' to go past outbuildings dated 1783. They look like old station buildings and bear the motto 'Honi Soit Qui Mal Y Pense' — now where have I heard that before?

At the end of the buildings, turn left up the concrete lane that runs behind Itchenor House. The house was built in 1783 to Samuel Wyatt's design and according to the wishes of the third Duke of Richmond, who was a frequent visitor here. His grace's main local concerns included the building of a hot sea-bath on the shore (now the Jetty House), the preparations necessary for 'electrions' and the militia and perhaps most importantly, provision for the future of his natural daughter, Miss Henriette Leclerc, who inherited the house on his demise in 1806. To the right of your view of the house is a fantastic cricket pitch surrounded by oaks and grazed by sheep; the square may not be up to Lords' standards but it's certainly well fertilised.

Soon the lane becomes a muddy track and in the ditches beside it is a steady flow of water, this is because the local water table has risen considerably in recent years.

As the track zigs left, there's a stile and a footpath sign on the right-hand side. Go over this (not the signpost, silly) and towards the sea you see ahead. This is the Chichester Channel which, hopefully, will be placid for you but which can be very stormy at times. One more stile and you turn right in the opposite direction to West Wittering if I may put it in a roundabout way.

To your left are mud flats and you can walk back to West Itchenor either along the shore or along the path. Be careful not to go on the mud, since its firmness is only apparent. The channel authorities wage constant war against silt and the nearly invincible Japanese seaweed. In the watery depths far from your eyes are oyster beds struggling for survival, after centuries of human interference. "But answer came there none — And this was scarcely odd, because they'd eaten every one", etc (from *The Walrus and the Carpenter*). What you can see is the abrasive effect of the wind on the land which leaves tree roots dangling in mid-air from the receding sandy banks. As you get nearer Itchenor, more and more boats flutter by — millions on a summer's day. There's even a rusting collection of old landing craft lying beached near the boatyards. With the recession, the profits of the boatyards here have turned to loss. It takes about six weeks to complete a boat but now there are fewer and fewer buyers. If things don't improve, they could have closed by the time you get there. . . .

Continue by the footpath beyond the boatyard and you eventually emerge by the Harbour Office. Turn right for The Ship Inn and the pint you deserve after all this praiseworthy effort.

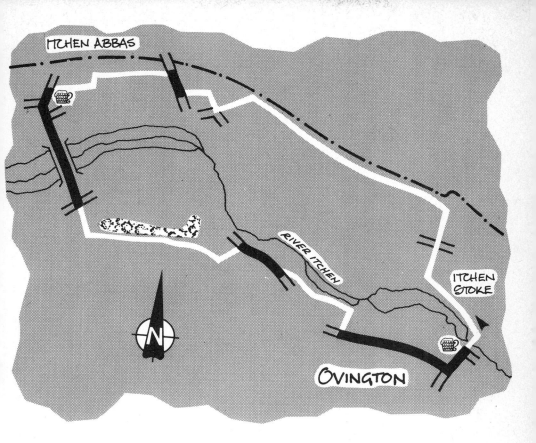

19   **Ovington**   APPROXIMATELY 4¾ Miles

The District

The ancient capital of England from the time of Wessex' predominance and up till 1150, Winchester was the seat of many kings, amongst them wise King Alfred and Ethelred, that ill-prepared head of state. Founded in capital fashion, Winchester Cathedral is the second largest in Europe and has apparently 'the largest early English retro choir' anywhere. This century, the rotten wooden foundations of the cathedral (which stand under water) had to be repaired to stave off imminent collapse and this task was carried out almost singlehandedly, it seems, by a man called William Walker, 'who wearing a diver's suit weighing 200 lbs, personally handled an estimated 25,800 bags of concrete, 114,900 concrete blocks, 900,000 bricks and squeezed 500 tons of grouting into the cracked walls'. The river is still a problem and visitors may only see the crypt, water level permitting. This Norman and Perpendicular building once the inspiration for a top twenty song, contains the graves of Jane Austen who died in 1817 and St Swithin, despite his request to be buried under open skies. His revenge takes the form of 40 days of rain, if it rains on his name day, the 15th of July. Things to see in Winchester include the Castle, The College, The City Cross by Godbegot House, the counterfeit King Arthur's Round Table, the museum in 13th century West gate, the Statue of ►

King Alfred and the cathedral window picture of Isaak Walton, author of *The Compleat Angler,* in which he sits reading the Bible by the River Itchen, one of his favourite angles ... this leads us upstream from Winchester to Alresford.

In the 12th century the pond at Alresford was enlarged by Bishop Godfrey De Lucy and became a 200 acre reservoir supplying water to make the River Itchen navigable so that the locality's wool might be brought downstream to the centres of Winchester and South-ampton. The pond has shrivelled since those halcyon days, but fish, birds and eels are still just as fond of it. Much of the water around here is used for growing watercress since the chalk streams maintain a steady temperature of 57°F, ideal conditions for the Hampshire half of England's watercress supply.

Ovington is a pretty village which stands at the confluence of the many branches of the Itchen in its valley. As you walk you may see one or other, or all, of 'pink willow herb, purple vetch, hemp agrimony, loosestrife, huge marsh thistles (beware of these) and yellow mimulus'. Striding amongst them are voles, shrews, moorhens, grebes, ducks and other giants of the animal world: I can read lists as well as the next person.

The path downstream marks the old Pilgrim's Way and leads to Itchen Stoke and Itchen Abbas, two villages set in beautiful country. Abbas has a church built in the Victorian Age and a Roman villa site.

Avington's major dwelling at the time

of the Domesday Book was a house called Afintune. This house moved site and was brought by the brother of Percy Bysshe in 1848 – it stayed in the Shelley family till 1952 and has in its time received visits from Charles II with Nell Gwynn and the Prince Regent, accompanied by Mrs Fitzherbert. Today it is occasionally open to less regal visitors and you, too. The cedars of Lebanon are magnificent, particularly near 'one of the most perfect Georgian churches in the country', which has beautiful mahogany woodwork from a wrecked galleon of the Spanish Armada. Now, from here ... swop 'O' for 'A' and you're back in Ovington.

How to Get There
By road take the A31 east from Winchester, turn left onto an unclassified road and you will find Ovington at a crossroad along here (approx 6 miles).
By rail to Winchester.
By bus take the Alder Valley 214 from Winchester to Itchen Abbas – Ovington is a short walk from here.

The Ovington Walk
You start the walk in the snug **Bush Inn** and when you've finished 'starting', turn left out of the pub and just before the junction with the road, turn left along the marked public footpath. This leads you to a footbridge over the crystal clear River Itchen. It's quite wide and glides smoothly if not particularly slowly. Swans and moorhens glide smoothly, but with a little less hurry. The bridge takes you over onto a strip almost in the middle of the river where rushes grow; you follow the footpath along the strip. Soon you have to turn right over another footbridge which takes you onto a lane that gently climbs up to the cluster of houses that is Itchen Stoke. Many of these houses are fine examples of rural architecture, notably The Shallows, a fine black and white, half timbered, flint and brick building. You emerge onto the B3047 by the green.

Turn right here and then left up the lane before the church. Walk up to the bridge over the disused railway line and just before crossing the bridge, turn left along the track keeping the railway cutting on your right. From here you can see across the Itchen valley to your left –

classic 'English' countryside. Soon the track dips down into the cutting and now you continue along the old railway line, where, naturally enough, it is easy, firm walking on the chalk, flint and grass surfaces.

Just by an old and disused BR workmen's shed the cutting becomes an embankment with field maple, oak and thorn climbing the banks. Make the most of the views while you can, for soon the embankment reverts to being a cutting. You pass below some farm buildings and under a bridge. There may be a large collection of old tyres here which you will have to negotiate — not really high enough to make you 'tyred', though. Enough of bad jokes. Just before the next bridge, head left up the newish chalky track to meet the track that crosses the bridge. Here turn left downhill, first between trees and then hedges. Follow this track down to the road.

Turn right along the road and almost immediately turn right again in order to cross a stile (in the loosest sense of the word) which is next to a gate with 'Guard dog — private' emblazoned on it. Walk up the left-hand edge of the field along the line of beech trees; the nice house (with rather aggressive owners) with its beehives lies across the paddock. So it's back up towards the railway line again, folks. But just before it, turn left through the gap or over the stile and follow the track and beech trees aiming to the left of the houses ahead. Pass the septic tank and follow the wee drive which is bearing you close to Baring Close(!) which runs between houses to a lane.

Turn right up the lane and on your left is The Cottage just after which is a thatched cottage, just after which is a drive, just after which is an unmarked grassy footpath which is just before a fire hydrant. Got it? Walk along this path between a hedge and the railway cutting. At the far corner of the field on your left is a huge beech, just waiting to trip the inattentive walker with its roots. Walk on between fences through beech and holly until the fence at the end of the beeches where both the path and the walker turn left. Both then turn right and continue to meet the tarmac drive of Littlehayes (whose sign is well nigh impossible to

The Inns

The Bush Inn, Ovington

A bush hanging outside a pub was a custom that goes back as far as the Romans. A branch of ivy was sacred to Bacchus, and Bacchus was sacred to the Romans as their god of wine; so a bush indicated that within one could find liquid refreshment. Simple. The pub lies on the Pilgrim's Way between Canterbury and Winchester, so there were many pilgrims for whom the sign of the bush was extremely welcome — after a long day's tramp, often in bare feet, there's nothing like a drink to wash away the dust and soothe the blisters. The River Itchen was navigable up to Alresford, so medieval bargees would have rubbed shoulders and swopped tales with the more devout drinkers.

Almost surrounded by water, this white painted and rose-clad pub has one largish bar and a 'sunken' restaurant, with three open fires in all. There are some copper pots and pans, but, more interestingly, a huge old smithy's bellows, an old butterchurn, two brass coffee urns and a strange trumpet-like instrument. The interior is as interesting as the exterior, with its pretty streamside garden of lawn and flower beds.

It's a Free House and stocks Ringwoods Best Bitter and Forty-Niner, Wadworths 6X and Courages Directors, all on handpump, with M and B Mild and two lagers on keg. There is also a selection of about 16 malt and grain whiskies, about 20 liqueurs, a selection of restaurant wines and English country wines, which include red-currant, cherry, damson, elderberry, parsnip, peach, apple, apricot and mead. If you can't find a drink you like in this pub, then you're reading the wrong book.

There's an à la carte menu in the restaurant and bar food includes soup, read). Walk on down between the school and its 'level' and molehilled games pitch, beyond which is a rather elegant Victorian built railway bridge.

At the lane, turn left and walk past Old Post Cottage and at B3047 go left to **The Plough.**

When you have 'ploughed' through your 'share' of the 'ploughman's' and 'tilled' your money and had a pint or two of course, leave the pub, turning right back the way you came. However, you turn left immediately past the Jubilee Tree towards Avington and Avington Park. St John the Baptist's church sits on your left in its beautifully kept churchyard. Indeed, it is in this churchyard that you can find the grave of one John Hughes who on March 19th 1825 at the age of 26 was the last man in England to be hanged for horse-stealing. For some reason, of which I'm ignorant, he was allowed to be buried in consecrated ground.

Follow the lane on past the old, and soon to be restored, mill with its sluices and weir and you may like to pause for a few minutes on the main bridge over the Itchen. This spot is particularly pretty and peaceful at dusk when the light, the water, the trees, the birds and everything all combine and conspire to persuade you that, yes, despite its countless drawbacks, England is one of the best places to be. Mind you, if you are here at dusk, you'd better get a move on as there's some way to go yet, and walking in the dark is inadvisable.

Walk on along the tree-lined lane over

all the bridges over all the tributaries and backwaters of the Itchen (on summer evenings, there can be thousands of midges and gnats here, which may give you some 'itchen' problems). After you cross the last bridge, you pass between grand gateways on either side of the road. Those on the left are dilapidated, but those on the right lead your eye along the avenue into Avington Park. Walk on further and at the junction by the huge yew, you can either turn left to go on with the walk or you can swing right with the lane for a short detour into Avington. If you have the time and inclination for the latter, you are rewarded with fine views of Avington House. This mansion was used by Charles II for his 'friend' Nell Gwynn because the Bishop of Winchester wouldn't allow her to stay within the diocese of that city, due to her sinful relationship with the king. It is still a private house, though it is open to the public occasionally. Avington is a pretty village and St Mary's church is very definitely worth investigation. If you have visited other churches mentioned in this book, then visit this one – the contrast is striking. It's not at all what you would expect in the heart of the country. Return down the lane to the junction by the huge yew and go straight on leaving the tree on your left to meet up again with the non-deviationists.

Almost immediately, you (all) turn right up the track marked as a public footpath. As you walk up, there are good views behind of Avington House and Park. When you reach the right-hand end of the line of trees, the track swings left above them as marked by the yellow arrow on the fence post. You are now walking along next to an earthwork – a rampart or low wall – and though it is clearly marked on the O/S map, it is not as clearly seen in situ. Indeed, if I hadn't mentioned it, would you know?

At the end of the line of trees, where the track swings right, you go straight on, cross a stile and walk along the edge of the field to another stile. Looking to your left as you walk along this straight stretch you can see across the Itchen valley – is the grass greener? Walk straight on to the copse, follow it and at its far end continue straight to the line of bushes, trees etc running across your path. There turn left down this line and cross the stile where this strip of woodland stops. Turning left after the stile, follow the fence as it runs down to a stile onto the lane where you turn right.

The river is close by on your left and you pass between a solid-looking farmhouse and its buildings. Where the lane begins to climb, fork left along Yavington Mead's drive. Just before this rather attractive house, turn left at the corner of the fence and follow the fence, turning right as it does until it leads you to the wall of the barn. Squeeze between the two, turn right round the corner of the building and at the next corner, go through the gate into the field.

Walk straight across this aiming for the stile and bearing in mind that by rights it is the stamping ground of horses and a rather tetchy donkey. The stile is closely followed by another, 6 yards distant, and in the next field, follow the bottom edge to a wee wooden gate in the far left-hand corner. Good glimpses of the river are to be had from this field. The path you meet runs, to the left, down to a footbridge over the river, but you turn right as the public footpath ahead seems to be closed. The sunken path runs up an avenue of ivy-clad walnut trees, which line your way like statues or slightly sinister sentinels.

Turn left when you re-emerge onto the lane which you follow past huge sycamores by Lovington's Drive. The lane dips and rises and then enters pretty Ovington, which if you have time to kill is worth a quick stroll. For this turn right at the junction. If you don't want to beat around the bush, turn left for The Bush and remember a beer in The Bush is worth. . . .

pâté, smoked mackerel, avocado, salads (ham and crab), shepherd's pie, spare ribs, curry, macaroni, spaghetti bolognaise and sandwiches (including salmon and prawn). What can be home-made is. If you can't find some food you like in this pub, then. . . .

The Plough Inn, Itchen Abbas

Set in beautiful country on the old Winchester to Alresford road, The Plough is a warm and friendly, though not especially old pub. Apart from its proximity to Avington House, one other event puts The Plough firmly on the historical, or in its case literary map. It was here that Charles Kingsley stayed while he wrote *The Water Babies*. Though he undoubtedly used the River Itchen as inspiration, it seems a river rather too shallow to be the actual river of the book.

A brick and tile building, it has two bars with open fires in both. There's fish netting in the public bar and, of more interest perhaps, is Mr Ellis' (the landlord) collection of plates in the saloon. He has at least 400 plates from all over the world, both old and new, valuable and worthless, attractive and not so attractive. This, in a way, is what makes it such an interesting collection.

What makes it an interesting pub (for the drinker) is the Marston's Pedigree and Burton Bitter (both on handpump) all the way down from Burton-on-Trent. There's also Mild, Bitter and lager on keg and a selection of 25 European wines.

There's an à la carte menu in the evening in the restaurant and bar meals include burgers, cottage pie, soup, beef curry, steak and kidney pie, bread pudding (go on try it) and butterscotch and chocolate sundaes. All these are home-made. There's the more usual ploughman's and sandwiches of course and you can take your food and drink out to the large garden where there are swings and slides for the kids and tables and chairs for adults.

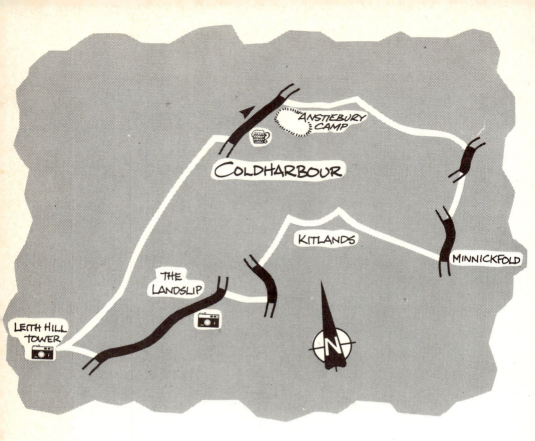

20 Coldharbour

APPROXIMATELY 3¼ Miles

The District

The village of Coldharbour clings to the steep escarpment below Leith Hill and its name means 'rough shelter for travellers' . . . literally, 'a dip in the ridge of trees'. There are six Coldharbours in Surrey. Half of the village consists of 17th century houses built to accommodate a community which grew up to serve the four great houses of the area, Leith Hill Place, Broome Hall, Kitlands and Anstiebury Grange; the rest is almost exclusively Victorian.

Little Switzerland (this part of Surrey) was 'discovered' by Victorians, who had travelled in Europe and who thought they saw Britain's answer to the alpine resorts of Switzerland in the surrounding woods and slopes. Coldharbour became particularly fashionable and new buildings went up roughly in proportion with holiday rents and prices. Pissarro's son came, saw and painted, and much of his work now hangs in the Tate Gallery as a souvenir of those halcyon days.

Coldharbour was self-sufficient up to the end of World War I, when the big households broke up in the general social upheaval. Up till this point, the church could rely on choirs of at least 30 voices and even a silver band supplied by the 'downstairs' members of the great houses. By the fifties, the village had all but died on its feet when commuting by car was invented and 'young marrieds' brought fresh blood to the community.

Today the majority of local jobs are provided by the Forestry Commission and the village racing stables.

Leith Hill's tower provides a marvellous outlook over to the Kent Downs, the Bucks hills and the slopes of Wiltshire, 'inexhaustible in beauty' according to Mathew Arnold. The countryside around Coldharbour has always been poor and wild; the latter quality attracted highwaymen, freebooters, gypsies and the equally unpopular broom squires, scoundrels who sold broom from the local commons as a cover for their criminal enterprises.

A report tells of a greengrocer from Dorking hiring a man with a blunderbuss to protect him and his wares as he drove his cart through the district. The geography of Little Switzerland also made it an ideal spot for smuggling and Coldharbour is said to have been 'up to its neck' in the contraband trade. As a reward for turning a blind eye to discoveries, excise officers would be left the items they marked with a chalk cross – this arrangement kept everyone happy. Before you go up Leith Hill to survey the beautiful countryside, so near yet so far from the conditions of London, you should know about its adders, one of which killed a tourist in 1876. More recently, a puma was reported on the loose in the vicinity.

At the other side of Coldharbour's green brake and red sand valley, is Mag's Well the place where a girl called Mag used cold water to cure herself of the itch (which itch, I don't rightly know). Dogs used to be sent there to get rid of the Mange and, should you suffer from skin complaints and 'scrofulous sores', it's just the place to go. Nearby Abinger has a clock over the road which says in writing, 'By me you know how fast you go' and its hours are struck by the conscientious figure of Jack the Smith. Dorking is an interesting town which has connections with George Meredith, Keats, Charles Dickens and Lord and Lady Nelson. Not far away, too, is Box Hill whose slopes contain the grave of an eccentric Englishman who chose to be buried upside down . . . and on the hill.

The walk leaves Coldharbour for Minnickfold, passes Kitlands and reaches the heights of Leith Hill before sloping back down to Coldharbour once more . . . all this at altitudes from 400 to

The Inns

The Plough, Coldharbour

Nestling amongst the scatter of roofs seen from lofty Leith Hill is The Plough, Surrey's highest pub at 780ft above sea level. Apparently mentioned in one of Dickens' novels, The Plough is carpeted and comfortable and the ideal place for families.

The outside walls are rendered white and there are two converted gas lamps to guide you in from the darkness at night. There are two bars with open fires and beams, old and new. Larger parties can sit round 6 foot tables and benches.

Food is available seven days a week and includes home-made steak pies with veg and mash, curries and pizza. Snacks and coffee are also served. The beer is all 'real' and you can take your pick from John Smith, 6X, Youngs Ordinary and Special and Badgers Best. In winter, Old Hookey, Winter Warmer and Old Timer will no doubt prove a warming experience. Kids are welcome in what Mrs Brown, the landlady, says should be considered an extension of her lounge.

1000 feet. The wooded countryside on the way is amongst the most beautiful in England and only the short (but horribly steep) stretch up Leith Hill is of difficulty.

How to Get There
By road take the A24 south from Dorking, turn right onto the A29 and then right again on to an unclassified road (approx 8 miles).
By rail to Dorking.
By bus a tricky one this, there are three post office buses a day to Coldharbour from Dorking, along with McCann's No 844 which only operates on Fridays (market day).

The Coldharbour Walk
Turn right out of **The Plough** and walk up the road to the junction by a white cottage. Turn right in the direction of Ockley leaving behind you the fine view of wooded valleys and crests to the north and east. Now to your right, in the angle of the roads, is the 11 acre site of Anstiebury Camp, which dates from 1800 BC according to the cursory excavations so far attempted. Used by the ancient British (male adults!) to store cattle, women and children while they went off with their bows and stone-tipped arrows to bully their foes, it once had fortifications 'much steeper and higher' than today's. It's likely too, that the locals once manned these palisades against the attacks of Vespasian's well drilled Legions. Hean Stige Byrig is early English for the borough by the highway (and 'Anstiebury'!) and the ramparts here stood guard over the ancient British road from Coldharbour to Dorking, a sheltered trackway cut 20 feet deep into the yellow sandstone. During the Napoleonic scare it was proposed that the camp should once more shelter the woman and children of the district, but this time against 'Boney'. Planted with beech in the late 18th century, this elliptical hillside fort hides its past glory under a bushel or two but its foundations and basic form are more or less intact.

Just before the 1:7 sign, slope off first left down a pockmarked track between fields, savouring as you go the view ahead. The many narrow strips of woodland give the illusion of continuity (vast forests seem to appear) — these are called 'shaws'. 12% of the area is covered by trees, a proportion which is very high . . . and so are you as the track begins to wind down between an old granary and a barn and then on through farm buildings.

Beyond them 20 yards or so down a muddy path there's a stile in the fence on the right. A downhill diagonal from here will get you to a stile in the bottom right-hand corner of a field with a singular equine specimen to gee you up on your way. Beyond the stile the wood begins and there's a hollow to your right as you bend to the left of a giant beech trunk before following a straightish path. In 40 yards or so, you cross another path, after which you carry on down with a fence to your left curving gently right. All around there are tall and slender trees and nearby rhododendrons are no wallflowers, either . . . parts of this walk are like a visit to the Botanical Gardens. Under a huge multi-trunked and straggle-limbed monster, whose reach you must elude, there is a stile by a holly tree and your entrance into a hump-backed field with a view. (To get to this point you will have kept on down with the fence to your left).

Head straight across the field and leave by the invisible stile which you don't see till you're near the large oak standing on its own. After this, follow the left-hand edge of the next field whose hedgerow is full of *troglodytes troglodytes,* the common wren. There's a stile by a gate before you turn right along a stony farm track with a chalky stream flowing clearly in the opposite direction to you.

By looking up beyond the steep fields to your right, you can see how far you've descended. Keep going along the track which bends right between two houses, immediately after which you go first left along another track; this means you have described an arc around the house with the small cupola on the left. Turn left at the lane past Minnickwood Cottage and the beaver-tailed tiles and crown chimneys of Minnickwood House. Rhododendrons and hollies fringe the roadside of this salubrious, secluded hamlet.

Pass Lower Minnickwood Place on your left and the road goes down between typical Surrey banks, dappled green and always cool under their treetop canopy. As the road twists half-right then left, there's a marked public footpath on the right of the bend. Take it and then fork right within earshot of a small nearby waterfall. This course of action leads you to a stile to the left of a gate, where a trickling stream of water runs after rainfall.

The stile is difficult to see at first and is not in good shape, so treat it gently as you clamber and drop beyond it to go along the left edge of the field. To the right is a steep slope and, ahead, a dark curtain of trees. It's interesting to note that you're still 400 feet or so up. Don't go left towards the stream by the break in the fence, but continue straight to the far end of the field. Next, follow the fence 100 yards or so up to the right to find a stile.

After this, head half-right for the stile by the gate under a large oak – it has no foothold and the gate lacks a strut or two but get over as athletically as you can to turn left up the track past Kitlands Cottage and its garden whetstone. Sandwiched between laurels and rhododendrons the track becomes pebbly as you follow it down left with the wall, passing Kitlands on the left. Through the gates snatch a view towards Capel. Where the lane rises you should spot doves on the farmbuildings to your right beyond a tiny fir plantation . . . some of the trees wear the woodcutter's death warrant, the white cross.

Beyond a pond on the marshy left, there are two tall lines of rigid evergreens which see you to the road. Turn left here down the road which soon swings right. When you see a stile to the left, don't go over it – instead look to the other side of the road where there's a public footpath sign for 'where you want', by a gorgon-like beech which is slowly ingesting what remains of a metal gate. Hurry quickly by it up a steep path and across a track into the woods. The path leads you a merry dance up the hill till you reach the road, a seat and a view. Above you is The Landslip.

Enough of all this sitting around! Turn left down the road and, once past the roadside 'handrail', turn right into the cavernous, wooded National Trust reserve. If you thought the trees were good before now they're positively magnificent in this vast cathedral-like space with its insistent birdsong, steep escarpment and overspilling azaleas and rhododendrons. You must now follow the road to your left, keeping amongst the trees if you wish.

Keep following the road through the evergreens till you reach the red brick entrance of a large house with wrought-iron gates on the bend going left. This is some distance along and just beside it there's a Surrey County Council Open Space sign saying Wotton and Abinger Commons and, to the right, a very steep path, take it, but take it easy. Go straight up with the path which goes leftish up a fearsome incline. It's lucky that the view is ample reward for the climb up this murderous slope; keep thinking this as you go up.

Now you're at the top and breathing heavily, let me begin, "If Box Hill can be said to be queen of the North Downs, then Leith Hill, Southern England's highest point, must be her consort . . ." or so they say. Apparently, and the extent of the view differs from day to day according to the prevailing meteorological conditions, 12 or 13 (old) counties can be seen from the top of the tower.

The tower was built by Richard Hull in 1766. Hull was the eldest bencher of the Inner Temple, a member of several Irish parliaments and a rich philanthropist to boot. Anyway, he decided to make 965 foot Leith Hill into a mountain (which is not to say that it was a molehill in the first place) and built the structure you now see on top of it. The platform of the tower is almost exactly 1,000 feet above sea level and thus technically speaking mountainous. Hull later chose to be

➤

buried beneath the tower, a case of folly under folly which, prompted half the neighbourhood to rifle it for its fittings and the other half to fill it with cement to prevent further outrage.

In 1844 Ordnance surveyors recorded that 41 London spires were visible from the platform here including St Pauls. However tall modern architecture and a cramped metropolis have whittled down the number. Restoration and the addition of a staircase came in 1863. Sip on a cup of tea from the new refreshment booth (the old thatched one was razed by arsonists) as you drink in the view over the Wealds of Sussex and Kent and seek out the glint of the Channel through the Shoreham gap in the South Downs. If your Latin is good you'll already know that the inscription on the tower dedicates the view not only to Hull himself but also to the neighbours and everyone else, for good measure. You can't be fairer than that!

Leave by the track to the right of where you came up – to the left as you turn out of the door of the tower. It is easy to get lost on the maze of paths which cover Leith Hill's green sandstone slopes, be warned and please don't.

At the major path junction in the dip, go straight ahead for the Duke's Warren and ponder upon this little appreciated face – experiments on earthworms in the 19th century revealed that the little creatures under study unearthed $7\frac{1}{2}$ tons of soil each year. One of the (Josiah) Wedgwoods of Leith Hill Place was married to Charles Darwin's sister and carried out this specialised investigation at the great man's request. During the war, this area was covered in barbed wire by the army for their own peculiar reasons and yet another thing you should know is that Leith Hill is tautologous, since 'Leith' itself means 'hill'.

Follow the main track avoiding turnings to right and left till you join a forest 'road' (unmetalled) where you keep right. Next keep to the right of the local cricket pitch, which comes as a surprise at such an altitude. Every Whitsun a cricket festival is held here when daisy-cutters replace wood cutters, stumps are drawn not left behind in the ground and sixes must be retrieved from the depths of the wood. Go past the metal gate at the far corner of the pitch and soon you're back at Coldharbour and the highest pub in Surrey.

If you want to see a church of Victorian Gothic splendour, turn right by the telephone box and head along the road past the clock on the old school and the friendly village shop. The line of houses across the grass to your right once thrived as shops and workshops in a self-sufficient community. Past the war memorial and seemingly 'out of town', you reach the church on the left which is loyally constructed from the soft and porous stone quarried on Leith Hill – this fact unfortunately means that the building is slowly crumbling as, each winter, water freezes in the masonry which subsequently flakes. The church was built in 1848 by a pupil of Pugin.

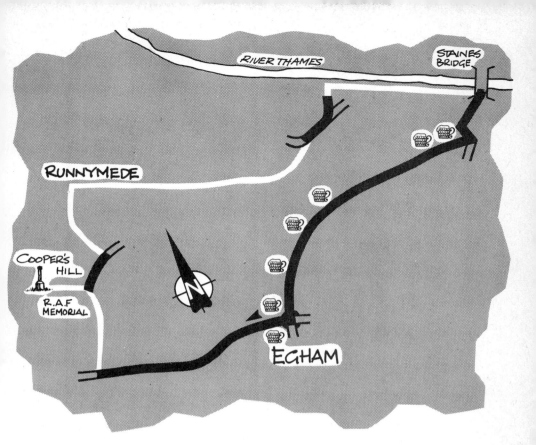

21   **Egham**

APPROXIMATELY 4 Miles

The District

Downstream from Windsor and separated from the Thames by famous Runnymede, Egham is a busy provincial town with a curving high street, numerous pubs and old roadhouses and 'a county air'. Egham began as the hamlet of a certain Mr Eig and, just before the time of the Domesday book, belonged, together with its 25 villeins and 120 acres of meadow . . . 'with 50 hogs for the pannage and for the herbage 25 hogs' . . . to King Edward. Subsequently the village, as was, passed into the hands of Chertsey Abbey, where it stayed till the monks were suppressed at the time of the Dissolution and the Crown took repossession. In the meantime, the meadow below the town made 'national headlines' and the history books when John set his seal on the Magna Carta at Runnymede in 1215 and 'granted' freedom under the law to the property owning classes. Clause 39 (of 63) states that 'no man shall be taken or imprisoned or dispossessed or outlawed or exiled or in any way destroyed . . . save by the lawful judgement of his peers'. Thus was established the profession of the lawyer.

Egham has many inns from the days when it was an important staging post on the important road to the South-West; English naval pre-eminence made speedy access to the ports of that area a vital priority. St John's Church has a 15th century lych-gate and a dubious reputa-

▶

tion; it has been described as being of 'simple and severe beauty', 'very ugly' and 'an interesting specimen of 19th century architecture'. Rebuilt in 1817, it apparently has eery and unusual catacombs. The poet Denham was a citizen of Egham; so too was the 18th century writer, 'Perdita' (Mary Robinson) who lived 'a fashionable life', which included writing poems in debtor's prison, becoming an actress and scandalising the nation by her affair with the Prince of Wales, later George IV. Painted as a young lady by Reynolds and Gainsborough, in later years she drove herself round town in a chariot shaped like a coronet. Interesting buildings in the vicinity include Great Fosters, an Elizabethan house with a moat, and the Royal Holloway College, which is modelled on the Chateau de Chambord in the Loire and was endowed by (and called after) a Victorian pill and ointment magnate, who wanted to promote education for women. It was designed so that each lady had her own two rooms and is now part of the University of London.

Cooper's Hill, eulogised by Denham, was planted with three walnut trees for the coronation of George IV (earlier the Prince of Wales, remember). Its other memorials are to the RAF designed by Sire Edward Maufe, to John F Kennedy in an acre of the USA which is this side of the Atlantic and to the Magna Carta, donated by the American Bar Association.

The Bellweir Lock near the town opened in 1817 and came to be so called after Charles Bell who earned £4 a month as its first keeper. The present workings were built in 1907 and still stand 'abouen Stanes brygge' like the first ones. There were two wooden bridges at Ad Stanes in Roman times and the present Staines Bridge is the 5th built since then . . . completed in 1832 by Rennie; tolls stopped being taken for a ride across in 1871. Virginia Water is not far from Egham and its eponymous artificial lake was produced by Cumberland, the Butcher of Culloden and Governor of Virginia, that former colony. Windsor has Wren's Guildhall and the largest inhabited castle in the world, which can be visited when Her Majesty is away from her favourite home. Eton is the home of the college where they fight battles on the playing fields . . . or something like that . . .it's partly open to the public which may account for the category of school it belongs to.

This is a fairly short walk encompassing the length of the High Street (7 pubs, 4 featured) and including both famous Cooper's Hill and the meads of Runnymede. Also by the route is the Thames and waterproof footwear is a must after rain. The walk is easy if you leave the pubs to the end . . . granny can be brought on this one.

How to Get There.

By road from junction 2 on the M3 turn right onto the M25 which will take you directly to Egham.

By rail to Egham.

The Egham Walk

Turn right out of **The Red Lion** in Egham High Street. This pub once had stabling for 80 horses and a thriving trade putting up weary travellers who were fearful of braving the packs of highwaymen and freebooters who once skulked Bagshot Heath by night. This original movement sets you on a course whose next port of call is The Crown, followed by **The Kings Arms,** just past Strode College and just before a roundabout. The High Street is not short of pubs.

Go straight across at the roundabout passing to the right of **The Eclipse.** If you visit all these pubs you'll know why the road here is called 'Tite Hill', though it probably won't bother you in the least. Keep going along the pavement with private Runnymede Park to your right, through the trees. Watch out for tall and upright Elms and Alder Close.

Immediately before Kingswood Rise, turn right along the parallel path and swing with it into the copse, to the right of a row of houses ahead. Soon the path bends left and you can peer over the corrugated fence on your right at rolling lawns and nasty looking Staines beyond – the results of Eton, Eg – and Ham in the vicinity? Geologically speaking the district is roughly divided into London Clay and Bagshot Sand on the higher ground and alluvial gravel lower down. As you emerge into a lane by Kingswood Halls of Residence (to your right), make a mental note that the walk later goes past this annexe of the University of London.

However, first go left up the lane for the RAF Memorial on Cooper's Hill, designed by Sir Edward Maufe. This is a tribute to the 20,000 allied airmen who died without burial during the Second World War: their names are listed on the premises. Two lines of sentinel trees form a driveway guard of honour as you go in. From the tower, there's a fine view of the Thames while you muse on these lines,

"On Cooper's Hill eternal wreaths shall grow
While lasts the mountain, or while Thames shall flow."

You can see Windsor Castle, the line of the Thames (which also marks the northern boundary of Surrey) and the hills of Berkshire beyond.

Turn left from the drive and left again to go on past Kingsdown Halls which is on your right. Where the potholed road swings right, go left under a giant tree and past a crumbled crash barrier that looks like it was used unsuccessfully against the hordes of Attila the Hun just before closing time. Keep on the resultant path through the woods for a short while, till just before you are level with the RAF Memorial, looming above to the left. Here turn down along the path to the right whose start is marked by splintered tree stumps. Roll and tumble with this path till you reach a paddock fence, which you follow after turning left. When your progress is impeded and obstructed by undergrowth, go left a little to resume course. Soon you reach a path which, if you turn right, will take you down between two marshy paddocks and onto Runnymede itself, England's most famous meadow.

In 1215 his Royal 'heinousness' King John did not sign the Magna Carta under duress here . . . that's because he sealed it, giving English 'freemen' freedom under the law. 'Bad John's' demands for excessive feudal dues and restrictions on the powers of the church were contrary to the laws of Edward the Confessor

The Inns

The Red Lion, Egham

The Red Lion dates from 1521 and is one of Egham's old coaching inns. The atmosphere is 'moderne olde worlde' with original brickwood lattice windows, beams, open fires and a steady jukebox beat. The inside is very spacious and houses a display of old coins and adverts.

'Hand-drawn ales' are available as are fresh and toasted sandwiches. Further to these, you can get a variety of hot and cold snacks; light lunches and 'a special of the day' which is always home-made. Shove halfpenny and darts can be played.

The Kings Arms, Egham

The Kings Arms was probably built in the early 16th century and is first mentioned in records of 1620; originally it was for the use of a local lord's private army. There is a ghost which is often heard walking around but which has never been seen. In the exterior wall is an ancient tethering ring and windows which have been bricked in. Inside there's an open fire in the single bar.

The present King of The Kings Arms is publican Ian King and he serves Directors and Best on handpump and other Courage beers on keg. Although it's a

and contrary to the interests of nearly everyone else. Under the leadership of Stephen Langton, Archbishop of Canterbury, the barons of England 'ganged' up on the king and forced him to set his seal upon a document which formalised the unwritten laws of the land and which probably marked the first regal and legally binding acknowledgement of the rights to liberty and property of 'freemen and barons' – not the serfs! Although there is a commemorative 'Gothic' cottage on nearby Magna Carta island, it is highly unlikely that the greater charter was sealed anywhere but here on the meadow. Reports of the time confirm that John arrived under heavy guard from Windsor, for each day's negotiations with the hostile knights who were camped out here by the Thames. No one knows exactly where it was sealed. If you look to your left by the road, you can see the entrance lodges designed by Edwin Lutyens and set amongst the trees are monuments to John F Kennedy and the Magna Carta. This area was once a duelling field and later, in the 18th century, Egham race course.

With the Windsor road approximately 300 yards ahead, go right. On the hill behind, you can see the airmen's memorial reaching for the skies and Shoreditch College brooding behind trees. You come to a slim stretch of water, home to a number of swans which glide regally across its shiny surface under a perfect stretch of English meadowland. In order to keep going, bear slightly left for the gate with the 'Private Fishing' sign. At water's end keep left and soon you will see a small circular pond on your right, less graceful than its predecessor. From here, keep swinging left with the hedgerow, aiming not for the road to your right but rather for the busy Windsor road, some distance ahead across flat parkland. Keep left and you should reach the road opposite the Citroen warehouse, a palatial mass.

By the road, go right till you're level with the 'Motorboats for Hire' sign and the start of Yard Mead. Cross the busy

small pub, The Arms claims to have the largest range of food in the area, from the ubiquitous cheese roll through steak to venison and calimari; meals, 7 days a week! The pub has four darts teams (including a ladies' one) and a juke box.

The Eclipse, Egham

The Eclipse stands on the A30 roundabout at the bottom of Egham Hill. Built in the thirties and named after the famous racehorse who won over £25,000 in stake money; including the 1881 Derby. In a long and distinguished career, the horse sired 335 winners and died aged 25 in Middlesex.

The Eclipse has a brick and timber frame enclosing a saloon bar with restaurant and a public bar.

Directors comes handpumped and other Courage beers are on keg; there's draught Guinness, too. The restaurant will cater for any needs not met by the snack menu (with home-made pies). Kids are catered for in the restaurant and there are up-to-date video machines and darts.

The White Lion, Egham

The White Lion offers the hungry customer a selection of sandwiches and snacks and a menu of hot foods, on which are listed pizzas, omelettes, sausages, prawns and more. Draught Guinness can be drunk and keg Courage Best Bitters and Tavern Mild can be likewise consumed.

Built on the site of an old thatched inn which was burnt down, The White Lion roared into life in 1930 . . . the pub has recently been given 'a face lift' leaving it with central heating throughout an 'all round' saloon (with open fire) and an L-shaped public bar.

road to go down this lane. In next to no time you will be confronted by a forest of masts and the flurry and bustle of boats and boatmen. . . . This change in the landscape can be accounted for by the close proximity of the Thames. Turn right downstream – hire a cruiser if the fancy takes you – and continue past well-kept gardens of 'bijou' riverside residences and the curious buildings which constitute that bizarre genre, Thames Valley Tudor. On this broad sweep of water you'll see people in boats (mostly famous television personalities) and various swans, ducks and idlers mucking about on the river. At Bellweir Lock you can marvel at the spray of plunging water and the smart uniforms of the lock keepers. Beyond 'Runnymede', a hotel for conferences if ever I saw one, turn right by the path up the parapet of Staines bridge and then right along the pavement to the roundabout.

Exit second left (marked Egham) past The Victoria and into The Avenue. This metamorphoses into the High Street and takes you past **The White Lion** and a stone in the wall declaring to the world that it is 18 miles from Hyde Park corner. Turn right opposite the fire station and roll back past The Catherine Wheel and the interesting church of St John's to The Red Lion and well-earned respite.

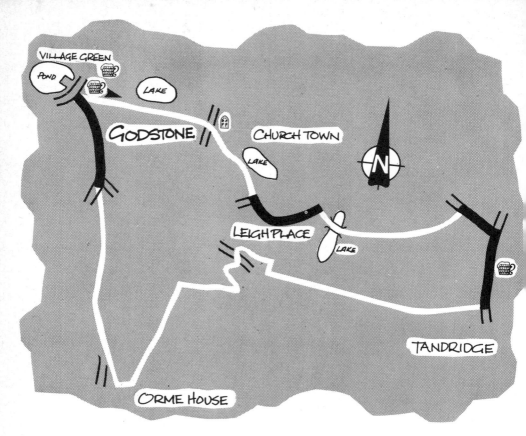

22 Godstone

APPROXIMATELY 4½ Miles

The District

"A most beautiful village" Cobbet.

Life in Godstone has always turned on its vital access to London and the South coast resorts. When the old (Roman) road was unaccountably re-routed westwards in the 17th century, the heart of the village moved from Churchtown to today's centre of Godstone Green. This new highway took over as the axis of the local leather trade, the lifeblood of the village coaching inns with 30 coaches a week and, upon my Thesaurus! the main artery for transporting the products from the soil of the district. The latter included fine silver sand, surreptitiously mined, or 'smuggled', and sold for hourglasses, for scouring and for use in place of blotting paper; hearthstone, which came in two varieties, soft white for whitening and hard dark for paving, furnace linings etc (this stone was also used in The Tower of London and Windsor Castle); fuller's earth which is used in manufacturing processes and lastly hops. By the time the railway came through the Godstone Gap in the 19th century the area was extremely undermined and therefore liable to both subsidence and economic collapse, since much of the underground stock was exhausted. It was therefore a mixed blessing that the local workforce could take to railway commuting and turn the village into a 'dormitory'.

Godstone Green is a vast expanse of grass with a history that is extensively

110

recorded in a village pamphlet called 'Godstone 1900'. The old quoits courts may have been re-marked for football, but the pond remains much as it was when 19th century ducks, that extinct species, were collected by drawing a string across the surface of the water from one end to the other. Meanwhile horse traders put their steeds out to grass on the common itself but only till 9.00 pm after which the silk hatted constabulary would impose fines. Early this century, the village cricket team was most demonstratively supported by the local barber . . . 2d a haircut . . . who travelled with them to all away matches in their 'two horse brake'. If they had won, the villagers heard the tune, 'See the conquering heroes', blaring from the barber's cornet long before the brake was in sight; any other tune meant disaster. Jack Hobbs himself played for Surrey against this team here and scored 172 after not being given out LBW on his third ball . . . the umpire, Tiggy Vigar, explained later that this was because the crowd had come to see the great man bat. This was in 1912. Other 'celebrations' held on the green include those for the Silver Jubilee and Diamond Jubilee of Queen Victoria, the coronation of George V and relieved Morris Dancing after the Relief of Mafeking.

In Churchtown, visit not only the church and almshouses but also Pilgrim Cottage, Tythe Cottage and The Old Pack House with its 'jettied crossing'; this was restored by Maurice Elvey the 20s film producer responsible for recreating the 'glories' of Balaclava on a nearby Surrey hillside. The (Samuel) Pepys family originated in Tandridge, which today is isolated, unlike in the past when it was an important parish, shaped

The Inns

The Barley Mow, Tandridge

Parts of The Barley Mow are 300 years old from the days when it was built as a coaching inn on a back road to the south coast. Customers go back in generations in a pub which has seen as much change inside as it has in the outside world; they have included Dennis Compton, the cricketer, Bert Wilcox, the well-known unknown and the alcoholic gamekeeper, whose ghost is now said (in some quarters, denied) to haunt his former haunt. In the days of spittoons and wall to wall sawdust (last century) he used to sit before the fire watching white mice come out of the fireplace – this was his own version of delirium tremens, pink elephants to anyone else and no doubt helped him pass the time of day.

Home of the Young Farmers Club and a rugby team, the atmosphere is jovial and hearty. There are seven bitters including hand-drawn Sam Smith and Wessex and top pressure John Smith, Courage Best, Fremlins, Tartan and another I forget. Additionally, there's snacks and hot food – plenty of it – and tables 'for proper eating'. There's a concrete garden out the back and kids can be taken there or into the restaurant.

The Bell, Godstone

Though modified in the 1700s and re-modified this century, The Bell dates back to 1393. The kitchen was a high pitched medieval hall and the sloping floors upstairs and original beams confirm the building's antiquity. The Bell, apparently, catered for 'private carriage trade' rather than stage coaches and had a reputation for good catering, which persists to this day: the menu includes sandwiches, snacks and tasty steak pie. Ind Coope 'real ale' is set for future long and thin round the Roman trackway which brought iron from the Weald. Once the site of a priory of the Augustine order, it now is said to have 'the darkest church in Surrey'.

The walk has lots to see on its way to Tandridge and the Barley Mow. From this second village, it returns by field, bridle track and roadside to Godstone's heart of grass once more. The going is easy, the paths well mapped out.

How to Get There

By road take the A22 south from Caterham, crossing over the M25. Godstone is at the intersection of the A22 and the A25 (approx $2\frac{1}{2}$ miles).
By rail to Godstone.

The Godstone Walk

Leave by the door of the Suffolk bar and head in the direction of Godstone and its village green. Cross the road by The White Hart and find the Bay Path leading to the local church – this is a public footpath. As you can see from the sign, The White Hart was established in the reign of King Richard II (the 14th century), received Goode Queen Bess and was honoured by several visits of Victoria, who stopped by for tea on her way to Brighton and had her horses changed at the same time. The name The White Hart, is probably a symbolic reference to Thomas Becket, the martyr. Beware of low flying swans as you continue along the Bay Path with a watery Nature Reserve to your left; this way you're soon brought out beside the church and Churchtown.

The first church here was small and wooden and this grew through Norman foundation work and medieval and Victorian periodic additions to become the church you see now; it was restored in 1872. Beside it are the lovely old almshouses of St Mary's (also of 1872). In Saxon times, Churchtown was called Walcnesstede (Walkingstead) since was an area where cloth was trodden in vats. . . The Saxons here made a living by 'fulling' cloth, a cleaning and condi-

tioning process using local fullers earth, still used in bleaching and purifying oils, pottery glazing, water paints and cosmetics.

Go up the steps to the church, under its broad lych-gate and your path goes to the right of the building and exits with stile in the direction of the pool, where two boys are said to have drowned after skating on thin ice, despite parental warnings. The trees remaining here are part of what was a 'pleasaunce', with rhododendrons from China planted by Major Rhode, possibly to commemorate his own name. The path by the water's edge goes to the right over delicate wrought iron bridges and then swings right to leave the pond.

Next, as you scamper up hill following the path, there will be a handsome building set among fir trees to your right. Make for the stile in the right-hand corner of this 'field' and go into the trees. After swinging left, swing yourself over a stile and turn down right in deference to the yellow arrow and despite the distractions of lovely 'folding' Surrey countryside. The path leads to a fairly odd metal stile which you can climb in as odd a style as you like, before turning left and making off down the track past late Victorian Leigh Place, whose brickwork is somewhat over elaborate. Leigh Place's history includes Sir Richard Lee, Lord Mayor of London in 1460 and again in 1470, and the tenancy of Sir John Evelyn – they lived in previous structures on the site.

Beyond the house and outbuildings, and in 40 yards time, turn right past garish marker posts, down a path between garden and field and towards lake, as you go there's a giant rush plant to tickle most of your fleeting body. Following the public footpath sign, go left towards Leigh Mill House, where gunpowder was once milled and flour, too. These days the water wheel remains, if not the demand for the products of the Mill which closed in the thirties, after a 'working life of 900 years'. Nearby is an earthwork mound which may or may not have been the Castle of Odo de Danmartin who founded 13th century Tandridge Priory. Odo or no, the hills here have resounded to the clash of arms since then, when film supremo Maurice Elvey, re-enacted the Battle of Balaclava for one of his epic films on the surrounding slopes.

Leaving the lake behind, turn right beyond Leigh Mill and go past a tennis court to a T-junction where you turn left, with affluence in evidence all around.

Now there's an artificial trout lake below right and, above right, a pair of creaking, squeaking trees, rubbing trunks elephant style. Take a gander at wild geese on the water and at a badly executed picture of a security guard and his best friend – the style of this warning is purest naive. Soon you come to a stile, so haul your bulk over and continue almost straight on and downwards a little to go along the left side of a sloping cornfield. To your right is the awesome spread of a large sewerage works (the site of The Battle of Balaclava?) and, when you join the path by a telegraph pole and houses simultaneously come into view, keep straight on now heading for Tandridge. The path becomes a track which arrives at the road opposite 'St Dennis Orchard' and 'Three' – turn right for **The Barley Mow.** Mr Elvey used Tandridge church as the setting for Gracie Field's wedding in 'Sing as we Go', whose plot involved our heroine in much maidenly basket carrying.

delivery and, at the time of writing, the two spacious bars (Norfolk and Suffolk) serve DD, John Bull and draught Guinness. These can be enjoyed inside on window seats to a background of red flock wallpaper and beams, while outside you can put your feet up in a grassy garden with not only fruit and vegetables but seats, too.

The Hare and Hounds, Godstone

The Hare and Hounds dates back 400 years but has been much modernised of late. It seems that its brick floor was laid by someone called Long Robin in 1766. It has a good selection of beers and an excellent variety of things to eat.

Leaving The Barley Mow, turn left down the road past the school, 150 yards after which, you turn right over a stile to follow the public footpath starting by the Tandridge village sign. The path goes down the left edge of the field and in the bottom corner head left between the bushes and then fork right after about 10 yards to go to the bridge with a stile at either end. From here go about 50 yards straight ahead to a yellow-arrowed stile and continue in an arrow dynamic direction up the right side of the field to a metal stile in the top corner. After this proceed straight across a fallow field, fellow, to find a three bar stile, after which you continue half right over a ditch in the middle of a line of trees to find a stile just to the right of the white building, which is The Wonham Hotel.

After rapid ascent and descent (no dissent now) turn left past the carts and entrances of the hotel, to find the public footpath sign beyond and to the right. Go through the gate marked and walk to the visible stile. Cross this, limbo under a lichen limbed tree, to the right following the boundary of the huge field right round to the top corner. Here there are two openings, take the higher, left-hand one and follow the deep rutted track to an awkward stile by a gate. Hurdle this (impossible!) and go left along the bridle path. To your left as you go is a view over farmland which flows to the distant heights of the South Downs. Follow the track to the road and before you get there Orme Hill House stands below left, this is a Gothic, preparatory and secondary school: you must go through a gate to reach the road.

At the road, turn right and follow it into Godstone, which is a fair distance away. To break up the journey you can climb Tilburstow Hill on the left or follow the public footpath to the right of the road (a course of action I recommend). When you get to the village (thank God for Godstone), you can go either to **The Bell** or make for **The Hare and Hounds,** which overlooks the large green or would do if it weren't stuck behind a large 'local amenity' . . . if, in doubt ask a local.

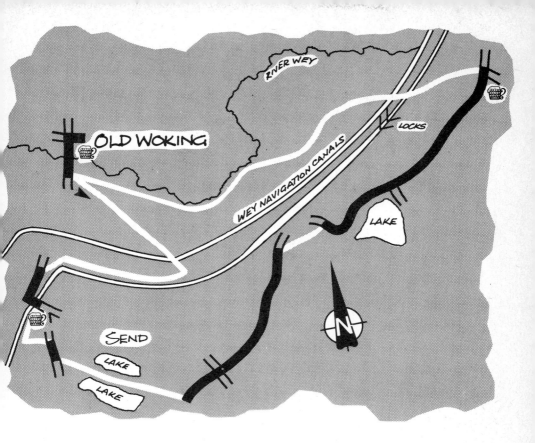

23 Old Woking

APPROXIMATELY 4¾ Miles

The District

Originally known as the Wye, the Wey was and is the most important river in Surrey. It was navigable for 20 miles upstream as far as Godalming and was fundamental in the development of Guildford. The river flows north out of the county town and, just before Send, a village of rather tasteless and drab residential development, it flows past Sutton Place. Built in 1523, it was one of the first unfortified country mansions (not that it really needed to be – it was protected on three sides by the Wey), and, until his death, it was the home of reclusive Paul Getty, one of the few men rich enough to be able to ignore the punitive English super-tax systems.

However, back in the 17th century, Sir Richard Weston was lord here and it was he who undertook the construction, in 1651, of the Wey Navigation, a canal which interestingly and deftly uses different branches of the Wey. With what seems like incredible speed, 200 men took only nine months to build this link between Guildford and the Thames and London. The effort was not wasted and the canal thrived by transporting timber, wool and grain downstream and road-building stone, coal, flour, meal and manure upstream. It's recorded that in 1664 amongst all the other traffic, 4,000 timber barges made the journey and, at the canal's peak in 1838, 83,003 tons of goods were moved along its waters.

➤

Woking is a pretty soulless place unless you count a railway station as a soul. In 1838, the London and South-West Railway Company, presumably with an envious eye on the success of the canal/river, built 'Horsell for Woking' station on what old maps call 'Woking Heath'. It was virtually the only building there and it was around this station, that this 'upstart town', as it has been called, grew up. Not only is it an upstart with no previous historical existence or importance, but also, it started up with astonishing speed. It expanded faster than any other Surrey town. All in all, it's probably to be avoided unless you are a Muslim, for it was in Woking in the late 1880s that a certain Dr Leitner, linguist and Orientalist, founded one of the earliest mosques in England in the grounds of his Oriental Institute. The Institute died soon after the Doctor, but the mosque thrived.

Old Woking however, is a different bucket of mackerel altogether. An Anglo Saxon settlement preceded a village mentioned in the Domesday Book, where it was listed as a possession of the Crown. This meant that its inhabitants were rather luckier than Mr Getty — they didn't have to pay taxes. It was described by Defoe in 1724 as 'a country market town . . . so out of the way that 'tis very little heard of in England' and it's perhaps this isolation and a consequent desire for a place on the map that caused eleven villagers to claim, in 1812, that they had all seen a grotesque double-headed monster leaping five times across the Wey from bank to bank and then, would you believe it, swimming off downstream. I suppose they got the snippet of fame they wanted.

The Wey then winds on through water meadows dominated by the ruins of Newark Priory, well worth a visit. As is Wisley Garden, a few miles away near Ripley. Surrounding Wisley village, it is where the Royal Horticultural Society does its research work. In its 300 acres are laboratories, greenhouses, a pinetum and a rock garden. There is a fantastic variety of shrubs, trees and plants, many rare in this country, and especially beautiful are the thousands of azaleas, camellias, roses and rhododendrons.

The walk leaves Old Woking, crosses the Wey and then the Wey Navigation. It then follows another branch of the Navigation to The New Inn. From there, it passes through Send and follows a lane past Papercourt Farm and returns to Old Woking across various branches of the Wey and the Wey Navigation. The going is easy, but due to the long stretches of water that the walk follows, it can be muddy, especially after rain.

How to Get There

By road take the A3 south-west from London, and then turn right onto the A245 for Old Woking.
By rail to Woking.

The Old Woking Walk

You start at **The White Hart** and when you leave, turn left out of the pub to the small roundabout. You turn left here towards Send and Ripley and walk along the pavement over Broadmead Bridge over the River Wey. Just after the last house on the left – 2, Hartland – turn left over the broken stile onto the marked public footpath. Head out across the field to the old pillbox and, passing it, continue in the same direction until you meet part of the Wey Navigation system. In this flat valley there are several branches of the Wey and its Navigation, so it's difficult to tell different branches of the Navigation apart. Anyway turn left along the bank, climb a wooden fence at the water's edge and soon, near where the pylons' cables pass overhead, you arrive at a wooden footbridge which you cross.

On the far bank, fork left along a path through the scrubby grass, over a wee concrete footbridge and onto another, this time elevated, footbridge across another, 'mainer' branch of the Wey Navigation. But don't cross this bridge: instead turn right along the towpath. You pass a concrete-batching plant, a scout hut and then masses of attractive bamboos on the far bank, while on your side, there are willows, oaks and a lot of nettles. This stretch of the canal is decidedly pretty with rushes and later, rhododendrons and holly bending over from the far bank and dipping into the brownish water.

Walk on up to the roadbridge and turn left over it to **The New Inn**. When you leave the pub, turn left and then left again to walk between it and the canal along the gravelly towpath, which is very wide here. Where it narrows by a brick bunker with a steel door and an abusive sign, turn left up the path between hedges of privet and holly.

At the road, Potters Lane, go right and just after a house on the left called Peny-darren, turn left along the marked public footpath. Follow the double drives and at the end, the footpath continues in the same direction between fences and soon, between lakes. On this causeway grow oaks, silver birch, willows, brambles and bracken and on the lakes cruise mallard, wigeon and mandarin duck. On the far side, after a path joins from the right, you perform a Z-bend and then walk between houses to a small road.

Here you turn left and, walking along with sports pitches on your left, you come to a crossroads which you go straight over, along Tannery Lane. As you stroll along, you have time to admire the fact that the vines of White Place Vineyard on your right actually grow in this climate of ours. You pass grand-looking Heath Farm with its protecting hedges of various firs and its fine black weatherboarded barn.

Just after the 'Single track road with passing places' sign, turn right through a gate into a field and walk half right along a path heading for the two poplars close to each other, slightly to the left of the black barn. You walk in front of The Crack Pulverising Mill Ltd and a workplace with a Union Jack door. When you meet the lane, turn right and follow it over a stream and on. When you pass Watermeadow Cottage (oddly it has a beach-hut in its garden) there is a lake to your right and when you get to 3, Prews Cottages, there's a gap in the fence opposite, so you can investigate closer, dawdle along the bank or simply sit down for a minute or two. Then return to the lane and go on in the direction you were heading before.

At the triangle, go straight on and soon you pass Papercourt Farm (the lane is now called Papercourt Lane). This farm gives you your third black barn to admire

The Inns

The White Hart, Old Woking

Originally a 15th century pub, it was greatly added to by the Victorians, who used it as a hotel up to the First World War. In fact, when he was Prince of Wales, Queen Victoria's son used to punt on the Wey and regularly used to pop in here for a drink or two afterwards. Perhaps more interesting, was the annual Leek Court that was held here. Visiting magistrates would preside over various petty cases and generally hand out a number of fines. At the end of the session, the drinking would start, and invariably the magistrates would re-fine the offenders if they didn't join in the singing and general merriment. Justice must be seen to be enjoyed by every citizen.

This two-bar pub is not desperately attractive but makes up for that with its warm and youngish atmosphere. Usually there is trad jazz on Friday evenings and either various live acts or a disco are laid on for Saturdays. The garden was described by Nigel Palmer, your landlord, as 'rustic', but looks to be pleasant enough in summer.

A Courage pub, it stocks Directors and Best Bitter on handpump and JC, Tavern, Mild, Blackthorn cider and two lagers on keg. On weekdays there's a selection of cooked food (grills and other pub grub) at good prices and there are other snacks (sandwiches etc) at all times.

The New Inn, Send

An old fashioned pub just by the Wey Navigation, The New Inn at one time used to be a hospital and mortuary, while the original pub was down the road a little. However, though its window boxes and its rendered walls make it old-fashioned from the outside, the inside is

— it's the best, if rather tumbledown. Ignore a public footpath off to the left and continue along the lane which is soon flanked, on the left, by massive oaks. The lane weaves between bungalows and houses and Barataria, the last house on the left, has four solar panels. Just after the telephone box, the lane meets the B367 and, to your right, is/are **The Seven Stars.**

Leave the pub and retrace your steps back past Barataria Mobile Homes and just after its long wall, there's a stile and a marked footpath going right. Walk along between the hedge and garage, crossing straight over a metalled track to another stile.

With your back to the stile, go half left across the meadow to a footbridge — cross it. From here, go straight on to a line of trees ahead and then turn left along the trees. They lead you to a National Trust-tended lock and weir complex of the Wey Navigation. Cross the lock on the wide concrete bridge and, ignoring the 'Towpath' sign pointing along the front of the lockkeeper's cottage, leave the building to your left and go to and over another wide bridge over another branch of the Wey Navigation.

Turn left upstream along the far bank and soon you come to a wooden bit of fence, which you don't quite have to swim to climb over; also it has barbed wire on it — not really the kind of thing one expects on a public footpath, what? Climb it anyway and then head across the meadow aiming for the nearest pylon to your right. Walk on in the same direction past it, until you hit (well, not exactly) the Wey.

Don't lose your Wey here. Turn left along its bank and follow it as path and river meander a bit, to a stile by a gate. Follow the river on upstream and then the edge of the field round to the gate, where you first entered. Turn right along the road back across the Wey (this is confusing) and right again at the roundabout for liquid refreshment after a refreshing liquid walk.

rather more modern. Four years ago it was converted to one large bar and refurbished throughout. It has an original beam, some old prints of coaching days, a little brass and by the door an aquarium with guppies and angel-fish. There is a large garden at the back.

Its beers include Friary Meux Bitter and Burton Ale (both on handpump) with DD Löwenbrau, Arctic Lite, Skol and Guinness on keg. Bar snacks include sandwiches, ploughman's, pâté and soup.

The Seven Stars, Newark Lane, Nr Ripley

There was a pub here from 1150, presumably as a second retreat for the monks from nearby Newark Priory of roughly the same date. However the present pub was built in 1927 and serves as a retreat for anyone over fourteen. It is a friendly two-bar pub with four open fires and in the saloon, a good collection of porcelain and pewter — there's some Minden china, a Doulton jug and beer mugs from Victorian days onwards. A 1916 beer take-away jug is a reminder of a past before canned supermarket beer.

You may be lucky, or unlucky depending on your temperament, to be in the pub on one of the many occasions (sometimes as often as two or three times a week), when strange chanting can be heard in one corner of the saloon. A ghostly reminder of some previous incarnation of the pub, the mixed voices of some previous incarnation of these former customers can only be heard in the corner itself. Though perhaps, it adds a little extra mystery if you know that Gregory Peck used to come here after filming *The Omen* at Newark Priory.

There's Friary Meux Bitter and Burton Ind Coope Bitter, both on handpump, along with John Bull, DD, a lager and a mild on keg. Food includes basket meals, various pies (the steak and kidney is home-made), sausage rolls, ploughman's and sandwiches with salads in the summer. Which is when it might be nice to take any or all of the above into the garden with its pretty flowerbeds.

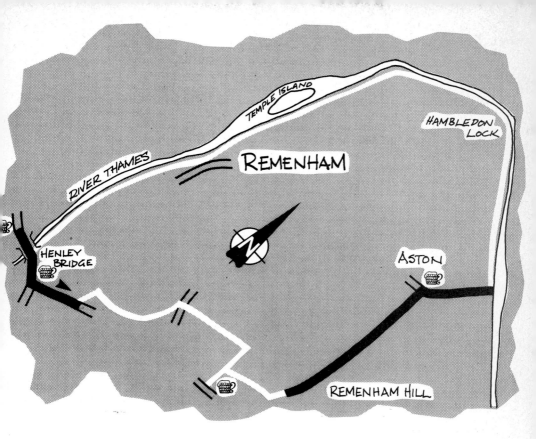

24 Remenham

APPROXIMATELY 5½ Miles

The District

Henley means 'old place' in early English and is reputed to be the oldest town in Oxfordshire. In 1829, the first 'varsity' boat race took place on the nearby Thames before a crowd of 20,000 and between rival crews of 'stalwart sons of Albion' . . . as usual Oxford won easily. Ten years later in 1839, the first Henley regatta was held with a view to 'producing most beneficial results to the town and being, a source of amusement and gratification to the neighbourhood and the public in general'. That year the Town Challenge Cup was won by The Wave Crew, with the Albion and Dreadnought crews deadheating for second place. Telling, new phrases soon appeared in descriptions of the town such as 'The Mecca of Boating Men', first cited in a local history of 1856 and still to be found in today's Henley guide, and the Regatta became one of the highlights of the English social calendar and the world rowing season. The Grand Challenge Cup, known to commentators as 'The Blue Riband of Eight-Oared Racing', is the top trophy in what is now The Royal Henley Regatta.

Henley-on-Thames is usually a quietly, prosperous town with a 'county' atmosphere; this all changes during the four days of the annual regatta when it becomes noisy, athletically social and very prosperous indeed, as people seek to outdrink and outdress each other, at

▶

the colourful riverside festivities.

The town has many lovely buildings, the best of which are Tudor, Regency and Georgian, partly on account of its proximity to London and the many wealthy Londoners who built 'bijou residences' not too far from their place of work. There are two 'miles' of importance; The Fair Mile, the town's northern approach, which is lined with outstanding architecture and The Straight Mile, which makes up the course of the regatta. St Mary's Church by Henley Bridge was founded by the Apostle of Wessex, Birinus, in 630 AD and must originally have been a wattle and daub structure; the present building dates from the 13th century and in its yard there's a fascinating chantry house whose lower floor was once used as a classroom by Lady Periam's Blue Coat School at the same time as the Grammar School made similar use of the upstairs. Having been on the main coaching route between London and Oxford, Henley has many old inns, the most famous being The Red Lion Hotel, which has registered Charles I and George III among many other famous customers. In 1642 Prince Rupert had a spy hanged on the Elm tree opposite The Bell Inn, now Rupert House in Bell Street.

Notable former citizens include J W Jeston, who won a prize for producing 8lbs 5oz of opium from a quarter of an Oxfordshire acre in 1823; Humphrey Gainsborough, the inventor brother of the painter; Ravenscroft of Ravenscroft glass and, perhaps most famous of all, Mary Blandy.

Beautiful Mary Blandy was the daughter of Francis Blandy, a wealthy solicitor and Henley's town clerk. Mr Blandy had the unfortunate habit of boasting of his daughter's large future inheritance causing suitors to come flocking like bees to a honeypot, until a golddigger called Cranstoun won poor Mary's affection. Apart from having Jacobite sympathies (this was the 18th century), Captain Cranstoun had one other obvious drawback in his prospective father-in-law's eyes . . . he was already married. Acting on information, Blandy sent him packing back to Scotland, but Mary was in love and continued to receive the Scot's correspondence, which included a 'love philtre' to be administered in her father's tea. This she duly did and dad duly died since the substance was, in fact, arsenic. When his death became public knowledge, a mob chased her till they caught her at Henley Bridge she was then despatched to Oxford, tried and hanged in 1752. Opinion turned full circle and a public outcry followed, provoking a popular song which ends: "Accursed-condemn'd-dragged to the scaffold's side – she fearless mounted and unpitied died".

The walk starts off from The Little Angel on the Berkshire side of Henley Bridge and goes to the Five Horseshoes on Remenham Hill. From there a stroll down a country lane leads past The Flower Pot on the way to the bank of the Thames, which marks the way back to Henley beside the course of the Regatta. The going is easy.

How to Get There
By road take the A423 east from Henley-on-Thames, Remenham is just over Henley bridge.
By rail to Henley.
By bus the easiest way to the starting point is on foot, over Henley bridge.

The Remenham Walk
Be good at **The Little Angel** before turning left from its car park up the pavement by the main road; direction, London and Maidenhead, description, A423. Ignore Matson Drive as you steam up the 1:10 slope, with a pleasant cricket pitch below to your left through trees. Wait till you've

passed the 'school' traffic sign, then turn left up the steps of the public footpath which begins beside Craigwell House. To your left you can see Henley, most notably St Mary's prominent and famous tower. From this point on, there will be very little road traffic to contend with.

Past 'Underwood' keep between the railings and on and past a private swimming pool and a neighbouring tennis court. As the railings disappear, keep straight through Remenham Woods. Emerge from amongst well controlled brambles straight on to and straight off a stony raised track; the path now slants leftish past rhododendrons, hollies, beeches and damp spots of marshland. Wooden fencing begins near where the wider track starts which takes you past a modern house with a tree house perched precariously in one of its garden growths, to a lane, Church Lane, and the entrance to Whitewood House.

Go left at the lane, then right in 10 yards time through a gate, past a footpath sign and along the right-hand edge of a dashed pebbly field. To your right is Remenham Place and its manicured hedging and to the left is cluttered Woodside Farm. Beyond and north you should see a glistening chink of the Thames before the gathering beech-browed darkness of the Chilterns. In the corner of the field, go to the right through a wooden gate and along a secluded, wooded path. To the left dimly discernible through trees is a house called Common Barn and it's also to your left that a 'bomb crater' gapes, before the path winds out by a track which will lead you to a busy road where you turn left for The Five Horseshoes.

Across the road, and opposite the building, is a well which used to supply the neighbourhood of Remenham Hill. It was 270 feet deep which is why the wheels at its head are so large. In the private estate beyond, owned by Park Place (once a nunnery, now a school) there's a network of tunnels (from Friar Park across the Thames) which were used by monks with dissolute habits to visit the waiting nuns. Past residents include Lady Hamilton and the grounds sprout a fascinating collection of trees imported from all over the world in the early 19th century.

▶

The Inns

The Little Angel, Remenham
There are two little angels on the outside wall of The Little Angel, which stands just off the London Road and beside a peaceful cricket ground. The inn is 15th century and has kept up to date by transforming what was the site of a funeral parlour into its present day car park. It was also on this spot that Mary Blandy (see above), is thought to have been overtaken by the pursuing crowd and her ghost is said to haunt the premises, driving cats mad and preventing occupants, who encounter an uncanny 'forcefield', from descending the stairs after there has been a domestic argument.

The Little Angel contains a ninety four seater restaurant with a daily changing menu and Victorian pictures and prints in a bar, which has crepuscular lighting and a basement atmosphere. To drink, there's handpumped Brakspears bitter and old ale, as well as draught Guinness, and vintage ports and a variety of wild cocktails to shake you up. Snacks include Farmer's steak pie which merited its own slice of fame in a write-up in *The Daily Telegraph*. In summer, lots of people sit out under umbrellas by the cricket pitch.

The Five Horseshoes, Remenham
In 1840 The Five Horseshoes was built as the staging post where they changed the team of horses after a steep climb from Henley's White Hart up Remenham Hill. The common land near here is where the Remenham Revels, an annual fair, were held. In 1936 the German national flag flew outside the hotel for perhaps the last time in this country before the Second World War, when their Olympic and no doubt Olympian rowing team stayed here for the Henley Regatta.

▶

Leaving The Five Horseshoes, go right along the road and first right back down the lane. At the white gate and gateposts under the conical conifer, bear right down the track past The Five Horseshoes' back garden. As the track goes private by paddocks, keep along the narrow path to the left between trees and hedgerow. This gets you to Aston Lane, formerly Ferry Lane from the days of local river crossings.

Go left down the lane. As you can see, the path ahead is narrow and bendy, so be careful of cars, which are, nonetheless, few and far between. Proceed along the steep-banked lane to sleepy Aston Village – past 'Highway' and 'Wistaria' and you can't miss **The Flower Pot** on its corner next to the village car park. The high-walled garden next to it flies a fluttering Union Jack and you will recognise this highly recommended hotel by the writing on the walls, 'Good Accommodation for Fishing and Boating Parties'.

Turn left from the pub and continue down Aston Lane past houses and to the river which prevents further dry progress in a straight line. The jetty of the old rope ferry still advertises The Flower Pot to passing boats, 'Mooring for Patrons Only'. Across the water is an ostentatious crenellated Victorian boatshed with a flag mast.

Turn left by the public footpath sign to cross a stream whose tiny trickle is about to become part of the 'sensual' flow of Old Father Thames. 'Thames' is an updating of the old English 'Tems', so schoolkids' spelling has a certain belated accuracy. From this point, follow the river upstream by the old towpath which runs by lush meadowland all the way to Henley Bridge.

On your way, you'll pass Mill End, a millhouse by no means run of the mill, since it was mentioned in the Domesday Book, and also because of the particularly wide torrent of its spectacular weir. Of the things floating on the surface of the river, most will be pleasure boats, barges, coots, dabchicks and great crested grebes. You'll also see Thames

In the bar itself you'll see postcards from all over the world, beer bottles from Venezuela, Kenya, Fiji and Australia and even a packet of Arabic 'Tide'. The Hanrahans once worked for BOAC and continue to receive souvenirs from all over the world, amongst which are some exceptional photographs of lions. If you're lucky (or unlucky) you may even see the ghost of a local scoundrel who died in the back bar during an argument over the division of some 'swag'.

Hand-drawn Brakspears and Henley bottled beers are on hand to assuage your thirst and your hunger can be treated to an à la carte meal or something from an extensive range of snacks. The garden out the back is large and children are well catered for at what is 'a family inn'. A word of warning – the bar area becomes very competitive at Regatta Time.

The Flower Pot, Aston

There has been a pub in Aston village for over 400 years and The Flower Pot has been in operation for 150 of them. It was built to serve locals, local ferry users and 'Fishing, boating and shooting parties', as its outer walls proclaim.

The hotel lives up to its somewhat eccentric name by containing an earthy mixture of humorous characters and a blooming good collection of monster pikes, chub and tench in large glass display cases. There are two bars, one of which has Victorian panelling, a coal/log fire and a lovely wooden bar with authentic old pumps.

You can choose to drink hand-drawn Brakspears Old Best and Mild, draught Guinness or 'old fashioned' Pimms, which is a speciality here. To eat there's steak and kidney pie, roast beef or a choice of sandwiches. Good weather makes it possible to sit out in a grassy garden, with a greenhouse almost overlooking the Thames . . . well, you can just see it. The Flower Pot is very much a traditional English country pub (a species almost extinct) and cannot be too highly recommended.

swans gliding along and these are apparently 'perquisites of the Queen's Dyers and Vintners Companies', a fact which makes them a protected species with heavy penalties on hand to deal with those who tamper with them. In summer banner flying barges crewed by men in the liveries of the City Companies come up the river for the ceremony of Swann Upping. The Dyers' swans are marked with one nick on the upper mandible, the Vintners' have two and the Queen's are privileged to go unmarked — an obvious case of swanupmanship.

Near the weir is Hambledon Lock, which was first built in 1773 to the design of Humphrey Gainsborough, the painter's talented brother, who also invented the tide mill and a drill plough. Travelling up the Thames used to be the best way of getting from London to Oxford and Bristol in the days of rough roads and no railroads. At that time, fly boats were drawn up and down the river by pairs of horses, who ran at full gallop along the towpath for half an hour at a stretch, before being replaced by fresh steeds.

Prior to the inception of the lock here, there was a 'flash lock'. This was a break in the weir where water ran swift and boats were either winched upstream against the current or allowed to hurtle uncontrollably downstream with it. Naturally, there were lots of accidents but few of them were fatal since, wisely, passengers would disembark and watch, fearful for their possessions, from the bank. So dangerous was a flash lock that barges with heavy loads, often transferred their cargos to pack horses, which would then reconsign their goods to the river beyond the Goring Gap.

Hambledon Lock today handles 39,000 boats a year, holds 409 tons of water and, at 17ft 6in wide and 135ft long, is the narrowest lock between London and Oxford. The river here is part of the Queen's Highway, thus travel is free — the snag is that boats must register and pay to do so, since the upkeep of waterways is expensive. The wooden piles

The Angel (on the Bridge), Henley

John Longland, Bishop of Lincoln and one time confessor to Henry VIII (he must have been a busy man!), was born in Henley in 1473, and, in his will, provided for an alms house on the site of what is now The Angel. In the cellar is the arch of a stone and flint bridge, which spanned the river in medieval times, although the present building is mostly 17th century or earlier. The bridge was the focus of much vicious fighting during the Civil War as the Parliamentarians defended the town against the Royalists.

'The most painted and photographed' pub on the Thames, The Angel has a traditional beamed interior, divided into 3 bars one of which has a large Jacobean fireplace. In another, there are photographs of determined locals drinking on the terrace in two feet of water during flooding. Famous customers, who have popped in for a quick 'one for the road', include the son of the Japanese Mikado, Grace Kelly, Max Miller, Douglas Fairbanks Junior and George Harrison.

You can drink Brakspears Pale Ale, Special and old ale (all hand-drawn), or top pressure Tankard as you gaze ever more fondly at the Thames from the terrace bar. You are advised to soak up all that liquid with pizzas, grilled trout, or other items from a wide-ranging menu, which includes hot and cold snacks. Children can be put up (with) on the premises!

▶

downstream of the lock are made of greenheart timber from Brazil and Africa and they're 30 feet long and anchored deep in the mud. Antiquated equipment (from the late 18th century) can make life difficult for the lock keeper here yet the waterway is in a very healthy state, as is obvious from the approving nods of the muscovy ducks, who choose to live round the lock.

When you get to Temple Island, the start of the Henley Regatta course whose building was designed by James Wyatt, you are also at the spot where the first 'Varsity' boat race began in 1829. At that time, the course was on a sharp bend which went from here to The Red Lion by Henley Bridge; you don't need a ruler to see that this is no longer the case. The strange snorting aquatic creature with eight heads and thirty two limbs is nothing to worry about as it is almost certainly a rowing eight out catching crabs in preparation for the Regatta. Half a mile on from Temple Island and across on the far bank, Buckinghamshire ceases and Oxfordshire begins – you're still in Berkshire. Apart from ducks and more ducks the local fauna and flora includes copiously weeping willows, alders, ash and lombardy poplars; rushes in thick clumps, a lifebelt in a tree and walkers out with thoroughly respectable breeds of dogs.

After the houses with matching ponds, go left over a stile to visit Remenham church. This village's population was decimated by the plague in 1625 and has never fully recovered. The church is early English and was built by the Montfort family in their capacity as local patricians not labourers. Look for the grave of Caleb Gould, a former Hambledon lock keeper in the late 18th century and early 19th century. Apparently, he, poor man, lived largely on a diet of onion porridge. Be that as it may, he chose these lines of Gay as his epitaph, "the world's a jest and all things show it,/ I thought so once but now I know it". As they say, it's hard to know whether to laugh or cry. Do neither, instead go back

to the path, turn left and continue along the towpath to Henley.

Across the water are large houses including Phyllis Court, originally built by Cromwell in 1643 and rebuilt by Christopher Wren. Its garden landscaping bears the inescapable hallmark of Capability Brown. On the same side, you'll also see elegant grandstands, topiary, a heronry (if you've got sharp eyesight), the waterside fronts of Regency and Georgian houses and lawns which slope down to the river bank.

Take the towpath past the Leander Club whose emblem is the hippopotamus, "the only animal that constantly has its nose in the air", and you'll emerge by Henley Bridge. The original bridge was swept away in 1774 and the present five arched model was erected in 1786 to William Hayward's design. The keystones were carved with Isis (facing upstream) and Tamesis (downstream) by Horace Walpole's cousin, Anne Damer, who lived at Park Place and was a friend of Napoleon, of all people.

Here, there's a choice, either go right into Oxfordshire to sample the hospitality of **The Angel** on the Bridge or, staying in Berkshire, go left and back to The Little Angel, where) they too can minister to your parched state with traditional English methods of irrigation.

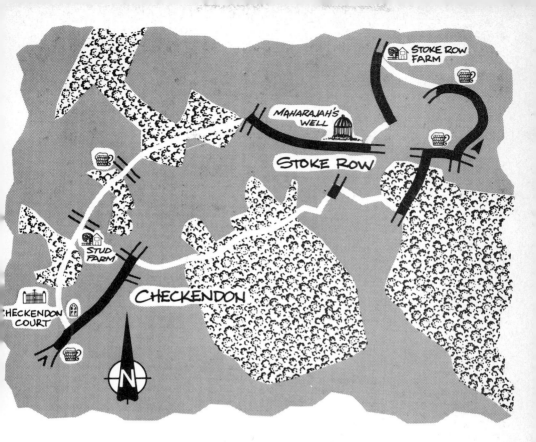

25 Stoke Row

The District

'But also a den of thieves and witches; a retreat for outlaws; the scene of orgies; a hide-out for heretics'. So the Chilterns have been described. The crime, licentiousness and non-conformity hinted at is probably mostly due to a relative lack of people and habitation on the Chilterns in the past. The few scattered and geographically isolated settlements were beyond the influence of the authorities, leaving the wild men of these hills to control their own behaviour, social, sexual and religious. This sparse settling was mostly due to the difficulty of farming this wooded chalk-ridge, cursed by a 7th century Saxon monk as 'the deserts of the Chilterns'. The difficulty of farming the land was mostly due to the almost total absence of that first necessity of life – water. That's not to say it doesn't rain – it does, but the chalk immediately soaks it up and sucks it down to non-porous layers of clay beneath.

What makes upland Stoke Row stand out from other villages is the way the water supply problem was dealt with. Edwarde Reade, from nearby Ipsden, was Governor of the North-West Provinces of India and, reminiscing there one evening, he told the Maharajah of Benares, of Stoke Row's chronic water shortage. Ten years passed before it crossed the Maharajah's mind again, whereupon he decided to remedy the situation. He paid for a well to be sunk the

368 feet necessary to reach the low-lying water. The winding gear was so well made, even old people could easily raise a bucket. Covered by an oriental cupola, it makes an odd contrast with the village's rather more traditional architecture and, as has been pointed out elsewhere, Whipsnade is not the only place in the Chilterns with an Indian elephant.

Checkendon's small and dignified church is worth a visit, though it's been said that the 'altar-cloth would disgrace the rites of a Solomon Islander', whatever that actually means. It also has one of the largest collection of brasses in Oxfordshire, for all you rubbers. Both Checkendon and Stoke Row boast what can only be called a fantastic range of pubs, and I can't recommend them all enough.

The walk goes from The Cherry Tree, round down the back of Stoke Row to The Crooked Billet and then via Stoke Row Farm back into the village. It goes along a road and paths to The Black Horse, and by path from there to Checkendon and The Four Horseshoes. It returns to Stoke Row by lane and woodland paths.

How to Get There
By road take the B481 north from Reading and then turn left onto an unclassified road at Rotherfield Peppard, Stoke Row is on this road (approx $7\frac{1}{2}$ miles).
By rail to Reading.
By bus the 7, 7A and 7B run regularly from Reading.

The Stoke Row Walk
This is a walk with four very good pubs, and I don't know how you could manage it, but I do advise you to visit all four if possible. They all have quite different characters, ranging from the rough-and-ready to the quietly urbane. Perhaps if you visit two of the pubs as you walk, and then later drive to the other two . . . but then that's incitement to drink and drive. All I can say, is that this is one of the few walks on which I can strongly recommend *every* pub, and all for completely different reasons.

The walk starts in **The Cherry Tree** in Stoke Row and, as you emerge from the pub drive onto the road, you turn left. You then turn left again, just before the green, down Newlands Lane. Walk down here, passing houses and cottages, firstly old and then more modern and mostly all pretty. The lane curves left along the edge of Bush Wood: there's an old gypsy caravan up in the field on your left. You arrive at **The Crooked Billet.**

Turn right out of the pub, and continue along the lane, now called Nottwood Lane. Where it bends up to the left, take the marked and narrow public footpath straight on, shimmying through a kissing-gate and along the back of the garden between fence and hedge. Shimmy through a broken kissing-gate and walk on to, and over, a metal barrier into an orchard used as a paddock, still keeping the hedge on your right. When you reach the corner, climb the stile on your right and continue in the same direction, now downhill, towards a set of two white metal gates. Pass through both and walk on up to Stoke Row Farm, going through a gate into its yard; leave the farm buildings and farmhouse on your right and walk up the stone-mushroomed drive to a metalled lane where you turn left.

On your right is a lovely, large, three-storey house with a walled garden — I'd pay £$\frac{1}{2}$ million to be a pools winner. Just after The Pond House's drive on your right, take the path through the white metal barrier up to the right. In the field beside you are two ponds and what look like two bomb craters, the result of either jettisoned bombs or gross inaccuracy. The path swings left by an octagonal building and emerges onto the road through Stoke Row. Turn right and then immediately right again, to walk up the path to the Maharajah's Well. The water hasn't been used since the late 1930s, though the Army did sample it in case it was needed in the war. Sadly, the Well, its mini-'bandstand' dome and the octagonal cottage have all fallen into disuse and disrepair. A Restoration Appeal Fund has been set up — please contribute to help save this unique, and somewhat amusing, monument.

As you leave the Well, turn right along the road and you now have to walk through part of Stoke Row. Most of the bungalows and houses are fairly modern but Bodgers and Giles Farm on your right are older and very pretty, and that's not to say the others are ugly. The garage opposite Giles Farm contains a beautiful vintage car, a Marshall diesel tractor and traction engines – do we smell a hobby here? The road dips and rises and, at the junction with the Checkendon and Woodcote road, turn half left along a marked public footpath that goes off into the wood past the further telegraph pole.

The path passes a fire warning sign and leads off into the wood, through large oaks and smaller firs. Following the distinct path through the middle of the wood, pass an old hedge on your left and a large building on your right. Where the path joins a track, go left along it in the same general direction as before until you leave the wood, emerging onto a lane. Turn right here and walk up to **The Black Horse**, an out-of-the-way sort of place, if ever I saw one.

Having nipped that thirst of yours in the bud, retrace your steps to just beyond where you emerged onto the lane from the wood and turn very sharp right up a flinty track. Walk in front of Bushmoor and head on along the track, along the edge of the wood (on your right). Fork so that you soon pass a plantation of Christmas trees on your left and at the clearing by a small half-timbered cottage, go left along a track, across the house. Just before the metal gate ahead, turn right over a stile and walk directly across the field aiming for the black barn, just to the left of a tallish house. At the fence, climb over onto the narrow fenced path that runs through training-grounds and paddocks for the horses of the stud farm; then climb over the stile onto the lane.

Directly opposite, the public footpath runs along the right side of a garage, through a metal gate, straight on over a wooden fence (with a stile-thing), across a small paddock, over another stile-thing, across the grass to a five-bar gate into the wood. Walk along the obvious path, passing a pond on your left and soon a field on your right. The path veers away from the field to a gate and a stile into another. In this next field, go diagonally right to walk past a water-jump (go on, have a go) to a stile over the railings. Checkendon Court is on your right and very nice it looks too. It's open to the ▶

The Inns

The Cherry Tree, Stoke Row

This pub is between 300 and 400 years old and was two cottages, with 100 year old additions. The pub has been in the Stallwood family for 60 years, or 3 generations, and Mr Stallwood's father and grandfather used to also make tent-pegs from local beechwood for the Army, the Scouts and Guides etc. The pub has played host to quite an array of famous people, including David Vine, Joe Brown, Simon Williams, Arthur Lowe (while filming), Dave Allen and especially Prince Philip, who came to Stoke Row for the centenary of the Maharajah's Well.

The pub has one bar, but you can drink in any of four different rooms all of which have open fires. A carpeted flagstone floor, old tables and chairs and old and very low beams all create a restful and rural atmosphere. Incidentally, a pub tradition says that if you hit your head on one of the low beams, you have to pay 2p to a fund, which goes to a local childrens' charity. There is lots of space in front of the pub for summertime drinking with a well equipped playing area for children. A Brakspears pub, its beers include Mild, Bitter and Best Bitter and Old Bitter all on gravity.

Food is simple and of the soup, toasted sandwiches and rolls variety, except on Sundays, when Mrs Stallwood has a day off from the kitchen.

The Crooked Billet, Stoke Row

This is the most unusual pub I have ever entered and I'm glad I did. It was originally not on the walk, but I was persuaded by Mrs Stallwood, in The Cherry Tree, that I *had* to include this pub. She was right.

There are twelve different meanings of the word 'billet' in English, but the name, The Crooked Billet, means a bundle of ▶

public on the first Sundays in May and August. However, to go on with the walk, you go left, down the path between railings and hedge towards the church. The path swings right and then left to Checkendon Court's drive. At the end of the drive with its sculpted yews, turn right to **The Four Horseshoes,** which is old and rural like the other pubs, but quite different from them all.

After all this pubbing, perhaps it's about time you visited a different kind of building – I suggest Checkendon church which I'm sure you can find for yourself. Though, it must be said that this wasn't the original site for the church. It was planned to stand in what is now called Devil's Churchyard. The church foundations had been laid in a place the Devil had previously earmarked for his own use, and so he cheekily moved the stones at night to the site of the present church. A little more historically, it's taken that the Normans built the church on a site of a wattle and daub structure probably erected by Caeca (hence Checkendon) after his conversion by St Berinus. The mural of Jesus and the Twelve Apostles in the apse was painted in the 13th century, uncovered in 1865 and then rediscovered recently. Eric Kennington was a local artist of note and there's an unfinished sculpture by him and a memorial window to him in the church.

Leave the church and turn left along the road. The old smithy (now Acorn Gates) is on the right, and it seems that many of the village's buildings are beautiful because of, rather than despite, their wonkiness. Walk past the recreation ground, and don't turn right at White Hall Cottage, but continue to a path off to the right, immediately after Swallowcliffe and immediately before Ardross Cottage's drive. The path runs between fence and hedge and then between a sheep field and a pig field.

The path enters a tatty wood, swings left over a fence to continue in the wood, goes over another fence (there is wood on the wire for your benefit) and goes

crooked wood. With the huge amount of beech and other trees around, this area has always produced furniture. Turning chairlegs etc required straight lengths of wood, which, once removed, would always leave bent and unturnable wood. This was bound together in bundles, to be used for other purposes.

The pub has no bar or beer taps. Mr Norman Harris takes your order, disappears down to the cellar and returns with your drink. If you don't want to sit outside, you can choose either the taproom or the parlour in which to drink. The parlour has a stove and is more comfy, with armchairs round the room and a table in the middle for games players. The taproom has old scrubbed tables (rare these days) and a very large open fire, which has a cauldron crane and an oven below, regularly used by the Harris' until recently.

They used to have a village shop in a room on the far side of the taproom and this 400 year old pub has been in Mr Harris' late wife's family since 1777. The atmosphere is warm, welcoming and very friendly.

All the beers are drawn by gravity from the barrel, and include Brakspears Special Bitter, PA, Old (4X) and Mild. There's also Henley's Strong Ale and Brown Ale in bottles and a standard range of other drinks. Sandwiches are available on weekends only.

The Black Horse, Burncott or Black Horse Lane

On an old Oxford to London road, it was a stopping-off point, if not actually a coaching inn. Now, however, while not really serving any community in particular, it serves the area in general. An old building of brick and flint, it has one bar and two rooms with an open fire in the bar. It has original beams, painted panelling, old locally made chairs and settles, and a lovely suite of padded armchairs and sofa, all of which go to make it a charming and yet wholly unpretentious pub. Run by the team of Mrs Saunders, the landlady, and her sister, it is scrupulously straight on through this wood of pine, oak and beech. Near the bottom edge of the wood, cross the path which goes up through the wood from a cottage on your left, and stay close to the bottom of the wood.

You enter a pine wood now which is much more organized, as they tend to be, and follow the path past a little bench and on down, still along the edge of the wood, to a fence by an old stile, which you cross. With the house on your left, cross the track, going slightly to the right of straight ahead, and on up through yet more trees, with fences on your left and right. The fence on the left veers away and then, at a 5ft trunk, you are shown the way by a white arrow on a tree opposite. Exactly 50 yards further on, fork left to stay on the path which leads you to a stile into a field.

Climb the stile and go diagonally right, to a fence and a stile out of the field, and onto a drive. Turn right here and, at the junction, left up the track which, were you to go right, would take you to Basset Wood and Wilmcote. Ignoring this useless information, walk on up until there are houses on both sides, and in between the first and second set of semi-detached houses on your right, there is a white barrier. Go through it and along the marked public footpath between the houses and their gardens and on.

By a shed, where a path goes off left into the wood, keep going straight on (well, very slightly right, if you insist). Leave the house ahead on your right and emerge onto the lane. Turn left here and walk up past the houses, to meet the road that goes through Stoke Row. Turn right, and walk back to The Cherry Tree, where you can curse the writer for his hellish instructions and then promptly forget both him and them.

clean and so, please remove any muddy footwear before entering.

All beers are gravity-fed and are drawn in the cellar and served over the bar. They include Brakspear's Bitter and Mild and Wethered's Bitter. There is no prepared food, but on warm days you can take your drink outside onto the terrace.

The Four Horseshoes, Checkendon

A pub with three different roofs, it is partly thatched, partly tiled and partly slated, and these various roofing materials show the different stages of the pub's development. The thatched section dates back to 1472, the tiled section over the public bar was added in 1520, and the slated section, which was stables before conversion to the lounge, was added in 1901. It's an unusual pub, if for no other reason than that its cellar is not underground. Checkendon is, I'm told, too damp to make it worth having anything below ground-level.

The 1472 section has its original brick floor and beams and, though large, the lounge is warm and welcoming with its large open fire, stag's head, fox's head and old prints. Hanging behind the bar is an amusing replica chastity belt. You don't see many of them around these days.

Very friendly Robert Massey, your landlord, stocks Brakspears Bitter, Special Bitter (both on handpump) and Old Bitter (on gravity), along with Guinness and lager on keg. There is a wide, and recommended range of food served from the bar.

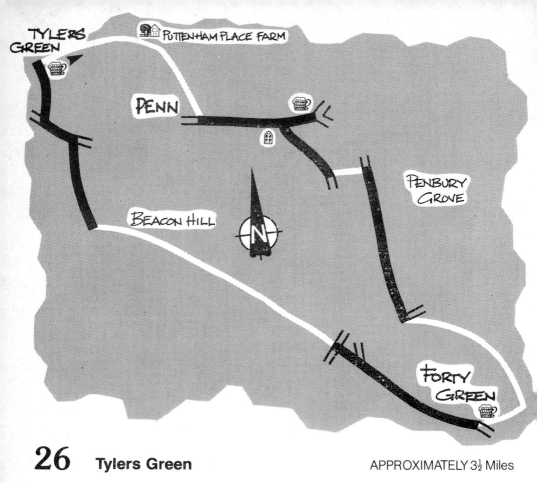

26 Tylers Green

APPROXIMATELY 3½ Miles

The District

High Wycombe, the second largest town in Bucks, 'lies along the deep valley of the River Wye' and has been an important centre of the Chilterns since Roman times. Once known as 'Chepping Wycombe' (or 'market of the Wye valley'), today's town leans more towards industry than market produce. High Wycombe's first big money spinner was the wool trade, whose craftsmen organised themselves into a guild, but this was rapidly overshadowed by lace-making and straw-plaiting, which lasted until the 19th century. Of today's main industries, furniture making began in the 17th century and to this day maintains a healthy output – the town museum houses a collection of Chippendale, Hepplewhite, Sheraton and Windsor pieces.

The Guildhall in the market place is a listed building and it is here that 'incoming and retiring' Mayors are weighed by the Chief Inspector of Weights and Measures. Now largely ceremonial, originally this was a genuine attempt to see how conscientiously the elected official had worked; any increase in flab counted unfavourably.

The National Trust owns every house in nearby West Wycombe and thus preserves many fine 15th-19th century buildings for posterity. Lovely West Wycombe House was re-modelled for Sir Francis Dashwood, Chancellor of the Exchequer in 1762 and a founder member of the Hell Fire Club, dedicated to the Devil and riotous assembly at West Wycombe Caves. A co-founder of this aristocratic and cultish club was John Wilkes, MP for Aylesbury, who when confronted with Lord Sandwich's statement "you will either die from the pox or be hanged", replied like lightning, "That depends on whether I embrace your principles or your mistress". Above the caves is St Lawrence's church, which has a golden globe atop, into which three members of the Club could squeeze and continue their hellbent poker playing late into the night. Despite a certain unpopularity, Dashwood undoubtedly threw some of the best orgies in the 18th century and yet left behind him, along with the nefarious tales, many fine buildings and an able and successful political record. The dripping caves used for the dark satanic rites are now well lit and open to the public.

Beaconsfield (say Beckonsfield) was, according to G K Chesterton, 'close to being an earthly paradise', but he was speaking of the old town sited on the crossing of two coaching routes – Aylesbury to Windsor and London to Oxford. Its inns include The Royal White Hart where QE1 stayed and rested her weary head. Apart from GKC, other notable Beaconsfieldians include Edmund Burke, the parliamentarian, Edmund Waller, the canny political poet who wrote eulogies to both Cromwell and Charles II; challenged by the King who thought his own devotion inferior, Waller replied, "Poets, sir, succeed better in fiction than in truth", Benjamin Disraeli and Enid Blyton – a famous five indeed! This century, Beaconsfield New Town grew up alongside Bekonscot Model Village (which you should visit) but has failed to achieve the latter's verisimilitude to idyllic post-war, country town life. The village has one inch to one foot scale half-timbered villas, churches, streams, farms, meadows, an airport and, of course, model villagers.

From Penn churchyard you can see a dozen counties and in the church itself is the painting of the Last Judgement, cheerfully called 'The Doom', below a 15th century roof which is 'one of the finest in the country'. Penn was described by Sir John Betjeman, for

The Inns

The Crown Inn, Penn

There has been a pub here since the 14th century, though the present Crown is late 15th, being created by knocking together two cottages. Other extensions were fairly recently added and blend in with the style of the old building. It's in typical Chiltern red brick and Virginia Creeper adds to its external attractiveness. It has two bars with open fires and a collection of old pewter and horse brasses. One bar was originally a coffin-maker's workshop before being incorporated into the pub.

It's said that Henry VIII came by horse from Windsor Castle to the Crown to visit his mistress, whose ghostly form, it's also said, can still be seen here, though not by the present occupants. What is more certain is that Ruth Ellis, the last woman to be hanged in England, used to meet her lover, David Blakeley, here before she shot him dead in London.

However, the pub's attractions are not just of an historical nature. Pubs, after all, are for beer and Brakspears Pale and Special Bitters, Courage Directors and Bass (all on handpump) put the Crown in the top league. There's also 3 lagers, 2 keg bitters and draught Guinness.

There's a wide range of snacks all the year round, hot and cold in winter and cold (pies, salads, sweets etc) in summer. And in the restaurant there's an à la carte menu and a cold buffet lunch on Sundays, April-October, and a traditional Sunday lunch on Sundays(!), October-April.

The Royal Standard of England, Forty Green

It's difficult to know where to start with The Royal Standard of England. So, I suppose the beginning is the most sensible. Parts of the building date back to reasons best known to himself, as 'The Chelsea of the Chilterns'. Not far from Penn, Jordans is a village round a green and the burial-place of William Penn, who, despite friendship with the King, was imprisoned many times for his free-thinking, Quaker beliefs, before he bought Pennsylvania, a mere snip at £15,000. Alongside him are buried his two wives, Mary and Isaac Pennington and Joseph Rule, the White Quaker who wore undyed clothing. The question is, was Penn named after Penn . . . or was it the other way round?

How to Get There

By road take the B474 north-west from Beaconsfield, Tylers Green is on the road (approx 3 miles).
By rail to Castle Street.
By bus the 363 from Castle Street (Chilternlink).

The Tylers Green Walk

You start at The Red Lion on the other side of the road from the pond on Tylers Green's green. As you face the pub, go left and then turn right along the marked public footpath between the pub and Old Bank House. This stony track leads down towards Puttenham Place Farm. Just before the farm though, at the large holly tree, fork right, away from the buildings and then turn right as marked, down towards a gap in the hedge. Once through this gap, turn left along the hedge and then, at the corner, turn right up the middle of the field where presumably there used to be another hedge,

now removed to save having to maintain it. This strip leads you to and over a stile, past a tennis court on your right and straight on to a second stile by a plantation of various firs. Climb it and walk along between fences to the road, where you turn left.

You are now walking into the straggling village of Penn. This village high on its hilltop may be relatively unknown but it has a much larger and more important offspring. William Penn and other like-minded Quakers from round here, packed their bags, crossed the Atlantic and founded Pennsylvania, a place free, for them at least, of religious ostracism and persecution. The road passes between Penn Court and the school on your left and the Old Vicarage and Holy Trinity Church on your right. The church with its squat tower is a medieval building justly famous for its unusual 'Doom' painting which dates from the late 15th century. A short distance beyond, on the left is **The Crown Inn.**

Having spent somewhat more than a crown (inflation is wicked), turn right out of the pub retracing your steps, until you turn left, just before Holy Trinity along Paul's Hill. Walk down past the houses and just before the Vicarage (the new one or just the other one?), take the public footpath up to your left. Cross the stile and walk along the bottom edge of the field. At the end of the Vicarage's garden, continue in the same direction, towards the trees of Penbury Grove ahead. Within the trees is a school. At the metalled drive, turn right and when you reach the white gates on your left, go straight on as marked, ignoring a public footpath that goes off to the right.

You should now be walking along the edge of Corker's Wood with its well-spaced beech trees. The path swings left and at the man-made clearing, go half right as indicated by the white arrow on the tree, skirting round the right-hand side of this open area. Ignore the arrow, by a depression, which points to another footpath going off to the right. You follow your path to the opposite side of the clearing from where you entered, to a track that descends through tall trees. Keeping the fence and field close on your right, go half right to a stile by a gate.

Nip over the stile into the field and,

following the rough direction of the arrow on the stile, aim for the nearest tree, near which you meet a track. This takes you down to a stile by a large gate and thence to another stile by another large gate. Ten yards after this second set, turn right along a tree-lined gravel track which dips down and then up to the left of a garage and past pretty cottages to **The Royal Standard of England** at Forty Green. Having scoured books on Bucks and having picked the brains of the *Daily Telegraph* Information Service — all in vain — here is my guess as to why Forty Green is so called. There was or is a field or meadow near here exactly or about forty acres in size. Boring, I'm afraid.

If you were to do your monarchical bit in the pub — by toasting the Queen, every member of her family and then the crowned heads of Europe for good measure — you'd probably get alcoholic poisoning; so exercise a little moderation and skip the Europeans. Anyway, when you have finished, leave the pub and turn right at Forty Green's wee triangle (One Fortieth Green!) and walk along the lane away from the letter-box by the corner of Woodslade. This quiet lane goes downhill and soon runs alongside the bottom of Gatemoor Wood.

After a while, you reach a fork: here go left uphill between tall beech trees. And 'where this little lane meets another (almost at the crest and at the far side of the wood), take the marked public footpath and bridleway which head off together staying in the trees of Gatemoor Wood. Now though, you are walking through holly trees and bushes. You meet a track and turn left along it. Because it's a bridleway it can sometimes be quite muddy, but undaunted you follow it through holly, oak and

the 11th century and bits have been added down the ages. With very good sense, an 800 year old building was bought and demolished to provide the authentic building materials for recent extensions. So, with the exception of a few conspicuous modernities (the cheese bar, the padded bars, and the easy-to-wipe leatherette bench seats and stools), the character of the pub has been preserved.

Previously known as Ye Ship which possibly explains the source of the pub's beams and timbers, it was given its unique name by a grateful Charles II. After his defeat at Worcester, he spent one of his last nights in England hidden in its rafters, after which he fled to France. Restored to the throne in 1660, he remembered those who had harboured him and now the pub remembers its undoubted debt to him (in commercial terms) by naming one bar the King Charles Room.

The pub is decorated with antiques and curios including bugles, old guns, old pictures, a ship's settle rescued from Edmund Burke's house which burnt down in 1797, and, interestingly, some stained glass from blitzed London churches, pieced together, repaired and added to the pub in 1962.

The beers are Marstons; indeed Owd Roger Strong Ale was brewed in the pub for over 400 years, until a time when Marstons took over the chores, and brewed it exclusively for the pub. Other pubs do serve it now. Both Owd Roger and Marstons Pedigree Bitter are hand-drawn from the wood. There are also keg beers and other drinks.

The 'Cheese Hostelry' offers a choice of twenty different cheeses to go with the home-made bread and home-made chutney from a 300 years old recipe handed down from one landlord to the next. There are also hot meals at lunchtime in the winter and you should try the home-made brandy pâté. Time your visit carefully to take full advantage of everything this historic pub offers.

beech, ignoring turns to left and right. At the end of the wood, the path continues between fields flanked now by smaller trees.

Walk along this sunken and again sometimes muddy path and just after the point where it begins to descend, you turn up to your left, slightly backwards, to a stile into a field. Follow up the right-hand edge of this field until, just before the corner, you turn right over a stile into the next. Head slightly uphill along the faint path across the field to a gap between the corner of a large garden and a line of trees. Continue in the same direction, keeping the garden's fence on your left and thereby passing the owner's blunt message — is this breed of dogs for sale, I wonder? You pass, on your left, a pond partly surrounded by trees, as you follow the fence up to and over a broken stile.

Walk between the two hedges and continue along the driveway passing Thae Cottage to the lane at Beacon Hill. Turn 'right' along the lane and pass Thatcher's Field (a punette for you true-blues). The lane runs down, passing the pond and a lovely natural, though trained and clipped, arch over Yew Tree Cottage's drive.

At the main road, turn left round Slade's Garage and, following the road, fork right along Elm Road, passing Stratfords, a lovely antique shop, and April Cottage, back to The Red Lion and your car.

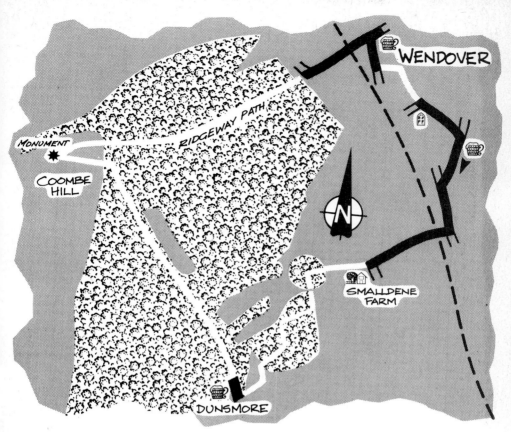

27 Wendover

APPROXIMATELY 4¾ Miles

The District

'A straggling, purposeless sort of place' – so said Robert Louis Stevenson of Wendover and it just shows how wrong even great writers can be. It is a very 'English' town in all senses. It lies on the northern edge of the Chiltern ridge, neatly plugging the gap between Boddington and Bacombe Hills where it seems to fit perfectly. The ancient Ridgeway and Icknield Paths pass through it and, straddling a stream from which it takes its name (Wendover means 'white water'), the town is warm, even cosy, with its brick and timbered cottages and houses, a lot of which have dormer windows. It has a restored 14th century church surrounded by chestnuts, limes, sycamores and two great yews; some very fine 16th and 17th century wall paintings were uncovered in Bosworth House and, while most have gone off to the Victoria and Albert and Aylesbury museums, two remain in situ; The Red Lion Hotel is an attractive 17th century inn and there is the manor of John Hampden.

Wendover seems to have had more than its fair share of connections with Westminster. As well as Canning and Burke, 'that great parliamentarian', John Hampden was also an MP for Wendover. Representing his home town and later all Buckinghamshire, he was a fierce opponent of Charles I's highhanded and yet underhand tax-gathering. Persecuted for

►

135

his religious beliefs, he almost sailed to America with his cousin and fellow Puritan Oliver Cromwell, but for the sake of English history, the boat didn't sail.

Having refused on principle to pay a small but unconstitutional tax to underwrite the King's naval expenses, he and his sympathisers were charged with high treason. The King himself led an armed force into the House of Commons in order to make the arrest but was forced to simply say 'the birds have flown', as indeed they had. This armed violation of Parliament was the worst and last mistake Charles I made in peacetime for it provoked 4,000 Buckinghamshire men to march on London. The English Civil War had started. If the ship had sailed, taking Hampden and Cromwell to America. . . .

. . . then, beforehand, they both would have had to apply to 'The Chiltern Hundreds'. Nowadays a traditional and obscure custom, it is what an MP must do if he/she wishes to resign his/her Membership for personal reasons. A Hundred was a Saxon administrative unit, which doesn't make it any less obscure.

And the last Westminster connection is that Chequers, the country home of British prime ministers, is just on the other side of Coombe Hill set in hundreds (no, not them) of acres of patrolled parkland. Given to Lloyd George and all successive PM's as a thanks offering for the ending of World War One, it was built in the 13th century, rebuilt in the 15th and used by Queen Elizabeth I to imprison Lady Jane Grey's sister, Lady Mary, who was in disgrace for secretly marrying Thomas Keys, her social inferior.

Coombe Hill is 852ft high and is the highest viewpoint of the Chilterns. It offers spectacular views over Cymbeline's Mount to the left. This is a mysterious hill and is supposed to have been the site of a last ditch stand in the path of the invading Romans by Cunobelin (his real, un-Shakespearean name), chief of the Catuvellauni tribe. His sons were slain in the battle. Myth also has it that if you run seven times round the hill you

may raise the Devil up from Hell. As others have wryly observed, this smacks of hallucination induced by exhaustion. As you swing your gaze to the right, the Vale of Aylesbury is laid out before you and about this, the afore-mentioned Mr Stevenson seems to have been more accurate, if no more interesting when he wrote 'the great plain stretched away to the northward, growing ever more and more indistinct until it became a hurly-burly of trees . . . and snatches of slanting road'.

The walk starts in The Wellhead Inn, crosses the A413 and goes to Dunsmore along a lane and paths; from here it makes its way to Coombe Hill and thence down Bacombe Hill back to Wendover and beyond the church, The Wellhead.

How to Get There
By road take the A413 south-east from Aylesbury, Wendover is on the road (approx 5 miles).
By rail to Wendover.

The Wendover Walk
Turn left out of **The Wellhead Inn** up Hale Road, past Wellhead Farm to the A413. Turn left towards London and Amersham, but don't worry, you only have to walk 150-200 yards along it, before you turn right up the lane to Smalldean (dene) and Scrubwood. The lane goes over the railway, under power-lines and on up between beech and holly. Soon you can no longer hear the main road's traffic as the lane gently climbs between hedged banks up to elegant Smalldene Farm. You can see its horse-shaped bush as you approach and when you can see the property properly, it seems an idyllic place to live. The house looks comfortable, there is extensive brick and black weather-boarded outhousing and as you peep over its neat beech hedge there are two spiral-shaped shrubs in the pretty garden.

So now that you know where the writer would like to live, turn right at the house and leave its black barns on your left. At the barn that seems to serve as a garage, fork left, up a sunken and sometimes muddy path, past the back of Smalldene Farm and on up through more holly and beech amongst other trees. As you walk you can amuse yourself wondering whether the holes in the banks belong to foxes or badgers – who knows?

By a disused gate, there is a crossing of paths and here you go left and then at the hand-painted sign 'Dunsmore', fork left as marked. The path climbs through brambles, over a fallen tree, over open ground by a line of fir trees to an arrowed stile, and on, as directed, along the right-hand edge of the hedge, to a gap in a line of trees, with a double arrow on one of them. Follow the right arrow, which means you follow the strip of beech trees, keeping them on your right. If you look over your shoulder here, there are good commanding views over Cock's Hill to the left, Halton Wood in the middle and Boddington Hill, slightly out of sight to the right.

Where this strip of trees meets the wood, you go straight on into the wood as arrowed, following the well-defined path that's clearly marked all the way through by arrows on trees. If I was a joking man, I might say something terrible about Robin Hood and inaccurate archery, but as I'm not, I won't. This is a spacious and noble little wood, with tall and graceful beeches rising from the flinty soil beneath (poetry prize, please sir). A set of two metal fence-stiles takes you across a fenced track and you continue following the arrows, passing above what looks like a bomb-crater and gradually descending diagonally to the far corner of the field you can see to your left.

You cross a bar-stile into a different section of the wood, now mostly oak, and immediately turn left to walk along the edge of the wood. In the corner, there's a stile, seemingly built for people under six stone, which you climb and then you turn right up the path that runs between fences. Both the wood to your right and the field to your left are inhabited by horses and you may see a couple of Shetland ponies casually and confidently socialising with larger breeds. Climb over the stile by the white bungalow and green caravan and follow the path as it runs along garden-fences until, at the end of the corrugated-iron fence on your left, you turn right over a stile and walk along the back of the cottage, out on to the lane and on to **The Fox**'s pub sign and just beyond, The Fox itself. Like the animal, this pub is quiet and reclusive but

The Inns

The Wellhead Inn, Wendover

As you might expect, this pub is close to a well – well, in fact, seven to be exact. It or some previous building on the site, was a waterhouse since 1620, drawing, storing and distributing the water from its wells, some of which are under the terrace. In 1887, it moved up or down market, depending on how you look at it, when it was granted its first licence as an ale retailer. Popular with the railway workers at first, it now welcomes almost anybody (over 14, of course), though sometimes Michael Aughton and his family are slightly disturbed by ghostly knockings on the door at quiet times of the day and night. It's thought the knocker is a woman: indeed the area is famous for witches (who presumably don't rest after death) some of whom forced the re-siting of the church. The pub is on the Ridgeway Path – maybe that explains the mystery.

It's a Free House and Stocks ABC's Trumans Tap on handpump along with McEwan's Tartan Mild, Tartan Exhibition, Scottish Bitter, McEwan's lager, Kestrel lager and Guinness on keg. Bottled beers include Newcastle Brown, Worthington White Shield and McEwan's Strong Ale, and canned beers include Red Stripe lager and Fosters and Schlitz malt liquors. There are also about 14 malt whiskies. When they changed from water to alcohol, they certainly changed!

A wide range of bar food includes home-made soup, steak and kidney pie, burgers, sausages, scampi and chicken (the last four with chips) and shepherd's pie, and there is a roast lunch every Friday. Not half bad, I reckon.

unlike the animal, the landlord serves good pints of Aylesbury Bitter.

Drag yourself away from The Fox, back to the lane, but rather than walking back along it, turn sharp left at Appletree Cottage along a tarmac path, past a notice forbidding cars. At the fork, with public footpaths going off left and right, go right, along the edge of the garden; then where you see the path go straight on across the middle of the field ahead, turn left along a broad and muddy track, keeping the line of extremely tall fir-trees and the fence below them on your right. You now have to follow the fence for quite a way. It changes from railings to a regular rectangular thick wire mesh and you ignore an open gate to the right.

You go on and on and, depending on your tiredness, on. It is an attractive wood, though, mainly of oak and beech, but with the odd silver birch. Soon however the character of the wood changes slightly and the tall, straight-backed trees give way to more sinister, gnarled and twisted ones. You pass a field with a small house on your right and a track, which you ignore, veers off left — still you stay with the fence as another runs alongside it, forming a straight and narrow path between them: stray ye not from it. The track that veered off left rejoins you and the fence bends slightly right, but you haven't finished with it yet.

When the fence stops altogether (there's a wire-netting fence going off to the right), turn left along a very broad earth track and after 50 yards or so, climb the stile ahead out of the wood and onto Coombe Hill — 'National Health Land', as a local told me! Noting the gruesome picture of the dog-savaged sheep, keep your dog on the lead or, better still, in your pocket.

Fork right at the National Trust sign and at the corner of the fence, go straight on to the Memorial. This commemorates the men of Buckinghamshire who died in the South African War. An imposing, but not especially beautiful monument, it does stand in an imposing and beautiful position. While most of the rest of this van-guard Chiltern promontory is heavily wooded, the crest of Coombe Hill is bare except for the odd tree. The views from here are astonishing. I'm told that on a good day you can see as far as the Malvern Hills a few degrees north of Oxford and the Cotswolds a few degrees south, and, surprisingly St Paul's Cathedral, in the opposite direction. Certainly the short view down across Aylesbury, the Vale of Aylesbury and most of Buckinghamshire is unrestricted and well worth all your effort so far, unless it's foggy or dark, that is!

Walk back, in roughly the same direction, except on a lower path and you will pass a small milestone which tells you you're on the Ridgeway Path. This is an ancient path that runs from Ivinghoe Beacon in the east to Avebury in the west. It has recently been reopened as a long-distance path and it's now possible to walk in the footsteps of old travellers going back as far as the Stone Ages.

You leave Coombe Hill's National Trust land by a stile incorporating a dog flap/gate, you go into and out of a small dip and then out along an open strip of land. Wendover is slightly to the left of straight ahead and here you are spoiled for choice — there are at least five parallel paths you can take. At the barrier, follow the acorn marker and stay on the main path through the woodland and out onto open ground again. Once through another wooden barrier, keep to a lower level just above the treeline and soon there's a dense thorn wood (with the odd silver birch) above and a more mixed wood (though mainly thorn) below. You are now descending Bacombe Hill.

At the bench, don't fork left, but go straight on to reach some chalky steps which you descend to the sunken path. Keep on in the same direction and shortly you will enter trees with houses on your left. Walk on through the barrier and down to the road, where you continue downhill, still on the Ridgeway Path, which is now, rather boringly, a pavement. The pavement goes under buzzing power lines and over the railway bridge. Go straight over the roundabout, down the High Street to **The Red Lion Hotel** on your right.

Having slaked that thirst of yours, walk back up to the roundabout and turn left along South Street. You pass, on your left, no 13 with its horse's head and, on your right, no 29 which seems to be a house for dwarves it's so small. No 29 is opposite a garage and just after this, you turn left down Witchell and then walk into and diagonally left across the recreation ground (skirting the cricket square, of course) and leave by the opposite corner.

Turn left along Chapel Lane (for that is its name) and just before the bridge, turn right, along the (now tarmac) Ridgeway Path. Follow it to the right, as it veers away from the stream at unprettily-named Sluice Cottage North and at the corner of the green, stay with it still, i.e. not turning right. You pass a large pond on your right and then emerge onto a lane at St Mary the Virgin, with its two great yews on either side of the porch. This church was to have been built nearer what is now known as Witchell Stream, where its cross-shaped foundation trenches had been dug. However, it's said that witches came in the night and filled in these trenches and so the church was built instead on its present site.

When you face the church's lych-gate, turn left along the lane, which leads you past Pebble Brook School to the junction with Hale Road. While the Ridgeway Path crosses straight over on its way to Iving-hoe Beacon, you turn right along the road back to The Wellhead Inn and reward.

The Fox Inn, Dunsmore

About one mile from Chequers, this red brick pub has played host to different prime ministers over the years. Its quiet seclusion and cosy warmth presumably make it an ideal pub in terms of having a relaxing drink without being mobbed, quite apart from its handy proximity. It is important for customers to respect the calm of the pub.

It has two bars, both with electric fires and its old oak panelling is decorated with the landlord's momentoes of his smooth-haired miniature dachshund breeding days and with lots of foxy artefacts – pictures, a small tapestry, door-knockers, brushes etc. In fact, The Fox Inn is on Fox Lane, contains all these foxy things and is run by a Mr Fox. There is a terrace and a garden, both with tables and chairs and the latter with ample playing space for children.

An Aylesbury Brewery Company pub, it stocks ABC Bitter from the cask, along with DD and Skol on keg.

The food ranges from the usual sandwiches (beef, ham, liver sausage, cheese, turkey and salmon) to the more unusual Hot Turkish pastie, potted shrimps and toast and pâté maison and toast. A pub to be quietly enjoyed.

The Red Lion Hotel, Wendover

A half-timbered building with brick 'nogging', The Red Lion is a lovely 17th century inn which justifiably dominates Wendover's High Street. In the lounge the original fireplace with chimney corners remains, as does the stairway which leads to the room where Cromwell slept one night in 1642. His soldiers had to make do with the street below. Robert Louis Stevenson was another famous visitor – while walking the Chilterns and writing *An Autumn Effect,* he stopped here sometime in the 1870s.

Youngs and Morlands Bitters are available along with a standard range of bottled beers and spirits. The Red Lion menu should be investigated. By the way a 'Fraddy' is a smoked haddock.

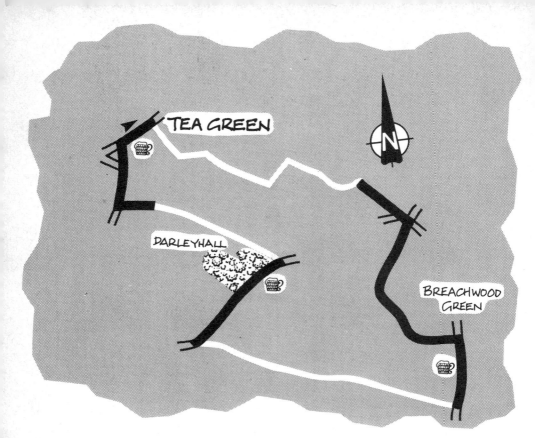

28 Tea Green

APPROXIMATELY 3¼ Miles

The District

Luton is a corruption of Leatown, meaning not very mysteriously, that it lies on the Lea, a tributary of the Thames, joining that mother/father of English rivers in London. Chaucer called it 'the sedgy Lea' and in his day, it undoubtedly was, though nowadays it flows through Luton and Hertford before it reaches very unsedgy Tower Hamlets. A large and growing town, especially since the war, Luton is now being hit hard (where isn't?) by the recession, particularly in its motor industries. It has an international airport, as famous now as the Martini (or is it Cinzano, or Dubonnet, or . . .) in the advert. However, in the past, straw-plaiting and straw-hat manufacture

(which still accounts for 5 per cent of the town's trade), were its quieter, more rural money-spinners.

Waulud's Bank, by the Lea, is evidence of a very early, in fact neolithic, Lutonian settlement. It's a wide, flat-bottomed ditch in which Ringo-Clacton (yes, Essex) pottery fragments have been discovered. Similarly, Dray's Ditches are evidence of Iron and Bronze Age locals. Swiftly we move forward in time, to one of the more outstanding moments in Luton's history, when the Danes were beaten in a battle here in 817 AD. Not a great deal of historical note has happened since.

One of the largest churches in England, St Marys was built in the 13th cen-

140

tury and enlarged in the 14th and 15th — its worth some of anybody's time, as is Luton Hoo, just to the south. This Robert Adam designed, but subsequently burnt and altered house, now mostly reveals the work of Mewes and Davis, the architects of London's Ritz. The house is a 'daunting display of Edwardian wealth' and treasures include examples of medieval religious art, paintings by Titian and Rembrandt, china and porcelain, tapestries and furniture, 16th and 17th century jewellery and a collection of Russian Imperial Robes. The house is set in a large park landscaped by Capability Brown — the views of the lakes being of particular beauty.

Tea Green, Breachwood Green and Darleyhall, are astonishingly unspoilt considering their proximity to Luton, and if you can forget the airport you can forget the town. On the chalk downs here grow hornbeam, oak and many, many, beech trees and, for some very scientific reason I'm sure, many a bluish butterfly flutters by the wild flowers, a very high proportion of which are also blue.

How to Get There
By road take an unclassified road east from Luton and then turn left onto another unclassified road at Wandon Green; Tea Green is on this road (approx 3 miles).
By rail to Luton.
By bus the 88 operates regularly from Luton.

The Tea Green Walk
Walk out of **The White Horse** and, as you face the green, you can see, off to your left, paradise — ''no'' (in cockney accent), ''Luton Airpor' ''. If you don't understand this, then you don't watch enough ITV. Anyway, turn right out of the pub along Lower Road — something of a misnomer as the road seems, to me at least, to be on very high ground. Be that as it may, just before you pass the white water-tower, turn right on the marked public footpath to The Heath. Walk down the narrow path between fences and, passing the pub's car park on your right, strike out along a strip of untilled land between the fields. This is the first of many strips you'll walk along. To save expense and time, hedges which would normally

The Inns

The White Horse, Tea Green
Over the road from mysteriously named Tea Green's green, this 350 year old pub has, in its time, incorporated a bakery and a shop and, until 4 years ago. the local Harvest Festival was held here in the absence of a church. It was perhaps due to the lack of any religious control in the village, that caused The White Horse to lose its licence 30 years back. It seemed that after the Sunday lunchtime drinking session, there would always be a brawl on the green. At some point someone objected to these Sabbath fights and the licence was withdrawn. You'll be pleased to hear it's since been re-granted. The pub has one large bar with two open fires, some 500 year old ships' timbers from another building, exposed brick, two old settles, some brasses and fox brushes. It's a warm and friendly pub and was used in TV's *Buccaneer* series.

Its beers include Whitbread Best, Tankard, Trophy, Guinness, Heineken and Stella Artois and there's mulled wine in winter — very warming after a cold walk. Snacks from the bar include sandwiches, ploughman's and pâté, along with pizza, gammon, chicken, sausage, scampi and haddock, all with chips (except, of course, the pizza). Speciality of the house are its American-style burgers.

divide the fields have been removed by the farmers. Though this means that you can see further, it does tend to create bleakness (hardly the case here) and there is the possibility of soil erosion without sufficient windbreaks.

About 20 yards before a burnt tree-stump, the strip bends left and then you continue in the same direction along a grassy track, with the long grass and brambles on your left. After 50 yards or so, turn right along a narrow strip down the middle of the field. Tankards Farm is on your right and, when you meet the end of a grassy track bordered by three largish oaks, go left along the strip. At the end of this strip, you go right along another. This one is raised and quite obviously a late hedgerow and it heads for the nearest houses of Breachwood Green. To your left is the gutted cone of an abandoned and largely uninteresting windmill. Still, for city-dwellers, it's a potent rural image, so perhaps it serves some purpose. It's been derelict for at least 25 years.

You pass three more oaks and a quadruple holly and, at the line of trees and bushes, you head alongside their foliage towards the gate by the nearest house and Windmill Road. Touching your forelock to the duck who lives in one of the gardens, walk along Windmill Road past the concrete, wooden and rendered houses to the junction. Here, turn left towards the telephone box and just before it, turn right along Brownings Lane. Luton Airport is ahead of you as you amble along this quiet lane, which swings left between a pond and a black barn. Just past the barn, look to your right at a lovely timbered and brick, but sadly rather tumbledown, shed.

As Brownings Lane swings right past the white house, it suddenly becomes Colemans Road. Undaunted, press on and soon, on your right is Medlow House, built in 1865 as a brewery, and Colemans Farm, where there was once a church and a school. John Bunyan, who signposted the way through hell to heaven, worshipped at the church and preached on the green between the two houses. Walk on down this peaceful lane and at the junction, turn right along Chapel Road. You pass pretty Fir Tree Cottage and Old Pump Cottage with its plough in the garden, and reach **The Red Lion.** Enter, order, drink and eat.

Satisfied, leave the pub and turn right to continue along Chapel Road. On the other side of the road is the really rather architecturally-odd Baptist Chapel. An impressive building, it houses Bunyan's Bible, though unfortunately it's generally locked (the building, not the Bible). Walk on past The Old Homestead and turn right along the marked public footpath to Darleyhall. Out along the strip. It turns left and then right and, at the corner of the fence, you go straight on, with the fence on your right. At the end of the fence, walk just right of straight ahead to two oaks together on another strip — follow this and stay on it as it goes left and then right. If you still want them, there are good views of Luton Airport and its almost continual traffic.

At the small rubbish tip, the strip turns right again and at the old gate post on your left, you turn left along the left-hand side of a hedge that seems to have escaped the busy bulldozer. At the

corner of the field, turn rightish down the path between hedge and bushes and, follow the next strip that gradually dips down and then gradually climbs the far side. Winch Hill Farm is up to your left on, yes, Winch Hill, and looks down across the beautifully contoured fields. At the corner of the fence, walk straight on, keeping the fence on your left. The views behind are just great. The fence leads you up to a lane, where you turn right and the road winds you down and up to Darleyhall and, more importantly, **The Fox**, where you can go to ground for a while and have a sly one.

Turn right out of the pub and walk on up the lane, between houses and the wood. At the far side of the wood, turn left along the marked public footpath by the double telegraph poles. You follow the edge of the wood, for a few yards on a track and then a path and, at the first corner of the wood, go straight on, following line of overhead cables, along yet another strip. You reach a gate, where you turn left and follow the patchy hedge – where the bulldozer did only a half-hearted job? – as it swings right.

At the bottom of the dip, go right and then left along the hedge punctuated by trees. When Tankards Farm is exactly to your right, nip through the gap and out onto its lane. Turn left along the lane, away from the farm and follow it between several holly trees and eventually out onto a bigger lane. Turn right and walk up, back into Tea Green and something a little stronger than tea at The White Horse.

The Red Lion, Breachwood Green

On the main road through the village, the pub was built about 1920 on the site of an old blacksmith's shop and forge. A pleasant two bar pub, it's centrally heated as well as having an open fire in the lounge. Mr Gregory, the landlord, tells me that there are very few pub-going villagers old enough to remember any interesting local snippets.

So you'll have to be content with the beers. A Greene King pub, its real ales are IPA, Abbot and Light Mild on top pressure along with a selection of keg bitters and lager. Food ranges from sandwiches up through basket meals and starters to full meals like T-bone steaks etc. For afters there's Black Forest gateau, or cheese and biscuits and coffee.

The Fox, Darleyhall

Succeeding an earlier building set a little further back from the lane, this 150 year old pub was built as such and has served as such, except for a 6-month spell in recent years after a previous landlord had died in a fire late one night. There's one largish, friendly bar with an open fire and a stove. With a few articles on the theme of foxes, a collection of limited edition bottled beers and a selection of porcelain heads as its only special decoration, the pub is modest and unpretentious.

A Greene King pub, it stocks Mild, Bitter, Abbot and King Keg on keg as well as lager and a standard range of other drinks. You can take your drink and your food (from a selection of rolls, burgers, sausages and scampi) out to the small lawned garden in good weather.

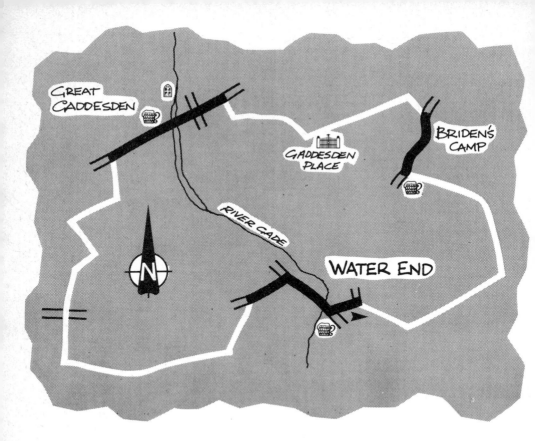

29 Water End

APPROXIMATELY 5½ Miles

The District

E M Forster described the area around Water End as 'England at its quietest . . . England meditative'. Homely Herts is one of England's smallest counties and has a high population unevenly distributed between densely populated and accessible towns and sparsely populated and isolated villages. First peopled by the neolithic farmers who arrived in 3500 BC after the tides of the Pliocene Age had receded for good (hopefully), Herts later became part of the Roman Empire and of the Kingdom of Mercia. Talking of dense populations, the local peasantry become known as The Hertfordshire Thickheads in the 17th century since they 'lapped up' stories of witchcraft and devilry like water in a drought. In Great Gaddesden (part of the walk), 3 parishioners were excommunicated at one point in the 17th century for 'being bewitched'.

Nowhere in Hertfordshire can you get more than 40 miles from Piccadilly Circus, yet, despite this apparent 'geographical disadvantage', the rolling dipping Chiltern hills here are the most heavily wooded in England. Fagus sylvatica, the beech, is the tree, whose shallow spreading roots are best capable of extracting nourishment from the poor chalk soil, and which for centuries has provided the hills with character and their human inhabitants with varied professions. The Steward of the Chiltern Hundreds was paid to protect travellers from robbery by locals who relished the cover of the woods and slopes. 'Bodgers' were nomadic carpenters, who kept the woods in trim and who carved beechwood chairlegs for the Chippendale factory, among others . . . these were added to other parts for assembly. Also to be found scurrying around the hills, is the edible dormouse, that particularly crunchy little rodent.

In 54 BC, when Julius Caesar led his cohorts across the Thames to attack Cassivellaunus, King of the Catuvellauni, he must have passed by what wasn't yet St Albans. During the later Roman occupation, Verulamium was honoured with the title of 'municipium', high praise indeed for a distant outpost of the Empire -- in fact, the only one in Britain, but something which did not stop it being attacked by Boudicca (Boadicea) in 61 AD at the time of the Icenian Revolt. In 209, Alban, a Romano British subject, was beheaded by the Romans and promptly became Britain's first Christian martyr . . . a shrine was later built which King Offa II of Mercia set an abbey on top of in 793. Watling Street (the main London road) was diverted to go past the abbey and this neatly ensured a steady supply of pilgrims for the abbey and trade for the town. At the time of the Dissolution, the abbey was sold to the townspeople, reduced to St Albans parish church and the great shrine of St Albans was smashed to pieces for tax purposes (Henry VIII's). In 1877, the abbey became a cathedral and the town a city by Royal Charter; St Albans Cathedral is the second longest church in England (550ft) and contains the Purbeck marble pedestal of the old shrine, reconstituted from 2,000 fragments. Nearby is the unique watching chamber from which

▶

The Inns

The Red Lion, Water End

A hybrid creature of 16th, 17th and 18th century styles, The Red Lion began life as a coaching inn in the mid 16th century. During World War I it was used as a bivouac by the Royal Artillery – officers in the house, lesser ranks in the barn. During the Second World War, General de Gaulle came to inspect the Home Guard here and was most put out that the tricoleur was not put out on display for him. Throughout the fifties, the golden era of British filmmaking, many film stars stayed at The Lion while filming in the vicinity: they, included Michael Wilding and Elizabeth Taylor.

The Red Lion has two bars, a games room, log fires, horse brasses and beams; on the walls are prints of Dickensian characters. The saloon bar is particularly elegant and opens on to a huge garden with a weeping ash (achieved through graft): here they're busy building an assault course to keep kids busy.

The beers (all hand-drawn) are Benskins, Ind Coope, Mild and Burtons, together with draught Guinness. To eat you can get fresh rolls from the local bakery which go well with 'the nutty flavoured' and reasonably priced trout of the River Gade. Home-made soup, pâté and chili-con-carne are also good value.

▶

monks observed pilgrims placing offerings in the 'healing holes' of the holy relic . . . this vigilance was a 'round the clock' job. Apart from the cathedral, things to see in or near St Albans include Gorhambury House for Chippendale furniture (remembering 'bodgers') and Georgian grace: Verulamium Park, for a Roman theatre, complete with stage, and a Hypocaust heating system; the 5-storeyed 15th century curfew tower, one of two in England, and the City Museum.

Nearer Water End is Hemel Hempstead, also on the River Gade. Part new town to rival Stevenage, part ancient borough from the time of Domesday, the town suffers from a clear case of urban schizophrenia. In the old town, a curving high street rises graciously to its church and Little Marlowes House, Old Marlowes House (in 'Marlowes' naturally), the Corner House and Henry's Banquetting hall (not a transport cafe) are buildings which can be visited for pleasure. The highspot of the new town is the shopping centre, if you like shopping centres. . . .

The walk goes from the outskirts of lovely Water End, up and away across fields to Briden's camp and The Crown and Sceptre. From there, it goes past Gaddesden Place on its way to Great Gaddesden, the woods on Pipers Hill and back to Water End. It's an easy walk with beautiful Hertfordshire scenery all along the way.

How to Get There
By road take A4146 north-east from Hemel Hempstead, Water End is on the road (approx 3 miles).
By rail to Hemel Hempstead.
By bus both the London Country 317 and the United Counties 43 run regularly from Hemel Hempstead.

The Water End Walk
Go straight across the busy A4146 from the car park of **The Red Lion** and head up the road in the direction of Flamstead and Markyate. 40 yards or so up, as the road bends left, there's a public footpath to the right; direction, Stagsend. Taking your cue from the sign, follow the sunken path which climbs the left edge of the field and bends gradually left. Soon you're striding between fields of corn and cabbages and, as you get higher, there's a small and 'quaint' house on the brow of the hill to the left across an undulating field of greens.

Nearing the top of the hill and having just passed under power lines, you come to a wooden gate on the edge of a wood. Don't go through it; instead, go left and follow the right-hand edge of the field towards the 'quaint house' mentioned before. This means you rapidly pass under the power lines again and you may have to go left a little to skirt the patch of newly landscaped wood which contains a giant tree nearly dead on its feet. (At the time of writing this area was undergoing council transformation). Keep along the edge of the field towards the house which was formerly part of the skyline. To your left is a view over peaceful, prosperous and therapeutic farmland lifeless but lifelike scarecrows dangling in the wind like gallows victims.

Go to the right of the ('quaint') house and you'll find a track which veers left past it and its old black barns. The soil here is full of flint pebbles and these were at one time used extensively in local buildings, not only for facing but also as wallstone. Hertfordshire's agriculturers have waged a constant battle, begun in Saxon times and continued ever since, against the poor quality of the county's stony soil. Much improved drainage and the use of modern fertilisers have led to the present high yields, so much so that Herts has become known as a corn-growing county.

At the crossing of tracks, go straight across and inevitably (if you keep going, that is) you will arrive at **The Crown and Sceptre,** at the end of a row of cottages. After all that 'poor stony' soil, it's probably only fair to shed your gum boots before going into the bar.

Having taken your pick of the 5 re(g)al ales available at this pub, which commands an entry in The American Good Beer Guide, go right along Briden's Camp's main street. Half of the name derives from General Bridonius, commander of an erstwhile Roman garrison, and the other half from the fact that both parties were stationed here. The Romans came early to Herts and stayed from the 1st to the 4th century. By the time they left, the Belgic farmers who lived in the area had, by imitation and compliance, achieved great leaps forward in their standard of living and their cultural 'niveau', including, no doubt, the provision of underfloor heating and vomitaria.

As you go, the local cricket pitch is across the road to your left as is an equestrian circle. A summer's evening here can resound to the thud of ball on bat and the clip clop of horse on track. Follow the road past the old red brick cottages, with moss-covered tiles and numbered 44 and 45 — suspiciously high for a village of this size. Soon you go left up Home Farm Lane past a black weatherboarded house. In about a hundred yard's time, there's a double wooden gate to the left which someone has failed to mark as the public footpath it *is*. Go through it, then along the left-hand edge of the field with Home Farm full-face across the grass to your right. Skirt the spinney and nip over or under a single strand fence in this field with old estate trees and the odd pheasant or two, too. Gaddesden Place comes gracefully into view ahead. I believe the building is up for sale — but don't get too close to it, in fact, head well to the right of the large house and just to the right of a prominent evergreen to arrive at the end of the field . . . within a stone's throw of the house; please don't try and prove this.

James Wyatt built the house towards the end of the 18th century for Thomas Hasley whose epitaph in the local church receals that "owing to the instability of human felicity, he was only able to inhabit his new home for 14 years". That doesn't seem too bad to me.

Just beyond the far corner of the field is a public footpath sign. Turn down right leaving the sign to the left, then turn left after a metal gate and go downhill (not signposted). Follow the fence on your left past a single strand fence and an old and now 'out of place' stile to pass under immense beech boughs and to a wooden gate in the corner. Through this, go right and follow the edge of the field to

▶

The Red Lion's landlord Ralph Jones makes parachute jumps for charity; so far the pub has raised enough money for three guide dogs. This pub is recommended, drop in yourself and see why.

The Crown and Sceptre, Briden's Camp

The Crown and Sceptre is a busy spot in a quiet village just off the walkway from Berkhampstead to St Albans. What was once the living area of a former landlady is now one bar with original beam work from St Margaret's church. An old clock by the bar was made by Steptoe, a well known Victorian clockmaker of Hemel Hempstead.

There are three coal fires to thaw you out and the bench seating is traditional. The same can be said of the beer in this Free House, which includes hand-drawn Abbots, IPA, Sam Smiths, Adnams (from the South Wold) and draught Guinness. Hot soups and ploughman's lunches are only available at lunchtimes and not on Sundays. There are tables outside in summer and there's 'no way' that this pub, featured in the American Good Beer Guide, would allow a juke box on the premises.

The Cock and Bottle, Great Gaddesden

Once known as The Fighting Cocks, the Cock and Bottle was originally built in the 17th century as a farmhouse.

Square built, with white painted walls, it has two bars, saloon and public, which have not been 'dolled up'. The Cock

▶

147

the road. (The public footpath actually runs at a diagonal across the field but there's no point in trampling down the crops). When you reach the steep-banked lane, turn down left. This valley has been inhabited since the Palaeolithic Age, instanced by the fact that many implements and tools of the time have been discovered here. You have been walking along parts of an ancient Neolithic (later than Palaeolithic) trackway and you may have noticed Hertfordshire Pudding stones used as milestones along the way — local legend has it that they are 'magicky' and capable of growing in size at will. Gaddesden's name comes from 'Gaetesdene', meaning 'the pasture of Gaete's people', 'Gaete' comes from 'gat', an Anglo-saxon goat. Any more questions?

Reaching a crossroads, go straight on into Great Gaddesden, a beautiful place "which owes much to its hillside position and little to its village plan". You'll pass a garden centre on the right and a football pitch for midgets with exceptional ball skills on the left. **The Cock and Bottle** stands on the right of the road, part of the cluster of the older village houses, which look out over the lovely meadows by The River Gade and a reedy pond packed with quacking ducks.

While in Great Gaddesden, visit the church of St John The Baptist. To do so, turn left from the pub, left across the car park and left at the telephone box. There is a large pudding stone marker in the churchyard which stands on the site of an old pagan religious circle and a later wooden Saxon church. Parts of the walls of the church are made of Roman bricks, possibly from the villa at Gadebridge near Hemel Hempstead. Within, there's a chest hewn from a single piece of wood with a slot for donations to the Pope and an organ which was renovated in 1971 after donations from local parishoners. This had to be re-renovated after lead was stolen from the roof and torrents of water came through the ceiling and gummed up the works. Today it plays as sweetly as it ever did. Looking back to

Gaddesden Place high on its hill, you will be interested to discover the graves of the Halseys, its former owners, all around you: Sic transit gloria mundi.

Leaving the pub, turn right up the road past the large black barns (again!) of Church Farm on the right and the tiny vicarage on the left. Just after the Victorian letter box (of 1861) in the wall to the right and the ageing splendour of idyllic Glebe House, turn left up the track beside and before Piper's Cottage.

Go through a metal gate and across the field to its farthest corner. Here there's a choice of two openings. Don't dither, take the left-hand one and then go right beside the right-hand hedge of the resultant field (past a tall elm stump over the hedge to your right and apparently giving you a 'thumbs up' sign or two). Look all around you for a proper sense of Dacorum (the latinate name of the district), the rolling Chilterns and unbroken Herts countryside: meanwhile don't bump into anything as you proceed in raptures. This is Piper's Hill. Ahead and slightly left is Potten End almost smothered by trees. You can still see Gaddesden Place behind and you can imagine the view it enjoys; after all, if you can see it all this time. . . .

When you reach the hedge (fairly soon), go through the gap and turn hard left towards the wood. At the edge of the trees, tread left a little to find a 3-bar stile. Enter with stile but don't expect the trees to be impressed. Go to the right of the small crater and follow the path to a point where there's a second stile on the edge of the wood to your right. Go left with the path here (not going near the second stile) and you'll come to a third stile by a field. Go over this and a fourth too, as you make a bee-line for the road. With Potten End now to the right on its hill, you should be able to spot a huge tree on the horizon.

Go straight across the road and follow the direction pointed out by the public footpath sign. There's no clear path so try your best not to damage any crops. In the soil you'll find a remarkable number of flint pebbles which can't do farm machinery much good — a flint with a hole in it is supposed to be unlucky. Halfway across the field, roughly level with old hangars to the right — judge for yourself —

turn left and walk towards the trees. You can still be watched from Gaddesden Place, by telescope.

Be careful of rabbit holes and their effect on your delicate ankles, as you follow the right-hand edge of the trees: collectively, these trees form the shape of a pointing hand. Once past the rubbish dump and level with a modern house, visible above you to the right, turn down left into the wood by a grassy track near the old and now useless stile. Thread your own way to the far end of the wood, so to speak, to the end of its pointing index finger. Further instructions will meet you at the tip.

Out of the wood, follow the line of oaks which emerges in the direction of Gaddesden Place. Below you is Water End sitting pretty by the glassy pond which adds reflection to the village's other aesthetic qualities. All around are shady valleys and sloping farm- and woodlands – it's not surprising so many Ealing Studio classics were filmed in the area.

Reaching the end of the oaks, go on a bit and look for the old stile to the left which takes you into a bumpy field with an old yellow van and a donkey with an appetite for life – yours! It is hard to ignore this beast as he gnaws at you as you pass through his territory; whether nuzzling or guzzling, angry, hungry or friendly, he finds you irresistable company. Bring a sugar lump or a spicy Victory V and make sure he's an amiable ass. Go over a stile in the bottom left-hand corner and turn right at the road to go past Jacaranda.

At the main road either go left into what is the largely 17th century village of Water End, a favourite spot for photographers and filmmakers, or turn right to go directly back to base past the lush and luscious watercress beds for which the district is famous. Go across a lovely bridge and the unwatery Water Endy end available in pints in Ralph Jone's 'Locker', otherwise known as The Red Lion.

remains an old fashioned country pub.

Beers are keg Watneys, Ben Truman and Special – restricted cellar space prevents 'real ale'. The menu is limited to rolls and pork pies and this pub supplies the mostly beautiful village with crisps in the absence of a shop. The scenery around Great Gaddesden is lovely.

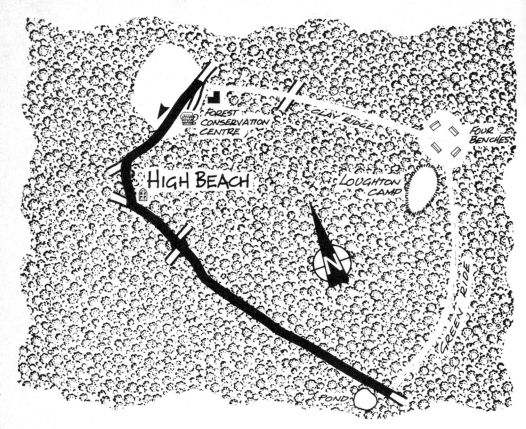

30   **High Beach**

APPROXIMATELY 2½ Miles

The District

Formerly known as the Forest of Essex and then Waltham Forest, Epping Forest stretches up in a band from the northeast of London. Twelve miles in length, and covering 6,000 acres of woodland, it is seldom over two miles wide.

The forest is perhaps mostly famous for its wealth of wildlife, not least the black fallow deer (although now much depleted in numbers), along with stoats, foxes, rabbits, hares, squirrels and a plethora of birds and insects. Sadly, badgers and red squirrels are no longer to be found. Conservation has been a serious problem in the forest as, over the years, people have eroded the conditions needed for the survival of the plant and animal life. A short walk soon reveals, even in winter, the plastic, glass and paper aftermath of human visitation. You are, therefore, requested to leave behind the wild flowers, shrubs and leaf mould; but to take home the litter.

Epping Forest Conservation Centre at High Beach provides exhibitions as well as answering queries and conducting public walks and lectures.

High Beach is one of the best loved and visited parts of Epping Forest. The lanes around here are canopied by oak, birch and beech and in autumn they are ankle deep in leaves. High Beach itself is a scattered village, not very big, but endowed with a surprising number of pubs for its size. One of these, Dick Turpin's Cave, is built over an underground hollow said to have been used by the highwayman. However this is one of those caves which is given a different location depending on which particular pub in the forest you happen to be visiting.

If you believed all the stories, this alcoholic highwayman would at one time have been a regular in every pub within thirty miles of London.

How to Get There
By road take the A11 out of Waltham Forest, High Beach is on an unclassified road off the A11, between Epping and Waltham Forest (approx 5 miles from each).
By tube to Loughton.
By bus there isn't one, so follow the High Beach Road north-west for 1 mile.

The High Beach Walk
A fairly short walk taking in the views of High Beach and the Sherwood Forest-like glades of Green Ride. We start at High Beach outside **The Kings Oak,** where, in summer, food and refreshments are sold from a kiosk. A short walk down the road to the right takes you to the Conservation Centre — a helpful place if you need orientation after visiting the pub, or simply background information on trees and forestry. Back outside The Kings Oak follow the road opposite directly away from the pub's entrance. To the right are 'Pillow Mounds', the original function of which is unclear, suggestions ranging from iron age kilns to rabbit warrens. Cross over the road and head on down the slope to where the alternative

The Inns

The Kings Oak Hotel, High Beach
To some it might seem pointless straying further than The Kings Oak, as the pub commands one of the best views of Epping Forest — indeed it's possible to gaze upon five different counties from the top of the building. It's a mine of historical information, being named after an oak tree that Henry VIII took refuge under, whilst waiting for news of Anne Boleyn's execution. Do not pity the rotund monarch and the doleful picture he presents — when he heard that the deed had (indeed) been done, he slapped his thigh and cried: — "the day's work is done/Uncouple the hounds and let us follow the sport". In 1881 Queen Victoria went to High Beach to dedicate some 5,559 acres of Epping Forest to her nation's people — there was such a scrum that a temporary grandstand was erected as a vantage point on the pub's roof. Other stories of more dubious origin include a cellar ghost called 'Jakey', who once steamrollered a barman with a barrel and a 'White lady' said to roam the top floor after a chambermaid had thrown herself out of a window. Perhaps she'd been pestered by good old Dick Turpin who is said to have been familiar with The Kings Oak — along with every other pub in Essex.

It's an attractive three storey building with tall windows and high ceilings and plenty of space inside. It's a Charrington house, with IPA and Worthington E, and offers an assortment of sandwiches, cold snacks and hot basket meals. If this doesn't suffice there's always the tea shop next door. Outside amusements include a large tree-filled beer garden, a car park with 60 parking lots and an empty swimming pool. The beach itself is thought to have been underwater at some point, as various skeletal fossils of (additional?) watering hole stands on the right-hand side. From here retrace your steps up the hill and turn right down Manor Road.

Take the left fork opposite the lion-topped gates of Arabin House. Tennyson stayed here for two years whilst writing his 'In Memoriam'. Peering through the trees to your left is the spire and clock of the stone-built church of The Holy Innocents. The inside is not a disappointment; look out for the cross shape beneath its high vaulted wooden roof and the majestic organ which was built in 1878. Leave the church, turn left and then left again round the churchyard. Continue past the old signpost, following the Loughton arm, eventually coming upon the Robin Hood roundabout and intersection with the A11. Across the way is **The Robin Hood Hotel**, for centuries a comforting sight as it signalled the end of a long day for haywains journeying to and from London.

Once out of the pub, turn left at the roundabout, signposted 'Loughton 1 mile'. To the right of this road is a wooded area known as Strawberry Hill. Eventually you'll encounter a pond off the road to the right, inhabited by mallards, weed and rushes (Earls Path Pond). The path running alongside the pond is continued on the left-hand side of the road. It is partially blocked by logs to keep out cars, but you should follow it to the left. It is in fact one of the most famous tracks in the forest – Green Ride. The Ride was laid at the time the forest was handed over for public use. Its original purpose was to accommodate a single visit by Queen Victoria.

Holly is much in evidence along this section, as are ferns and horse droppings. At the bottom of the slope to the right runs Loughton Brook, and beyond that Staples Hill.

Cross the bridgeway and continue up the track; the gradient steepens upwards here but the going is only slightly more difficult. At the top of the slope to the left are the remains of Loughton Camp. This is an ancient earthwork which, now being covered with forest, is not easily picked out. In fact it's impossible without straying from the track and wandering around in the trees for a while. A clearer example of an iron age earthwork, Ambresbury

Bank, is to be found a little further north in the forest. It was constructed between 300 BC and 10 AD, and is traditionally known as the place from which Boadicea set forth to lose her last battle with the superior Roman armies.

Retaking the path after, no doubt, a fruitless search for the ancient earthworks, you soon stumble across a clearing, marked by four log benches, where another track crosses Green Ride. At this point go left along what is known as Clay Ride (as the name suggests it can be very muddy in winter).

At the very end is the busy A11 and, across this, the path is marked by a single white stick protruding somewhat anonymously from the bank. Not far into the trees on the other side, you should encounter a riders' gravel chip path, which you should follow to the right.

At the next green sign to the left of the track (horse riding on gravel or wood/chip only) bear left up the track in the trees at approximately 10 o'clock. This brings you out onto an area of open common land next to the Conservation Centre at High Beach and a stone's throw from The Kings Oak. Across the road to the right is a roadside servery where, at almost any time of the year, a hot cup of tea and sandwiches can be bought.

Incidentally ordnance survey maps have only recently adopted the 'Beach' spelling of High Beach. It may also be correctly spelt 'Beech' as the origins of the word are unclear. Although the most obvious association is with the tree that is so prevalent in this neck of the woods.

sea creatures have been unearthed here.

The Robin Hood Hotel, Loughton

Believe it or not, unlike nearly every other pub on the outskirts of London, The Robin Hood is not a former coaching inn. It functioned originally as a 'hay house'. The hay carts stopped off overnight on their way from Bishops Stortford to the Haymarket in London. The old road used to run further into the forest and only in more recent times has the pub stood on what is now the busy A11.

When the new road was built it was constructed at a higher level than the ground around it and, as a result, the pub's original ground floor has now become the cellar (fully equipped with windows and doors). Some of the old beams and wood panelling in the pub date back a long way, though the present landlord has made many alterations. Its olde worlde character is, however, maintained by the open fires, ageing beams, odd bits of saddlery and cart wheels. The large collection of world currency pinned over the bar is from the landlord's naval past.

Two hand-drawn bitters are on tap — Directors and Courage Best Bitters. Also on draught are JC, Guinness, Blackthorn Cider and two lagers. There is also a wide choice of over thirty Scotch whiskies. Food at the bar is average bar fare — in the pie and sandwich league. The large garden at the rear of the pub is particularly pretty in summer.

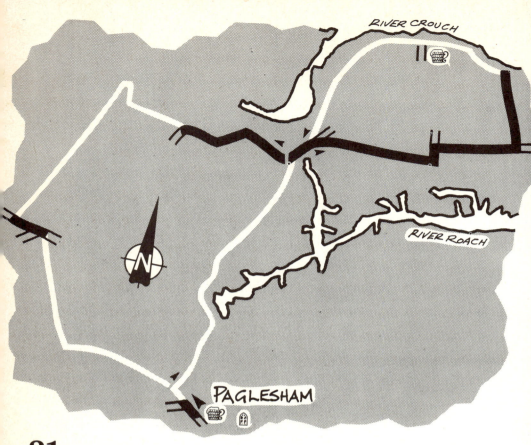

31   **Paglesham**

APPROXIMATELY 4¾ Miles

The District

The character of Essex folk seems to have drastically changed since the first stirrings of English history. Then, it was the land of King Cunobelin, Shakespeare's Cymbeline and every child's nursery rhyme hero Old King Cole; it was the land of Boadicea, the Queen of the Icenii, a warrior-queen fixed in the national memory for her lethal hubcaps; it was the land of Caratacus an early English and anti-Roman guerrilla leader; and it was the land of Brithnoth of whom I have never heard, but who was doubtless of great importance. The Roman capital of Albus Longa, far-flung outpost of their empire, was Colchester, until Boadicea sacked it in AD 61: the Romans wisely moved their capital to London.

And yet nowadays Essex seems the epitome of peacefulness. Beyond the sprawl of Greater London, it is a quiet county with a distinct agricultural identity. Market towns, riverside towns and coast towns dot a region of modest halls and mansions and warm and pleasing, often weatherboarded, houses.

In the last two centuries it has seemed a county of extreme passivity. London decided it wanted a nearby seaside town and Southend-on-Sea was created by filling the gap between the coast, Prittlewell to the north, Leigh-on-Sea to the west and Shoeburyness to the east. Voilà Southend! It is London's Blackpool and nothing was done by half-measures.

It has the longest pier in the world (1½ miles with a railway along it), its floral clock is enormous, it has a vast (and really exciting) amusement park round the Kursaal, and it stretches for seven miles along the coast (the Golden Mile is the place to be at night). It exists for fun and excitment and has been, and still is, a great pleasure to a great many Londoners. Quiet and restful it isn't. Southend isn't too bad an example, but everybody meekly looked on as the county suffered badly at the hands of savage developers. Jazz-age ribbon development extended tentacles deep into Essex and the fill-in created a dreary suburban uniformity. Nobody seemed to care. It must be said that now, people do care and new developments at last have a degree of imagination and individuality. Things look brighter now, but the damage must remain.

Despite all this though, Essex has a surprising amount of unspoilt countryside. And the Essex shoreline of grey muddy creeks and marshes, which surround the islands formed by all the rivers north of the Thames, has fortunately created a large area of only limited potential, in terms of 20th century industrial and technological growth. Farmers use all the land they can and the substantial remainder is left to nature. These islands betray their Viking roots with names like Havengore, Foulness and Wallasea, as indeed does Paglesham, or Packlesham as it can also be written.

Paglesham, Eastend, reaches down to Paglesham Reach on the Roach, is famous for its yacht-building, and was famous for its oysters. This trade has died out here, as perhaps has smuggling. Boat-building and farming are reflected in Eastend's pub name — The Plough and Sail, so perhaps drinking is reflected in Churchend's pub name — The Punchbowl.

The walk starts in Paglesham, Churchend and goes via ditch, creek and lane to the Ferry to Burnham landing-stage on the Crouch. Then, via sea wall, lane and farmland, it goes to the outskirts of Canewdon. It returns by ditch and field to Paglesham, Churchend. It is flat country and the going is easy.

The Inns

The Punchbowl, Paglesham

Perhaps the oldest pub in the vicinity, The Punchbowl dates back 550 years or more. It was three cottages, probably lived in by ploughmakers and sailmakers (old local trades) and many old boats' timbers have been used in its construction. Another old trade was smuggling and there are many tales of smugglers being caught and summarily hanged on nearby elms; indeed a man named Bligh was hung, drawn and quartered here.

A weatherboarded tall building, it has one long bar which is jam-packed with treasures. According to Mr Lyon, the landlord, there are between 750 and 850 items of antique value, which include much pewter and copperware hanging from the original beams, pipes, mugs, Toby Jugs, a 1691 waterclock, Wimbledon plaques, two 1828 Burmese elephants (!), carriage lamps . . . the list goes on.

It's a Watney's pub and stocks London and Stag Bitters on handpump along with Wilson's Great Northern Bitter, Special and Ben Truman on keg. There are also lots of whiskies and about forty (French, German, Italian and Californian) wines. Lunch can either be an à la carte meal or from a wide range of bar meals which

How to Get There

By road take the B1013 north from Southend and then turn right onto an unclassified road at Rochford. Continue along this road, turning right after Great Stambridge and then second left (approx 7 miles).

By rail to Rochford or Southend.

By bus the 10 and 10B run regularly from Rochford and Southend.

The Paglesham Walk

Spoon yourself out of **The Punchbowl** and for a quick look at Churchend, Paglesham, turn left and walk past the row of weatherboarded cottages with nicely warped tile roofs. You reach the corner of the churchyard where there are steps for mounting horses. Beyond, of course, is the church itself, a fine, mostly Norman building being restored at the time of writing, and at the end of the road is the village/farm pond with ducks and swans. However this is not the way the walk goes. So, to start the walk, retrace your steps back through this one-sided hamlet, past The Punchbowl, past the house just beyond and turn right just beyond the house over a concrete footbridge: then head left between the edge of the field and the stream. On this flat-as-a-pancake land, it's hard to tell whether a water-channel is a stream or simply a drainage channel – you'll have to see if you agree with the various names I've given them. My word is not gospel.

The ditch you're following joins a bigger one (don't cross), and amongst the wee trees on the banks you may be lucky to see a solitary heron mournfully looking out over the reeds, leg crooked and all. Follow the path you're on to a crossing of streams and ditches and climb up onto the bank ahead. From here you get your first view of the creek, which to the south meets the River Roach and to the north the River Crouch, thereby making the land away to the east an island; in fact it's called Wallasea and is one of the six islands of 'the Essex Archipelago'. Of course the creek is the haunt of sea, river and creek birds far too numerous for a full list, but look out for terns, dunlin, curlew, knot, oystercatchers and watch out especially for the dark-bellied brent geese which are partial to the eel-grass of the area.

Turn left along the ridge of the bank/dyke/sea wall, walk to and over a stile. When you can cross the ditch to your right, do so and follow the well-defined footpath along the edge of the field through the long grass. A wood off to your left prevents you from seeing the lorries whose every gear-change you can distinctly hear as they negotiate the bendy roads between the timber yards at Baltic Wharf and retailers inland. At a corner of a stream, go in the same direction as before with a ditch on your right. As you swing half left now, it's more marshy on the right and the path wiggles between a muddy hole on the left and a ditch/stream on the right. It follows the edge of the ditch and goes under telegraph lines – so you are still walking along the edge of the field. Once under the lines, the path goes rightish towards the nearest telegraph pole and then goes along the right-hand side of a ditch. At the far end, you cross a wooden footbridge and turn right along the road.

Follow the road, flanked on both sides by streams. On your left are big mooring buoys – blocks of wood fixed together into large cubes which bristle with hooks and eyes. A large barge wallows in the mud beyond. The road passes through the dyke/sea wall and as the road curves right, the caravan park and the timber yard are on your left and rather a lot of cabbages are on your right. You are now on Wallasea Island.

At the corner by Bambergers, it looks, in misty weather, as if the telegraph poles march off ahead, as if the field disappears to the horizon and nothing. Indeed Wallasea Island was covered by water in The Great Tide of 1953. Except for a few trees peeping above it, the sea wall cuts off the mainland. When you meet the No Through Road that goes straight on, go left to Essex Marina and The Wardroom Hotel. Walk down the drive through the avenue of trees, past prefabs on your right and into the boatyard. Walk straight on past the warehouses and workshops and arrive at the Marina itself which is more like a small village with its shops etc. Climb the steps to the left of the Marina office to see the Crouch at the 'Ferry to Burnham' landing-stage.

Burnham is downriver across the little jetties that prevent the boats of all descriptions from floating out to sea. Turn left, pass the telephone box, go down over the slipway and along towards the larger wharf which may or may not have some Scandinavian shipping attached. Walk along the sea wall, behind the Baltic Wharf and on, until you see **The Creeksea Ferry Inn** with its Barracuda Disco . . . (on the Crouch?). Refreshed, continue along the sea wall in the same direction as before. Great barges used for mooring lie like beached whales on your right and the caravan park with its swimming pool is on your left. The sea wall swings left, away from the Crouch, and soon there are more wooden buoys on your right in the marshy creek. Climb the stile and turn right along the road.

The road goes right, left, right as, one supposes, do your feet. The first right is where you emerged onto the road before and the left is by Lion Wharf, which sounds impressive but isn't: it's a small building on your right at the head of the creek. Then there's another right and at the next left, you leave the road and take the public footpath straight on, over a metal and concrete stile and along a track towards the silo and other farm buildings. The track passes through these and ten yards after, you swing right to skirt a small plantation of Christmas trees. Walk along the edge of these trees to a bridge over a ditch by a dead and ivy-clad tree.

Turn left and walk along the edge of the field, and when you meet a track, go right, along it. Follow it as it bends left and when it meets another track, turn left uphill. This track runs straight as a die past a wood on your left and then past Lambourne Hall on your right. It is a 15th-16th century building with a fine red mansard roof. You reach a metal gate by a pond and the track takes you to another gate onto the road where you turn left. In so doing, you are leaving Canewdon, the hill of Cana's people, which rises behind you. Canewdon's church on Beacon Hill has served in its time not only as a spiritual beacon for its congregation, but also as a more practical beacon for sailors: I mean, it has doubled as a light-

include scampi, steaks, and duck. All in all, a good pub, but beware the Doberman.

The Creeksea Ferry Inn, Wallasea Island

On the River Crouch, this is a Tudor-style pub with an 'olde-worlde' public bar with a stone fireplace and a large saloon which overlooks the river. In the summer, it's much frequented by people from the nearby caravan park and has music and dancing in the Barracuda Disco on Fridays and Saturdays. It's a Watneys pub and serves a selection of basket meals, as well as the more usual pizzas, pies, salads and sandwiches. Of course you can take your food and drink onto the riverbank and watch the river flow.

house. If the congregation ignored the church's ecclesiastical messages, then, at the east end of the churchyard, there was the village cage, a whipping-post and a set of stocks (dated 1775) to put them right. Canewdon obviously saw itself as a troublemakers' village, for not only did it possess this triple threat, but the stocks can hold three offenders at a time instead of the more usual two.

The road is now called Creeksea Road and just after the first house on the right, take the marked public footpath over a stile. The path goes half left across the paddock to a fence/stile and over into the field. Here turn right and soon you have to bend left at the ditch on the right. Cross the bridge and continue along the edge of the ditch. Just after a line of five trees, the ditch takes you left at a clump of dead trees. At the next corner, cross the ditch where you can and continue in the same direction, now along a track. You pass a line of healthy trees on your left and leave the track when it veers round the end of the line: here, you go straight on, now along a stream on your left. The stream winds and meanders – so do you. Another stream joins – this you cross by a plank, you landlubbers, and then again follow the original stream. You meet another branch of the stream and this one you follow, crossing it by a bridge a few yards along. It's now on your right and you now follow it, retracing your outward path (for such it is) back to the concrete bridge, Paglesham, Churchend and most importantly The Punchbowl.